A PASSI EDUCATION - THE STORY OF A HEADTEACHER

BY

CHRISTOPHER R. GOODWIN

BSC (HONS) NPQH

Dedication

This book is dedicated to Tony Marsh – good friend and teacher.

To my wife Liz for all her diligent editing and the love

To Pete Smith – who shares the vision.

To Sean Smith – a friend and colleague

To Mr. Tranter (Rydens circa 1966) who inspired me.

To all those other great teachers I have worked with who inspire others!

To all the students I taught in the course of a long career – You made it all worthwhile.

This book is also dedicated to my children and grandchildren. They represent the future. When I see them I know the world is in good hands.
My hope is that the generations to come will be better than us. That's the way it should be.
That is the power of education.

Long may we continue to build a better world through education!

Contents

Foreword   5
Chapter 1 – Headship – beginning the perfect storm and
      other disasters   13
Chapter 2 – More about the catastrophe at the beginning   23
Chapter 3 – Second time of asking   31
Chapter 4 – Relationship, ethos and philosophy   37
Chapter 5 – The purpose of education   52
Chapter 6 – PSHE and drugs   57
Chapter 7 – Managing people   72
Chapter 8 – Relationships   80
Chapter 9 – The curriculum   93
Chapter 10 – Inspections   100
Chapter 11 – The pastoral system   108
Chapter 12 – The whole child unwrapped from 'red tape'   113
Chapter 13 – Great lessons – great teaching   123
Chapter 14 – Knowing your students   133
Chapter 15 – Open doors and open minds   141
Chapter 16 – Managing change   145
Chapter 17 – Work ethic and effort   148
Chapter 18 – Those that can't do!   153
Chapter 19 – The government and politics and worst
      experiences   155
Chapter 20 – The tick-box culture   161
Chapter 21 – Assemblies   165
Chapter 22 – Time management   167
Chapter 23 – Banding, streaming and comprehensive
      education   171
Chapter 24 – My early years   175
Chapter 25 – Outside interests   178
Chapter 26 – Dealing with bullying   179
Chapter 27 – Grammar schools and selection   182
Chapter 28 – Restorative practice   186
Chapter 29 – Academies, free schools and religious
      schools   189
Chapter 30 – Inspirational teachers   192
Chapter 31 – Safeguarding and health & safety   197

4

Chapter 32 – Assessment and marking   203
Chapter 33 – It's the little things that count   207
Chapter 34 – Starting school sets the tone   211
Chapter 35 – Individuality or uniforms?   215
Chapter 36 – Parents!!!   218
Chapter 37 – Private education   227
Chapter 38 – Training and politicians   231
Chapter 39 – Rock 'n' Roll Head   238
Chapter 40 – Finance   240
Chapter 41 – Publicity   242
Chapter 42 – Back your staff   245
Chapter 43 – Attendance   247
Chapter 44 – Student Voice   249
Chapter 45 – Governors   250
Chapter 46 – Specialisms   251
Chapter 47 – Politics and education and austerity   253
Chapter 48 – My own classroom Ofsted inspections   256
Chapter 49 – Appointments and promotions   257
Chapter 50 – Leadership and management   260
Chapter 51 – The precariousness of Headship and the
                 tyranny Ofsted has become   262
Chapter 52 –   How to pass an Ofsted Inspection   266
Chapter 53 –   The future of education   267
Chapter 54 –   Retirement   269
Appendix 1 – What qualities a Headteacher requires   271
Appendix 2 – What really works in the realm of education   273
Appendix 3 – What is neither effective nor desirable   280

Foreword

I am very proud to have taught at Beverley Grammar School for thirty six years including fourteen years on the Senior Team followed by five years as Headteacher. During that long career I taught with numerous brilliant colleagues who I respect and admire as educators and friends.

I have also taught thousands of students and they have taught me. It has been a privilege working with such fervent, interesting students. I have fond memories and miss them all. I can honestly say that I never disliked a student although some were trying! They made my working life worthwhile.

When I first started at Beverley Grammar School it was in the process of changing from a Grammar to Comprehensive school. I believe in comprehensive education and I feel that I have proved it can work far better than any selective system. My heart will always be in that caring community that was Beverley Grammar School.

Haim Ginott inspired me. I implore every teacher and educator to read his work. He was a Jew who survived the horrors of a concentration camp. He saw the gas chambers that were designed by qualified engineers and children who were murdered in cruel experiments by highly skilled doctors.

He, like me, was more than suspicious of education.

He believed that the primary purpose of education should not be to instil knowledge but to encourage kindness, empathy and compassion. In this way the world might be free of highly educated monsters and psychopaths like the Hitler, Pol Pot and Mao.

I agree with him one hundred percent.

Teaching about maths, reading, writing and how to pass exams is pointless if we are not teaching our children to be caring human beings.

That should be the first aim of any teacher.

Leadership is about empowerment. If a leader doesn't enable their staff to take risks and grow they aren't worth their salt. A good leader should encourage all their staff to reach their potential.

A school is like an ocean liner. It builds up a head of steam and gets carried along by its own momentum. It cannot stop or change course abruptly. You have to guide it and plan each change of course well in advance. It takes all the 'sailors' working as a team for it to run smoothly.

Headship is like a race down a steep snow run on an old tin tray. You have limited control and your journey is perilously at the mercy of events and obstructions that cannot all be foreseen.

Yet a Head sets the tone for everything that happens in the school.

The art of Headship is to sell your vision so that the whole community is pulling in the same direction.

Paradoxically a Head is largely impotent. As a Head you have far-reaching responsibilities but limited power. There are good things about this. Many Heads proceed to Headship out of a desire for power, control and money. They are ambitious and can be overbearing, ruthless, and self-centred. At least the system limits their desire to exert a regime of fear and control

A Head has limited control over poor teaching. The kids may deserve better but there are no quick fixes. Headteachers are prevented from exercising much power by a series of legal requirements. These can be frustrating but on the whole having restraints is better than having a tyrannical Headteacher. A Head therefore has to eliminate poor teaching through example and by supporting and leading their staff.

You always find when you reach the top that you're actually in the middle. A Head is in the middle of everything pulled by the governors, staff, students, government, local authority and parents, you soon find you are not 'in charge'. You have to juggle everything to keep all the balls in the air.

It is said that the fact that someone wants to be a politician should automatically ban them from standing; the same thing is true of Headships. Those that think they know what they are doing are usually the worst. If a Head starts Headship by asking for more power or money it is likely that they are doing the job for the wrong reasons.

The only reason to become a Head is a passion for trying to make the world a better place. Education is the only way of achieving this. After all, education has to be better than war, religious hatred and sectarian violence.

. Education is all things to all men/women. To politicians it is a way of maintaining social order, reinforcing class or enabling mobility and addressing the economic needs of the country. To many it is purely about careers while to others it is about expanding minds, opening horizons and creating wonder. I'm very much in the wonder and awe camp. I am also of the repairing damaged kids persuasion. All my students were equally important and equally valuable. I hope I succeeded in making some of their lives better. That's what I set out to do. Their chosen career and economic value was secondary to their self-esteem and happiness.

Before starting this I checked on 'Rate my Teacher', a scurrilous website that has given a voice to some rather dubious individuals, but one which reflects how some others see you. It offers a modicum of objectivity. It was a little unsettling to see oneself described as an obese penguin from the CIA but on the other side there was also the recognition of the care and respect. It showed a career that was not entirely wasted.

I worked in Education for thirty six years and prior to that I was largely a victim of it for twenty plus years. My experience of schooling gave me the impetus to get involved and change it. My disgust at the education minister and the Tory attempt to belittle all the achievements of recent decades and drag education back to the appalling 1950s is my main reason for writing this. Children should be valued as human beings and not seen as mere economic units for the employment market. Education that is not developing all aspects of human empathy, and creativity as well as expanding minds is wrong. Most leading fascists have been highly educated - after a fashion. It was their empathy, compassion and warmth of spirit that was allowed to atrophy. Any education system that fosters elitism and the smug arrogance that stems from it should be resisted by all caring people. A system that ignores the promotion of human feeling and sound moral and ethical values in order to focus on exam league tables and economic performance is flawed. The society created would be cold and bitter.

I have fought against that limited view of education all my life.

I have fought for the warmth and light.

In my teaching experience I have known students with lower intelligence, destined for poor grades and lowly jobs, but possessing a range of qualities that left me humbled. I have known highly intelligent individuals, destined for top jobs, who were mean spirited and likely to create misery. My job was to bring out the best in both and my hope is that both types left school better equipped to make a positive contribution to society.

Education is a nebulous thing. We are building the future and the future is not only concerned with careers and wealth; it is also about families, societies, relationships and supporting those less fortunate. How to build a better world should be our curriculum. How we repair damaged children should be our imperative. How we foster positive human values should be our main aim. Teaching and learning, exam results and league tables are almost superfluous in the face of such paramount challenges.

This is why I believe the most important subject, and the most difficult to teach, is PSHE (Personal social and health education). All too often it is poorly delivered, pushed to the shadows and taught by reluctant exponents who happen to have some free space in their timetable. This is a travesty. PSHE is about life, about preparing students for a better world, dealing with the big issues of responsibility, respect, tolerance and empathy. PSHE, like the pastoral system, is about guidance, interaction and development of those qualities that raise the sensibilities. It should be given centre stage, pride of place and only taught by the very best of teachers with the most advanced skills. Anything less is short-changing the future. A school lacking a vibrant PSHE programme is like a robot with no heart. It is pointless.

The only way to address the world's problems is through good education.

As a probationary teacher I set about taking on the hierarchy of the school and changing the beast that was the current school. It was poor and not meeting the needs of all of its students. I wanted a revolution. You don't have to be in senior management to have a power base to promote positive change. I fought for change and managed to bring in a number of improvements. However, after twenty years of influential input from a lowly position, I realised that the best way of changing the system was to do it from the top and seized my opportunity to move into senior management.

I did things my way. I did not follow the rules. I was the sand in the Vaseline. The senior team found me a major problem. I refused to compromise. I did it the way I felt was right for the students and my own philosophy. And this method was highly successful. In the whole of my time in teaching I did not have a single report or inspection putting me below excellent. On the school's first Ofsted inspection, in which it achieved 'Satisfactory', all my areas were Outstanding. Over the next three Ofsted inspections, two as Deputy Head and one as Head, all my areas of responsibility were deemed 'Outstanding'. Being a maverick, and not following the rules, does not necessarily mean you cannot gain recognition. Risk taking is a big part of the game. Covering your back is a weakness and a flaw. Doing what is right, even in defiance of the orders from above, is an imperative. You have to follow your conscience.

Duke Ellington supposedly said that there were only two kinds of music: good and bad. The same is true of education. Bad education is destructive to minds, spirits and society. It should be banished even when it produces perceived results. My own maths teacher in secondary school always achieved a 100% pass rate with his classes. I passed maths from his class. Yet nobody was more successful at destroying a subject. To a man we came out of there hating Maths.

I have always questioned the education system. It seems crazy to put people together grouped by age. That never happens in normal social interaction. This is asking for trouble, particularly during teenage years when hormones are rampant and brains are melting and becoming rewired. It reinforces lots of negative behaviour patterns. It is almost as bad as grouping people according to ability, but not quite. I think we need to bring our best minds to bear to find a better way forward.

The present Tory Government of 2014 is bereft of ideas. What is proposed, a plunge back to the dark days of the 1950s emotionally challenged society, would be a disaster. We have to come up with something better than that. We have a wealth of psychology and sociology to fall back on. Politicians have the wrong agendas. They are ruled by their own political dogma. They always make a mess of it.

I only served five years as a Head. This is something I now regret. I was never personally ambitious and was severely lacking in self-confidence when it came to formal situations. One thing that was obvious was that there were going to be many formal situations and they came with the post. I ducked it for too long and was content with deputy headship. Consequently I came to Headship too late. As a Head I became used to the formal situations and overcame my anxiety attacks. One thing I have learned from life is that you should always push yourself and try to extend your reach. To not do so is perhaps to leave yourself with an unfulfilled life. You never know what you could have achieved.

I guess I'll never know. I would have liked to have served as a Head for longer and really set my philosophy into full operation. The school was motoring. The cherished beliefs, that I had spent thirty six years establishing, were bearing fruit. The atmosphere inside the school was warm, friendly and buzzing with energy. We were a positive, can-do, all inclusive community. There was a lot of love.

If you review the full panoply of responsibilities involved with Headship, as with many other jobs, it becomes obvious that it is not possible to carry out the whole role effectively. You are responsible for everything twenty four hours a day, seven days a week. You have to know every rule and regulation inside out. You are expected to represent yourself in the most exacting of circumstances without legal representation. To achieve this you would need to be in ten places at once, have a myriad of skills, be super intelligent and be able to read and hold in your memory a mass of legal documentation sufficient to fill a library. As with all such roles you learn to prioritise, deal with the pressing, delegate and relax in the knowledge that you are always exposed and could flounder at any moment from circumstances largely beyond your control. The stress is enormous. I was threatened with prison three times during my short stint. You can go two ways. You can become anal and try to nail everything down, creating a bureaucratic mediocrity or you can hold on tight, guide the tin tray over the bumps and away from the trees, experience a spectacular journey and enjoy the adrenaline rush.

Outstanding can only come as a result of going for it and reaching as far as your spirit will allow. All the checklists in the world cannot create a single spark of originality or flash of genius. Inspiration comes from passion.

Headship is a lonely place but it can be exhilarating when you have the support of the community you have helped create. Sometimes it all comes together and is transcendental. Those are the moments we live for.

As far as I am concerned mediocrity should never be an option.

What follows are my views on education and the mechanics of how the school came to become Outstanding while prospering as a friendly, supportive community in which everyone was loved and valued. I have sprinkled it with illustrative anecdotes from my own experience. This is about how to become Outstanding.

I believe with all my heart that we can mend broken kids, soften the arrogant and aggressive, and use education to change the world into a tolerant, peaceful place that works in harmony with nature.

When education is practiced properly it soars. It should work to take humanity out of the morass of war, poverty, environmental destruction and religious intolerance into a new age.

This is no idle dream of a helpless romantic idealist. This book is about good education.

Good education requires great Headteachers.

Chris Goodwin 16.11.2012

Chapter 1 – Headship – beginning the perfect storm and other disasters

The start of my sleepless nights began before my first term of Headship even began.

Having reached my mid fifties I was beginning to look ahead to taking an early retirement so that I had time to do all those things I'd been wanting to do, such as writing. Much as I loved teaching there was no denying that work left little time for my creative endeavours. I yearned for a more bohemian lifestyle. All my life I have fought against the conflicting interests of my biological clock and the timetable of work. Left to my own devices I gravitated to working late at night. As the evening progressed I tended to become more alert. In my younger days I would happily type my books from 10.00 pm until 2.00 am or even 3.00 am and then pay heavily for it the next morning when the alarm went off. I'd somehow manage on four hours sleep a night, with a little catch up on the weekend, as much as family life would allow, for three months or so until I'd completed the book that had been sitting in my head.

Throughout my working life I'd go to bed wide awake, sleep well and wake up feeling dopey with tiredness.

Retirement might just sort this out.

Then, out of the blue, Gerry, the Headteacher, retired and I was thrown into a dilemma: should I apply for the Headship or not?

Was I too old?

'You'll only regret it if you don't,' Liz admonished me. She was always the voice of reason. 'What harm can it do? You probably won't get it anyway. You know you won't be happy working for a new Head.'

She was right.

I had been happy working as a Deputy under Gerry. He gave me almost complete freedom to do my own thing. I could put my ideas into action. I was happy even though I was beginning to get bored. I'd got most things sorted and there was very little challenge in the role anymore. I was craving change. I'd been talking to Gerry about bringing in some major changes and had even drawn up plans for the introduction of vertical tutoring and the disbandment and restructuring of the Curriculum Team and Pastoral Team. I needed something to get my teeth into and keep my interest. In my head I was going to work for another three years and then retire. The idea of working for someone else whose views might not mirror mine, who might even start undoing all the stuff I'd put in place, was unsettling. I'd worked in the place for over thirty years and come to think of the school as mine. I could see the initiatives I had brought in bearing fruit. I couldn't bear to see them dismantled. I did not take much persuading.

I decided to apply.

The only problem was that the government had just made it mandatory to have, or be on the course for, the new NPQH qualification of Headship and I hadn't even applied for it. I checked with the website and found that I had just missed the deadline to get on the course by a few days; I was unable to get enrolled before the interviews. I applied for the next course which began in June. It was now February.

I thought this might well preclude me from being accepted as an applicant but put on my application that I had applied for the NPQH course and that I would be willing to accept the position subject to being accepted on the course. It was the best I could do.

My application was accepted. There were no objections from County at that point and my application proceeded.

My references from Gerry and my fellow deputy Dave were incredible.

My work record at the school was impressive. The number of initiatives I had successfully brought in and seen bedded was exceptional and fully backed up by inspection reports.

The negative side of things was mainly concerned with image. I knew this was the main factor from previous shenanigans around my appointment as a deputy head. I was a short scruffy individual who did not sit easy in a suit. I was also extremely maverick in the way I did things. I was not one for following rules and regulations or adhering to procedures. I rather did it my way.

People had trouble seeing me standing on the stage at public forums looking like a Headmaster. I could not blame them as I had trouble seeing myself that way. This was made worse by the fact that these were precisely the attributes Gerry did best. He could shine on a stage, talk for England and project charisma. These were things that did not come easy to me, yet I knew I still had all the ideas and energy to take the school to another level.

Liz took me in hand, decked me out in new suits, ties and shirts and created a more palatable image. It wasn't me but it partially filled the hole in what I had to offer. After all – this was a game.

I progressed to interview where I had to work at overcoming the image of the past and selling the 'new' me.

I had nothing to lose. I spoke from the heart and told them what I believed in and what I would do for the school.

The interviews took place in March.

The three day interviews were very exacting. They grilled me on all aspects of my philosophy, achievements and intentions through panel after panel, performance after performance. I had no problem with any of this because I had loads of experience and ideas and did not bother preparing – I just spoke from the heart and was relaxed about the whole thing. I had nothing to lose.

A more difficult part of the exercise involved being taken out to an evening meal. Prior to the meal candidates were told the title of the presentation they had to give to the whole governing body the next morning. The whole idea was to create enormous pressure and observe how you reacted. I ate my meal, sipped my wine, smiled a lot and made intelligent conversation as my mind churned over how I was going to handle the presentation. It was important that I remained relaxed and took my time even though I was straining to get away and begin work on the presentation for the morning.

I got through it without swearing or spilling wine over anyone. I used the right cutlery and even managed to crack a few jokes in a seemingly relaxed manner.

The next day I delivered my presentation and laid out my passion and philosophy with as much enthusiasm as I could muster.

That evening I waited at home with Liz on tenterhooks.

The chair of governors rang and told me I'd been successful, adding as a rider that it was subject to me being accepted on the NPQH. As this was a formality this seemed unimportant.

We celebrated.

It was exciting to think that I was going to have the opportunity to put my philosophy to the test. Would I be able to successfully sell the vision? Could I get the roof on the building I had designed and constructed or would the weight pull it all down? There would be no excuse. I would have a free rein. There would be no Headteacher to mull over my ideas with and give them the yea or nay. I would be my own master.

Psychologically Headship is totally different to deputy headship. As a deputy you can put forward the most radical ideas. Someone else takes ultimate responsibility. They oversee it; if the Head says 'no' it doesn't happen; if they say yes they take responsibility. As a deputy you are free to drive as hard as you like. You also have someone to talk it through with, to rub off the rough edges. As a Head you are on your own. There is no-one to pick up the pieces.

It is like doing a tight-rope walk without a safety net.

It was suddenly overwhelmingly daunting.

I remember Chris Woodward the England rugby coach being interviewed following England's victory at the world cup.

'How do you select the best team to get the fifteen best players out on the pitch?' an interviewer enquired.

'You never get the best players on the pitch,' Chris Woodward replied. 'You get the best that will perform on the day.'

The interviewer looked bemused.

'If I was to put a long beam down on the gym floor and ask the team to run the length of it most of them would do so easily,' Clive explained. 'Maybe the odd one would lose their balance and fall off but they wouldn't find it too hard. But if I was to place that same beam between two skyscrapers and ask them to run across it it's a different kettle of fish. The actual task hasn't changed. The fear of failure has become so much greater.'

'That's the same as running out on the field at Twickenham,' Clive continued. 'The expectation is enormous. Everything you do is filmed and analysed by millions. The pressure is unbelievable. Some of the most talented players are overawed by it. They freeze and under-perform. My job is to help them deal with the pressure and perform to their potential. That is why you pick the team that can perform best under that pressure. They are not always the best players.'

Headship is like that. The danger is that you may freeze and play safe by following all the rules.

Headship, if you strive for excellence, is about risk taking and giving full rein to that quirky individuality. Playing safe always creates mediocrity.

I didn't know if I could do it. The responsibility was suddenly frightening.

One lesson life has taught me is that you should never give in to your fears. Your subconscious is your worst enemy. It is always whispering in your ear telling you that you are going to make a fool of yourself. The trouble is that it knows you so well it knows all your weaknesses and never holds back at pointing them out to you.

'When you stand up there on that stage your hands will shake and your voice tremble. You'll look a fool,' it whispered in my head. 'You'll forget what you want to say and far from inspiring people you'll be ridiculed.'

It was this fear of failure that creates pressure.

I put my notes in a plastic wallet so any shaking was not so visible. I practised speaking so that I could control my voice and always took a glass of water on stage so that I could take a sip and control myself. It helped.

You have to stand up to your subconscious and tell it sternly to shut up.

Your subconscious holds you back.

I don't just mean that in terms of career development; I mean it in terms of life experience. There is no feeling as good as conquering your fear, doing something you dread and doing it well. This is true for bungee jumpers, sky-divers and people in all walks of life.

The fear of public speaking holds many people back. Don't let it. I have seen 'Heads of Year' delivering their first assemblies shaking and stuttering only to find, a year later, those same people have become confident and at ease on a stage. If it really bothers you, go on a public speaking course.

Don't allow yourself to be beaten by your own self before you even start.

The danger of not taking risks and pushing yourself is that you stay in your comfort zone. That is fatal. You get bored and shrink into yourself. I've seen teachers who had the ability to do so much more, decay into cynical individuals who spent the latter days of their career going through the motions. They grow to hate the job and can't wait to get out. Yet these individuals had so much more to offer and they owed it to themselves, as well as the kids they taught, to push harder.

By the time I finished I was confident on any stage but I never lost my nerves.

This is true of many performers. Many great comedians and musicians get themselves in a complete state before they go on stage. Then they walk out on the platform and become the epitome of relaxed self-assurance. You feel nervous because you care.

Even giving morning briefing was a nightmare for me at first. The start of a new school year staff meeting or staff training days were things I worried about all summer holiday though I doubt any of the staff noticed what a mess I got myself in. The outside was projecting calm humour while the inside churned and raged.

I was glad I took risks and made myself confront and overcome my demons.

You don't ever want to end your life with regrets.

During the summer term I began preparing for taking over the school.

I was told there were a few concerns regarding my application. Seemingly County had now objected because I was not on the NPQH at the time of my application.

I thought little of this at the time. I would shortly be on the course, which would fulfil the need, and I had a letter offering me the post subject to getting on the course. It seemed water-tight. I had more pressing things to think about. I had a school to prepare for September. I had to pick up the reins of Headship and manage the change-over.

Out of nowhere, three weeks before the end of term, I was informed that as County had formally objected I would have to reapply for my post. I would have to put in a fresh application and go through the whole process again and this would have to be overseen by officers from County to ensure it was all above board.

I was dismayed.

Here I was gearing up for a take over and suddenly I was no longer Head. What sort of start was that?

I could not see why the governors did not stand up to County and say 'no way'. They had appointed me fair and square. But they didn't. They backed down.

Then the school had an Ofsted inspection in the last two weeks of the summer term. It was all hands to the pump and complete mayhem.

All my hopes of a smooth transition were thrown into complete disarray. There were no cosy chats with the outgoing Head. There were no leisurely meetings to sort the nuts and bolts out. We were all rushing about getting the documentation and sorting the requirements for the Ofsted. In the midst of this I was in discussion with my union, the governors and County regarding my Headship.

The upshot of all this was that we achieved a second Outstanding Ofsted report and all my areas of responsibility once more came out as excellent. This was a really nice way for Gerry to leave and it cleared the way for me. I no longer had an Ofsted inspection looming over me for a while. It gave me time to do my thing and get it right.

The big downside at the end of that term was that the NUT union informed me that they unwilling to back me. I gained the distinct impression that they were not so bothered about Headteachers. I was on my own. I had to reapply for my job. I would only be a temporary Head in September.

County provided me with no mentorship, training programme or support. Nor was I allocated a fund to facilitate this.

There were huge knock-on effects to being a temporary Head:

My first task in September was to inform the staff that I was not actually the Headteacher; I was merely acting Head and would have to apply for my job. This, of course, led to everyone questioning whether I was still going to be around at the end of the term; did they have to do what I told them?

In their eyes I was not Head. It stripped me of credibility and all authority. I was a lame duck from the first day.

The second effect was that I could not appoint a new deputy head to replace my former role as I might have to drop back into that position if I failed to secure the job. This meant that I was still doing the bulk of that deputy's job while I was trying to pick up the reins of Headship. Fortunately I did have one deputy – Grahame.

My workload was colossal and further compounded by me starting the NPQH and having to carry out an enormous amount of work entailed in that plus my own stupid decision of wanting to continue my teaching load. I continued with A Level Biology teaching and my Y11 PSHE commitment.

I was determined to set an example. I was determined that no member of staff would work harder than me.

It was an ambitious and foolhardy decision that I soon came to regret.

No-one did work harder than me. I was driven like a maniac. I was regularly doing 80 hour weeks with no lunch or breaks.

At the start of my Headship, and much to the chagrin of the bulk of the staff, we had brought in a five period day to replace our four period day. We had to do this in order to give the range of curriculum options for the students. The previous Head, knowing what an upheaval it would bring, and nearing the end of his career, had knowingly left it to me to introduce. It was not the easiest thing to do at the best of times and the disaster of my uncertain situation made it trebly difficult. This was not the pleasant honeymoon period it could have been. We were straight into full-blooded confrontation.

This major development had been introduced with full staff consultation though the whole process had been messed about and curtailed due to the situation regarding my appointment and the Ofsted inspection coming at the end of term. Consequently the staff felt it had been rushed and rather imposed. They were up in arms because it increased their workload and worsened their work/life balance.

Despite the fact that we gave them more generous allowances of preparation time they did have a bit of a point. The lessons were shorter but they had to prepare, teach and mark more.

I think if we had taken longer over this consultation and talked it through more the staff would have been won over. They were a dedicated, caring staff and they would have acknowledged that, despite slight worsening of their conditions, it was definitely better for the students and the school. Without the proposed introduction of the five period day we would not have achieved an outstanding Ofsted with all the many benefits that brought for the school. We were told that by the Ofsted Registrar. These outstanding Ofsted inspections were essential for the survival of the school. They attracted the students to the school and it was student numbers that generated the cash. Without those outstanding inspections we might have been facing staff redundancies.

However the staff were not looking at the big picture. They viewed it from their own narrow perspective. They just wanted things to be the same as before. All they saw was that it had been good under the last Head and now it was looking a whole lot worse. They were railing at the workload without looking at the broader picture or the long term benefits. It made for a fraught start.

This was further compounded by the introduction of a new IT Management system. Unsurprisingly we had gone for a different system to all the other schools. It gave us an integrated attendance, behaviour and curriculum package that would enable us to develop our systems and incorporate them. It looked brilliant but was quite complicated. It had meant a lot of change and a lot of staff training.

That too impacted on workload.

Staff do not like change. People were struggling to understand the complicated system.

You could not have conceived of introducing as much change all in one dollop. It was far from ideal but in reality there was not much option. This was the time to do it. It would have been foolish to delay.

It would have been a lot easier if I had not had my own problems to contend with. It also would have been a lot easier if the new system had not completely crashed at the beginning of term leaving us without registers, teaching groups or registration groups. We were thrown back to paperwork and chaos.

That first week could not have gone much worse. Staff were muttering about my survival and what sort of Head might they get come half-term when the new Headship interviews were to take place.

My stress levels were through the roof. I was working all hours, going to bed exhausted with a head full of problems, concerns and worries and unable to sleep.

Each day was like an insurmountable nightmare. It looked as if I was heading for a breakdown.

Fortunately we got the ICT management system back up and running and that settled down. Grahame my deputy had only been with us for a year but he pulled more than his weight and rose to the challenge. Between us we did the necessary planning and made it work.

He was a stalwart. I could leave the curriculum, stats and ICT management in his capable hands and not have to worry about it.

We were a team though I don't think he was completely aware of the mayhem that was going on in my head. Liz was worried that I'd have a heart attack or stroke. My kids were worried about my health. I was trying to hold it all together and get through it.

Through all this turmoil and confusion I had to stand on that stage in front of staff, the school and the public and project calm confidence, charisma and leadership. Welcome to Headship.

Chapter 2 – More about the catastrophe and other disasters

It is true to say that the start of my Headship could hardly have been worse!

I think it was George Washington who said something on the lines of 'Most men can cope with adversity; to see the real character of a man give him power.'

On my first day as a temporary Head I had arrived early in the morning before the caretaker had even begun to unlock the place and stood in the driveway surveying the school as objectively as I could.

What I saw, when viewed dispassionately, was not too good. The iconic pavilion was almost derelict. Its windows were smashed in and boarded up, paintwork was a disaster with bare rotting wood exposed, tiles were missing and it looked ready for demolition. Inside the place it was no better. I knew the old boiler was broken, the roof leaked and it was a mud streaked wreck. The smell of the urinals pervaded the place and the showers did not function at all. It was still used as changing rooms but with no heating and in such a mess that it could not go on for long.

The pavilion was the first thing you saw as you came up the drive and used to be the pride of the school. It was a ruin. It set the tone for the rest of the school.

In the holidays someone had gone round with something like a hammer and smashed three huge windows in the technology block, two in the English block and two in the sixth form block. A corner flag from one of the football pitches was actually sticking out of one of the broken windows where someone had rammed it through. Even the relatively new blocks were in disrepair.

It looked a mess.

I looked round at the beautiful grounds with their established horse chestnut trees in full bloom. The sun was shining, flowers blooming and fields looked a picture. At least the grounds man was a star.

It was quite a challenge. There was a lot to do.

I was overcome with a feeling that it was all my responsibility. If I fell short then the lives of all the students and staff would be affected. I was responsible for their futures. It made me feel sick.

At that point I didn't know the half of it.

From day one, as I tried to cope with the storm that had overtaken me and keep my head above water, below the surface an even more serious set of challenges were circling like great white sharks silently rushing in at me to tear me apart.

The finances were busy going awry.

I inherited the school with a £90,000 surplus. This meant that for the first half of the term I did not have to concern myself too much with the finances. I had enough on my plate. I was struggling to establish myself as an acting Head with all that entailed; doing the work for the NPQH, keeping up with my former deputy's work, introducing the new initiatives against heated opposition, doing justice to my teaching and trying to plan for the forthcoming Headship interviews. As everything was going pear-shaped this was proving more than difficult. I only just managed to keep up with my teaching commitment. It was getting all too much.

I felt I was floundering. I had taken on too much and had reached saturation. I'd found my limits.

The finances were not a priority. I wasn't proposing to spend anything apart from a window pane replacement programme. It could tick over in the background. Or that was what I thought.

Unfortunately it couldn't and this became apparent following my successful second interview and my appointment as Head.

The school had suffered from falling roles. It had its lowest number of students for some considerable time. Fewer students had returned to the sixth form and year 7 was nowhere near full. More students were moving out than coming in, every single year group was depleted. While this made for pleasant small teaching groups that pleased the staff it meant that there was far less money coming in to the school than had been predicted.

This had been compounded by a staffing crisis. Three staff were suddenly on long term sick leave, including a nasty accident in the swimming pool while on holiday abroad. They required expensive cover staffing. Effectively we were paying twice for the same amount of teaching. On top of this a boiler blew and had to be replaced.

The government had been negotiating with the unions and the new contract involved revised teacher contact time, workload and emergency cover only teaching. The idea was sound – teachers should be in the classroom teaching; mundane tasks such as photocopying, displays, filing, supervision of exams and typing should be carried out by clerical and support staff. This had resulted in us having to employ more support staff and outside teacher cover for absence. Teachers would no longer cover lessons for absent staff except in emergencies.

As a consequence the wage bill had shot up over night.

After half term there was a brief lull. The five period day had settled in even though teachers detested the extra workload. The SERCO ICT management system had begun working and staff were beginning to get to grips with it. Things were looking up.

I sat down with my bursar Pat and went through the finances. I had a picture of where we should be from previous discussions with Gerry. It didn't seem to be there. We had a black hole. It appeared we had gone from a surplus to a deficit of nearly half a million. It sent chills through me.

There had to be something wrong here.

I rang up Gerry. We'd always got along really well and I knew he'd be supportive. He said to ring if I had anything he could help with.

He was very reassuring:

'Don't worry,' he chuckled. 'It always looks bad this time of year. It'll settle down. There are always bits of money here and there that start coming in. It'll look better in a while. Don't worry about it.'

I sat down with Pat and went through it with a microscope. She fed in all the monies that were likely to manifest and we still had a black hole of £450,000. There had to be something I was doing wrong. I rang Gerry back and asked him to come in and go through it with me. There had to be something I was overlooking. It couldn't get this bad so quickly.

He came into school, immediately sparking rumours that the governors had asked him back. We went through the finances. No matter how he looked at it there was no other result. We were looking at a massive black hole.

I went to the staff. They were cynical. They saw it as a management ploy to get more out of them. The unions were adamant that they were not going to provide cover. We had to stand by all the hard won agreements on working practice. They thought my fears of staff redundancies were scaremongering.

I sat down and explained the situation to the governors hopeful that they would see that this was none of my doing. A set of circumstances had conspired to create the perfect storm. I could not anticipate staff illness and boilers breaking down. The falling roles were unexpected. It had come together to create a catastrophic deficit.

My sleepless nights were now full of sweaty nightmares as my mind churned over and over how I was going to get out of this hole.

This was the reality of Headship.

I arranged a meeting with the education officers at County Hall. They had an emergency fund that could perhaps bail us out. The boiler and long-term staff absences met the criteria. A bail out could at least get the deficit down to manageable proportions and buy us the time to address the problem.

The school had history with County. We were grant maintained and been at loggerheads with them right back to the days when the school had initially resisted becoming a comprehensive thirty years before. There had been a major confrontation. County did not like the fact that being a grant maintained school gave us a lot of autonomy. We were highly successful and yet did not buy in to county programmes. It rankled with them.

We'd always born a grudge because we knew we didn't get a fair crack of the whip. Our buildings were dilapidated and it was felt that county starved us of money. Other schools fared a lot better.

None the less I went along to County Hall with what I felt was a good case. As a new Head I was sure they would want to be supportive.

I was ushered into a plush room with oak panels and red leather seats. I spread my paperwork and handouts on the polished wooden table and began to explain out tale of woe to the director of education, his deputy, a senior supervisor and the head of finance. It was quite an intimidating array. I outlined the falling roles, workforce agreement, long term sickness and broken boiler. I asked for emergency funding from the fund set up for just such contingencies. I asked for a loan to see us through and offered them the plan I had come up with to address the short-fall.

I had spent time and effort over the three year plan I had drawn up. I had looked at staffing levels, including not replacing a second deputy, and had schemes to get more bums on seats. I was confident that in a few years I would pull it round. It was all detailed and costed out. It looked sound.

They listened and studied the plans. They fired questions at me and gave me a hard time.

I was still sure that as a new Head, only in post for a matter of weeks, they would want to support me and the school. After all they had the interests of the students at heart as much as we did. Perhaps they just wanted to give me a hard time to ensure I took it seriously.

I endured the ear-bashing in the expectation of getting a sizeable chunk of our debt written off and a loan that would enable to address the deficit in a controlled manner over the next three years.

I was asked to go out and wait.

They conferred.

I was called back in.

No they would not give me any contribution towards the boiler or staff absence from the emergency fund. Further to that they were not prepared to loan money. I had to come up with a plan that would address the shortfall by the following summer – forget the three years I had come up with. They demanded that I instantly invoke redundancy proceedings and look to shed at least five teaching staff if not more.

They were going to send their finance manager in to go through our finances. If I did not come up with an approved plan to instigate redundancies they would have no option but to take over the governing body and enforce their own plan.

I basically had until the next summer and if I had not solved it they were going to take over the school.

I sat there stunned. I could not believe what I was hearing or the attitude with which they were delivering it.

If I introduced a redundancy programme I knew I would lose the support of staff. They were furious enough at having to swallow the five period day. To dump more work, fear and worry on them would have caused morale to collapse. I'd lose the school.

I was in my first term of Headship and I was looking at the possibility of losing the school. That kept going round my head.

I stared back at them with fury building up inside.

I told them in no uncertain terms where they could shove their ultimatum. I told them with plenty of choice words that I didn't need their help and stormed out.

Welcome to Headship.

I went back to school with fresh determination. Fury had fired me up. I stopped the building programme that had been started by Gerry. This money came from a special Government building fund and could only be used for building work but by devising a scheme for extensive building modification and remodelling throughout the school I could use the building money to refurbish and replace furniture. By doing this I reallocated all the money from repairs and maintenance to help plug the debt. It came to about a £100,000 saved. I then clawed back some money spent from capitation on building work the previous year. I cut capitation by 10% and started stripping out every budget I could get my hands on. Every penny counted. I went back to the unions to discuss cover. They refused to budge. I introduced more cover for the senior team. We tried to reduce supply needs as much as possible. I did not advertise for the new deputy. On top of my workload I was now doing more cover than anybody else. I was living on adrenalin.

I put my plans to the governors, (though I think I may have forgotten to tell them about any possible take over!) They were very supportive.

There was no way I was going to allow the school to go under.

By the time I had finished with my measly penny pinching austerity drive I had rescued £250,000. We had got below the £200,000 we were permitted to carry over. Not only that but I had managed it without having to lay off a single member of staff.

County would have to wait if they wanted to take us over.

I turned my attention to more long term solutions.

I could not use the same tactics twice. There were no building programmes to rob next year. We were cut to the bone and there were only two possibilities left: increase student numbers to gain more income or reduce staffing to cut costs, staffing being the bulk of the budget. You could not save much any other way.

I knew that if we reduced staffing it would snowball into disaster. Classes would have to be merged, class sizes would rocket and morale would go through the floor. Once teaching and learning were affected results would plummet, student numbers would drop and we would be in a downward spiral.

A Head is always, no matter how good a school is, one step away from a spiral down into the abyss. All it takes is a financial crisis, a bad set of results or a poor Ofsted. One of these can lead to the others.

I could not bear the thought that I might be the Head to preside over the school as it plummeted.

It was down to me to come up with a plan to attract students in. We had to fill all our year groups and attract students into the sixth form. Our survival depended on it.

I put my energies into doing that.

To attract students in you had to be outstanding, which we were, and you had to sell that to the public. That required a publicity campaign and good PR.

We had to quickly knock the school into better physical shape, get it painted up so it looked good, improve our results and sell it to the public.

I wanted every parent to see that we were a caring community school. I was not prepared to compromise on that for anyone. We were an open, caring friendly school in which their children would be happy and flourish. Not only that but they would be successful into the bargain.

I was not going to pander to the education establishment by focussing purely on results. I was banking on the fact that parents wanted their children to go to a school that focussed on the whole child, where their sons were not going to be bullied and would be cheerful and thrive.

I was not prepared to sacrifice my principles on the altar of dogma. I had introduced my philosophy as a teacher and a deputy. I was now going to live or die by proving it to be correct.

I was determined to run the school on my lines or not at all. I knew I was right. There were more important things than results. However, if I got those things right the results would improve as well.

I set about getting the pastoral, support, attendance, rewards and informal curriculum to function properly.

Education should be fun. I wanted staff to take risks in the classroom and feel secure knowing they would have my support. I wanted passion and energy in the lessons. I wanted active learning.

I wanted a happy school.

I wanted my door open all the time so anybody, student, cleaner or teacher could pop in for a chat.

I smiled and greeted students every day. I smiled and greeted staff. I smiled and greeted parents. I had to mirror what I wanted. I smiled even though inside my stomach was churning and my thoughts reeling. I was in a constant state of panic. I was working fourteen hours a day.

But I knew what I wanted!

I wanted praise and recognition to ring out from every classroom, from every corridor and every assembly. There could not be too much praise and recognition. That simply was not possible. People thrived on praise. It set the tone I wanted for the school.

We were a community. The staff and students were exceptional. I wanted them to know that. Whatever problems we might be facing behind the scenes I wanted the school to be brimming with laughter, full of wear-what-you-like days, concerts, charity events and extra-curricular activities.

Get the ethos right and everything follows.

I would not settle for an ordinary school with ordinary targets – we were to be extraordinary – or bust!

At that point the first thing to bust felt like it was going to be me!

Chapter 3 – Second time of asking

That first half term of my temporary Headship was a nightmare. I had no authority, credibility or self-esteem. The staff were convinced I was going nowhere and they would soon have another Head to deal with. Out of necessity we had brought in too much change too quickly. I was struggling with the commitment to the NPQH, which carried a considerable and unwelcome workload, and always ahead of me was the spectre of my interview. I had no alternative but to apply for my own job and go through the whole nerve-racking business of Headship interviews again. The union had let me down badly and refused to take up my case. They told me it was best to do another interview in order to give me credibility. They may have been right but it did not feel like it. I felt let down by everyone. I'd been given the job. I had the letter to prove it. I had been completely upfront and this had dealt me a heavy blow.

There was animosity and rebellion about the five period day I had introduced and almost delight every time the new 'Serco' computer management system broke down, which it did with monotonous regularity.

I was working myself into the ground, not sleeping and beginning to doubt that I could do the job. Maybe I had reached my level of incompetence? I knew I did not fit the usual model of a Headteacher.

I was beginning to doubt myself as a leader and manager.

The NPQH was exhausting. I was attempting to compile the huge number of files necessary. I was going on the courses. There were reams of files of evidence I had to gather together. Where was the time coming from?

It was the last thing I needed on top of the new role of Headship. I had no personal assistant, only one deputy and a big teaching commitment. On top of that I had to do a whole National Qualification of Headship in a short time. The deadline was unrealistic in the circumstances. The thought of it was making me panic. There was so much hanging on it. If I failed it I was shown up as a fraud and I would have to live with that forever.

The final assessment was going to take place in November. I had to complete the whole course in twelve weeks.

The pressure was building.

My job was advertised. I had a moment of soul-searching in which I wondered whether I really wanted it. But I was too far in now. There was no way I was going to back out. I applied again.

The interview date drew nearer. To add to the pressure County appointed someone to oversee every aspect of the process to ensure it was scrupulously fair. There were six applicants selected for interview and I knew there was no way this was going to be a shoe in.

I reviewed my reasons for introducing the two huge initiatives I had started the year with. It had certainly been ambitious to start with two big school-changing initiatives at the start of a Headship, let alone in the mess-up I found myself. I had started the process full of bravado and brimming with enthusiasm buoyed up with the euphoria of having been appointed Head. I had believed I could do it. Being a lame-duck had made it that much harder. The staff openly questioned my authority.

I stood back from it and reviewed my reasoning. If I was going in to the cauldron of interview I had to be sure that what I was doing was right. I had to believe in it.

I had introduced the five period day in order to broaden the curriculum. It enabled students to take more subjects. They had twenty five lessons a week instead of twenty. The benefit to them was enormous. It also meant that they could gain more passes at GCSE and that was good for them and the school.
Already the benefit to students was obvious.
There were a number of downsides. The lessons were shorter and this really did not suit practical subjects like science, technology, art and P.E although it did suit subjects like modern languages. Some of these down-sides could be alleviated by good time-tabling and others by modifications to lesson planning.
The workload for staff was increased substantially. They had more lessons to plan, deliver and mark. They had to modify their

lesson plans to address the shorter periods. I knew that was not easy and had given them generous non-contact time in order to alleviate the effect. I had not appeased them and I was still fighting a huge groundswell of bad feeling.

I weighed it up and was still happy with it.

I knew that it had to happen. Without it the students would have suffered and there was no chance of getting another good Ofsted inspection. I was convinced I was right.

I reviewed the Serco management system. It was different to systems in other schools but it was much more complicated which was why it kept breaking down. It did a lot more and integrated the attendance, behaviour, rewards, recognition, pastoral care and subject assessment into a whole oversight that enabled better tracking of student progress and the pin-pointing of support (both behaviour and academic) to where it was needed.

The down-sides were that it was so complicated it kept breaking down and it was difficult for staff to operate and understand. It had big training implications and a steep learning curve. But I knew that these were the teething problems of those early days. It would settle and open up a raft of opportunities.

I wanted all my students valued and supported. I knew that when the bugs were ironed out it would be an immensely useful tool for supporting students and that when staff had become used to working it there would be no further workload issues.

I was determined to press ahead despite the staff back-lash and the effect that might have on securing the headship.

The initiatives were right for the students; right for the school and in the long term would prove right for the staff.

I had to ride the unpopularity. It bolstered my resolve.

You would imagine that going through an interview a second time would make it easier – far from it!

My first time through I had been swash-buckling and passionate. I had nothing to lose. If I did not get the job I was happy in my role. If I did not get along with the new Head I could simply retire and do my own thing. I'd put in enough years. I would have been teaching for thirty two years.

That interview had been easy. They couldn't grill me. All I had to do was lay out my wares and explain my philosophy and achievements with verve and belief. I'd sailed through it.

This time it was fraught.

I was no longer a deputy, full of confidence and at the top of my game; I was an acting Head who had been battered by ten weeks of hell. I had the staff in uproar, a financial crisis and the school teetering. I was utterly exhausted and my self-esteem had never been lower.

I knew there was at least one candidate who might give me a good run for my money and I knew that the governors could easily be swayed. I'd been through that on a number of occasions in the past particularly when I had been knocked back as a temporary deputy and they had appointed an outsider.

This time I had nowhere to go if I failed. I could not go back to being a deputy as a failure. That would never have worked. I would have to retire.

I am not quite sure how I got through that second Headship interview.

This time I had nothing to gain; I could only lose. My nerves were shot to pieces, workload was unbelievable and my stress levels off the chart. Yet there could be no excuses. I had to go in to the interview and perform.

I knew the governors were receiving reports of staff unrest. That didn't help. The more vociferous were making their views known. It was also obvious that there was a strong candidate who was excellent. She would push me all the way. Even my deputy was taken with her.

I had to put everything to one side, stand up and seize the moment; I had to be calm, lucid, passionate and display the vision, management skills and leadership that had got me the position in the first place.

There was no way that I did as well at that interview but I did well enough. I had also gained my NPQH after a further gruelling interview and presentation and so I was duly appointed as Head. Now the staff knew I was in charge. My name finally went up on the door to my study and was carved into the oak panels in the Hall.

I was official at last. I was the Headteacher.

The worst was yet to come.

There were huge psychological reactions to being a Headteacher. I could feel the shift as soon as I was appointed for real. I was used to students calling me sir but was thrown when colleagues I'd worked with for decades started doing it. At first I resisted and reminded them to call me Chris. After a while I realised that it was fulfilling a need. They needed to call me Sir. They needed someone in charge who was controlling things. It made them feel right. I had to fill that role.

The second thing was the strange reaction of my friends. They had coped with me being a deputy but to them headship was a different kettle of fish. They did not know how to react. It was as if I had become a different person. They saw me in a different light. Some actually began to treat me differently. Some stopped communicating. Some treated me with greater respect. There was even a snobbish element that I found distasteful.

The third issue was how I was now considered to have moved up a notch in the great strata of society. I was now worthy of notice. I was now to be approached for the Masons, Rotary Club and Colonel Blimp's annual dinner party. I had suddenly become someone important.

At first I found it amusing. But beneath that I was appalled. It was revealing of the whole way this rotten system operates. This network of almost secret, exclusive 'Old Boys' pulled the strings, scratched each others' backs and maintained the status quo.

I made it quite clear that I would have nothing to do with any of it. I would not be attending dinners or any exclusive clubs. I considered them part of the canker that rots the whole stinking society.

I stood for fairness and equality. I live by it and I will die by it!

I survived the first term. From there on it had to be downhill – didn't it?

Chapter 4 – Relationship, Ethos and Philosophy

If you want to be a Head you have to have balls – balls to stand up for what you believe in – balls to do what is right. The vultures of reactionary establishment will pick your bones clean unless you are prepared to take them on and outmanoeuvre them. Failing that you can simply opt in, follow the rules and regulations to the letter, and settle for mediocrity.

Following the rules is no way to create excellence.

In 1978, at the suggestion of my wife Liz, I applied for and was accepted on a teacher exchange programme to the good old USA. In 1979, having been teaching for four years, we set off, three young children in tow, to teach in Norwalk Los Angeles.

My introduction to the school was a prolonged staff meeting discussing gang activity, guns, knives and what to do when petrol was poured over both exit doors from your classroom and set alight. It made me wonder what I had let myself into. Norwalk had the highest gang related killings in the whole USA. In my first week there an innocent boy was executed in the park opposite the school in broad daylight. He was chased, caught, bent over the bonnet of a car and shot through the head because he was wearing the wrong colour sweatshirt. He was new to the area. It was a case of mistaken identity. He did not even know about the gangs let alone what colours they wore.

During my second week I was taking roll-call. Every lesson started with a roll-call. The school was paid by the number of bums on seats per day. If you could get a student in school for just a few minutes the funding was secured. The first task was to ring in for the office to chase up absentees. They had twenty five secretaries poised to do this.

I called out the names and checked off the register.

'Heeey' a girl called out. I looked up. A slim blond girl was standing in the aisle, legs splayed and two hands held out in front of her pointing a handgun directly at me.

It is quite amazing how quickly your mind works when faced with a life-threatening situation.

I had only been there a few days. I could not possibly have annoyed anyone that much. I was the new Englishman. She was after scaring the shit out of me. I was expected to panic.

The whole classroom was watching.

'Put it away and sit down,' I instructed, looking her straight in the eyes. Inside my heart was doing thundering impersonations of Ginger Baker's drum solo in Toad but I knew it was imperative to keep calm.

I continued with the list before me, never raising my eyes from the page. When I had finished I looked up. The girl had sat down and the gun was no longer visible. I organised the class and strolled over, in as nonchalant a manner as I could muster to the girl who was now getting on with her work as if nothing had happened.

I stood over her but she did not look up.

'That was remarkably silly,' I told her in a quiet voice. 'If I had pressed the button you would have been arrested and out of here.' There was a panic button on my desk. If pressed trained security guards would have rushed in and dealt with things.

'It wasn't loaded,' she replied in a surly off-hand voice.

'I might have had a gun in my drawer. I didn't know yours wasn't loaded. I could have blown you away.'

She looked up at me with a look of amusement. The very idea was completely comical.

'Don't ever do anything like that again,' I said and walked off.

It made my year. If I had followed procedure her life would have been different and I would have had a shitty year.

Teaching is about relationship and choices of action.

I will repeat this a lot: - teaching is all about relationship. Without a nourishing relationship based on mutual respect between students and teachers you cannot achieve good learning whatever system you deploy. Learning stems from relationship. Relationship develops from attitude and personality. A teacher has to give and share of themselves. They have to care. It is the hardest and most worthwhile job in the world. Without care and compassion the classroom is a prison for both teacher and students.

Nothing can work unless it is based on a clear philosophy that is understood by all concerned and agreed by the majority.

Within every institution there will be a number of dissenters who do not agree with the stated philosophy. These dissenters need to be won over, disarmed or dismissed.

There are some bullying teachers who seek to run their classroom with a rod of iron, shouting in students' faces and intimidating everyone. They firmly believe this is how it should be done. They see themselves as the strong authority figure. What they say goes. According to them if kids did as they were told there wouldn't be any problems.

What they don't seem to realise that if everyone behaved like they do the school would be unbearable. I was brought up in a school like that. It bred belligerence, rebellion and anger.

Students would store up their pent up frustration and fear and take it out on everyone else in a hierarchy of displacement behaviour.

When I first arrived at the Grammar School in 1975 there were fights most break-times and a cold, macho atmosphere. Bullying was rampant. This is the result of too much classroom intimidation and too rigid systems.

The bullying teachers thought themselves strong. They controlled their classroom. There was no dissent. It ran like clockwork. Many of the students admired the control exerted and respected the order. One thing students do not like is a teacher who does not control a class. A class has to be controlled. That is fundamental. My point is entirely based on how this is done. Bullying should not be an option.

The bullying teachers openly spoke disparagingly of other teachers and undermined them whenever possible.

For the teachers in the wake of these classroom bully teachers life was hard. They would receive a class all pent up and frustrated. The resultant disorderly lessons were merely viewed as evidence that everyone should be adopting a forceful approach. Their view was 'Students needed to know, in no uncertain terms, who was the boss'.

I experienced my share of classroom bullying when I was at school and I know how it made me feel. Back then I simmered with anger, fury and resentment. The fact that, as a small boy, I was impotent to answer back or stand up to the teacher bullies made it worse. I resented them and hated them with a vengeance. I used every means to undermine, disrupt and oppose. I adopted sullen and open disdain. There was nothing I enjoyed more that standing there looking those teachers straight in the eye, replying 'Yes Sir' in a slurred, sneer of disrespect that would send them incandescent with impotence. I took immense pleasure from making them apoplectic through a display of controlled defiance while doing nothing overtly wrong. It was all about attitude. No amount of intimidation or punishment was effective with me. The pleasure I gained from getting through to them was ample compensation for any punishment they dished out. This hatred even went as far as puncturing tyres with a penknife and scraping car bodywork I am ashamed to say.

Indeed my hatred for those 'little Hitlers' was so great that if one of those three evil bastards from my childhood classrooms were to walk into a room, unlikely I know, as they must be all long dead by now, I would have great trouble controlling my fury. Just thinking about them raises my blood pressure. To this very day if I was asked to put a list of the worlds most evil people it would, of course, include such beasts as Pol Pot, Stalin, Hitler, and Vlad the Impaler, but it would also include those three teachers.

It seems incredible to me that they should still engender such bitter hatred fifty years on. But I still hate them with a passion. These were people who were supposed to be my role models, my carers, my teachers. Instead they were terrorisers and arrogant abusers of children. All three of them were traumatised ex-soldiers who thought children were lesser beings to be abused at will. All three of them deserved lengthy prison sentences for systematic child abuse.

It made my blood boil when I heard the government talking about bringing ex-soldiers back into the classroom to restore discipline. Yes, that's just what we need - a good dose of bullying intimidation. Let's bring back the cane while we're at it, and don't stop there, we can go the whole hog and run a series of approved schools and compulsory conscription. Put the miscreants in stocks and get the whole school to throw rotten fruit at them. That'd bring them back into line.

In my experience classes and individuals have a psychological snapping point. They stand up to the classroom teacher tyrant and take them on. The students challenge the teacher's power and their perceived right to intimidate. Sometimes this is down out of sheer fury. Sometimes it is a realisation that the bullying teacher is operating on sheer bluff – there is a limit to their power. If a student refuses to be intimidated they are powerless.

I have seen deputy heads in nose to nose confrontations, incensed with fury but having to back down. I have seen classes openly defiant and sneeringly disdainful to the point of complete chaos in the face of extreme threats from a castrated teacher. They become uncontrollable. I have seen individuals caned and leave the room arrogantly laughing and basking in the glory from their fellow students.

There is a limit to the power of intimidation.

There is no limit to the power of love.

The only thing I learnt from my childhood experiences with the education system in which bullying and violence were embedded; boring, repetitive memory retention and endless copying were the methodology, and cold strict discipline and heartless control was the order of the day, was that there had to be a better way.

I was going to prove there was a better way!

It seemed to me that the system was obsessed with control and the destruction of the individual. We were crammed into a routine and made into faceless robots.

As a child I had refused to be a cog in such a vicious, heartless machine.

I had refused to be a clone in a militaristic uniform.

I had refused to be broken by petty rules and systematic intimidation.

I rebelled.

Now my rebellion had made me a Headteacher! There's irony in that!

I remember Patrick McGoohan bringing out a series called 'The Prisoner'. I adored it. To this day I have a sticker on my desk that proudly and defiantly states: 'I am not a number I am a free man.'

I became obsessed with devising an effective education system that was fair and respectful and one that worked better than that vicious sausage machine.

I wanted enlightened education.

I was sure that most parents did not really want their children to go to institutions that terrorised them and trampled their spirits into blind compliance. They wanted their children to be liberated, inspired, loved, filled with self-esteem, and raised to their potential.

They did not want a factory that churned out exam results but reduced their children's personalities to mindless automatons.

I was also sure that (particularly the parents of students who would not get into selective grammar school system) they would not want a system that wrote off ninety percent of kids so that the esteemed ten percent could prosper.

I believe elitism creates resentment and failure.

I believe it could be done in a different way. My vision is of a comprehensive system with mixed ability teaching that promotes equality and breeds success.

A teacher could run a classroom with authority and respect without having to become a bully.

We could provide a loving, caring, respectful environment based around awe-inspiring lessons and creativity in which the whole child could develop into a beautiful adult.

Human beings have a history of cruelty, viciousness and destruction.

The world we have created is fuelled by aggression, violence, selfishness and greed. It is a world of exploitation, war and power largely dominated by psychologically damaged males.

It is my belief that the bullying environment we bring our children up in contributes to this.

If human beings, if nature, has a future we have to become civilised; we have to learn to live together in harmony and peace; we have to look at the bigger picture and put things right on the small stage. Schools are instrumental in changing the world. Without an education system based on love, compassion, empathy, tolerance and the development of the whole child I really believe we have no future on this planet. In thirty years time 7 billion of us will become 14 billion, nature will be consumed and we will then destroy each other with our own hatred as we compete for ever dwindling resources.

There is an alternative.

Enlightened education is the only answer.

The basis behind everything is philosophy. You have to start there. You sort out your philosophy and everything else evolves from that.

The philosophies I applied in my career were simple and basic. They stemmed from my upbringing, my beliefs and my experience. Above all my experiences in the world of education have added spice to my views. They are the same values I bring to all of my life: I did not need any religious moral code to arrive at it. It is pure common sense:

Everything should be fair

All people are equally valuable

Living things should be respected

Everything can be made better

Education should be fun and expanding

That is all. Everything stems from this; all the systems in the school; the way lessons are run; the way miscreants are dealt with - everything.

There were many dissenters. These included some of the 'old guard' who had become disillusioned and now saw it as a fairly well paid job and did not really care; the arrogant who saw some students as worthwhile and others as scum; the unimaginative who saw things in black and white and who believed that what the school really needed was a series of checklists and a set of intransigent rules – as if all students and incidents could be crammed into a mould; and the bullies who believed that what the buggers really needed was a dose of good old fashioned punishment and discipline.

One thing I was sure of was that you could not run an establishment using draconian control to enforce your views. It was no good espousing one set of values and living by another.

As a Head you had to be strong without being a tyrant. You had to live by the values you were putting forward. The philosophy was a living thing. There were no easy, overnight methods for dealing with the myriad problems and obstructions that prevented everyone pulling together to create the perfect school.

You had to argue your case and seek a degree of consensus. I was determined not to force my views on others.

From day one I set about freeing the students from the strictures of a failed system. That failed system was the 1950s model which had so utterly failed me and my fellow students; a system that enabled a chosen elite to prosper at the expense of the rest; an education system that was one great mind-destroying memory test drummed in through numbing repetition and tedious copying and memorising of facts.

Education was too important to be at the beck and call of politicians. We had to wrest it back from them and instil it with life and vitality.

Back in college me and my best friend Pete Smith, who later went on to found 'Wild Science', were of the same opinion – that the education system was boring and unfair; it reduced people and subjects down to less than what they were and needed overhauling. Pete dropped out to do it – I dropped in. I wanted to see if the madmen could successfully take over the institution.

The first step was to transform the philosophy into a working ethos that could begin to permeate the whole school. I had introduced this as a senior teacher and lowly member of the senior team fourteen years before I became a Head. The result was a stated ethos discussed and shared with all staff and students which took the form of a mission statement:

A friendly, open caring and successful school

A school offering equal opportunity for all

A school which values the complete development of all students and staff

A school committed to the continual raising of standards

This was thrashed out through repeated meetings with lots of healthy argument. As far as I was concerned it had to stem from my philosophy. That's what I fought for. As long as the caring, fairness and development was in there they could have their standards. For me the standards would come out of the process. If our students felt valued, respected and cared for and experienced lessons that were fun and thought provoking the results would follow. We did not have to focus on teaching and learning; we had to focus on excitement and challenge. If students were engaged and excited by education learning would take place.

OUR VISION FOR THE FUTURE

We aim to be a school where:-

- The education process is enjoyable to all concerned

- Students and staff are able to flourish and fulfil their potential

- Students, staff, parents and governors show mutual respect and support

- We are proud of our current achievements as well as our past tradition

- We always strive to improve standards and raise levels of achievement

- We have an open admissions policy up to an agreed admissions limit

- Our Joint Sixth Form continues to thrive and develop

- We retain the character and benefits of a small school

- We foster and develop positive links with the community

It was a start. The important thing was to involve everyone, value their input and be prepared to compromise so that they had ownership while remaining true to the basic philosophy. The fact that it involved everyone in putting it together meant that they all had a vested interest in making it work. Many of the potential dissenters were brought into consensus. We had fun, respect and care agreed by all staff. We could build on it.

The way to disaster is to impose change or philosophy. That results in lip-service. If everyone is unhappy or pulling in different directions nothing will gel.

The staff of any institution are made up of a great number of personality types. In order to be effective these have all got to be harnessed and unified. I found this out early on when introducing school dances. School dances had been unruly, troublesome affairs that the staff hated and refused to give up their time for. I wanted to reintroduce them with live bands. I made my case that the students deserved them and they would energise the school. Some were swayed over by my enthusiasm and argument that the kids would love them and it would feed into better relationships. I discovered that if I brought in an intricate, well thought through system that demonstrated I had addressed all possible eventualities, provided adequate cover and a range of patrolling likely to prevent trouble, all done with charts, lists, teams and detailed organisation I won over a number of the more logically minded who were sceptical of enthusiasm. They pawed over my intricate diagrams, rotas and arrangements, offered improvements and we were away. It was a lesson to me.

It is all about detailed planning, open discussion, compromise and taking account of the range of different views and personalities. You can never win them all over though but gaining a majority gives you credibility.

From the moment the vision was passed by the school everything that took place in it emanated from those words no matter how difficult that became. If it wasn't open, caring and friendly it wasn't worth a fig. If it wasn't fair it had no place. If lessons weren't fun and challenging they were worthless.

For my part as a Head this meant doing lots of things that made my life a lot harder but demonstrated clearly that I believed those words were more than words - that I believed in every letter of them. They were probably things that most people never noticed, took for granted or thought were plain daft.

As a deputy and a Head I was Mr open, caring friendly.

The most important thing I did was to smile and greet each and every student as often as I could. I positioned myself at the beginning of the day in the corridor and said hello to everyone. Gradually the majority, who had sidled past in silent embarrassment, began to smile and say hello back. It was friendly and respectful. It was nice. No matter how stressed and unhappy I felt I tried to project a positive attitude and quiet assurance. I can't begin to tell you how difficult this was at those times when your stress levels were through the roof, your morale and confidence was rock bottom, and you didn't know if you were going to survive the week.

I toured the school saying hello to staff and students and asking how they were. I was not checking on how well they were teaching or what they were doing but in the process I picked up how they were feeling and the mood. I could tell by walking into a classroom and sensing the atmosphere if things were right or not. I got to know the potential of my staff and who was underperforming.

I treated non-teaching staff with the same respect as teaching staff. We were all one team working for the good of the kids. They were equally important in creating the atmosphere and learning environment of the school. They were human beings of equal value to everyone else. They were doing a range of sometimes unpleasant jobs, pressured jobs, and difficult jobs, often underappreciated and certainly incredibly poorly paid. They deserved equal respect.

I talked to all staff in a friendly informal manner.

I talked to students and staff who held diametrically opposed views to my own. I gave them a platform and listened. I argued forcefully but I did not impose my views. I did instruct them how I wanted students talked to and dealt with though. I wanted them treating with respect. Shouting at students was strongly denounced.

My door was always open so that staff and students could drop in without appointment. If they were upset it was important that I gave my time and listened. I could then address problems and comfort people. It meant that most things could be nipped in the bud before they started to fester.

I politely insisted on certain standards, shirts being tucked in, ties done up, students not pushing and shoving, an orderly passage in our crowded corridors. I wanted a degree of smartness with a modicum of individuality. The students still had their bracelets, weird hairstyles and accoutrements. We could have standards without it becoming claustrophobically draconian. I knew from my own school days that pushing too hard on this led to student anger and rebellion. They resented it. It did not promote the harmony of relationship I was seeking. Yet there was room for a compromise. We had to have certain standards and they had to be enforced. If I did that enforcing, in a polite reasoned manner, then the staff would as well. If we had a polite orderliness then there was a good environment for learning. Students might not like this but would accept it if it was done well. Most staff ducked confrontations with students but I felt that as long as there were collectively agreed rules we should abide by them. If I had my way I would have done away with uniform altogether. There are countries were the education is extremely effective without having to resort to the de-individualisation of uniforms. I hate uniforms. However, the minor confrontations established authority so that when bigger issues arose the authority was already firmly recognized and subsequent behaviour patterns fell into place more easily. I was careful not to allow this to become heavy handed or disrespectful. It was not a power tool. This was an area I had rebelled at whilst at school. I could understand the feelings of the students. But I also knew that it gave them something to rebel against.

I signed each and every one of hundreds of certificates by hand. It would have been easy to save myself hours of mindless signing but I was mindful of the DJ Alan Freed. He had always played his records in the studio while they went out on air. Other DJ's would turn the sound off. He explained that, when questioned as to why he did this, 'the listeners knew when you weren't listening'. I think they did. They could tell if you cared and were enjoying it or not or merely going through the motions. For me, if a student was prepared to put in a term's worth of sustained effort the least I could do was to recognise that with a simple signature.

I tried hard to not just focus on the staff and students I liked best but to give time to the ones I didn't like quite as much - the miserable and dissenting. Only through open communication could you change people. If persuasion didn't work imposition would merely inflame. The only way forward was through open dialogue. If dialogue was suppressed there would be a worthless dictatorship that would be destined to achieve mediocrity. No matter how frustrating or antagonistic someone was being they had to have the opportunity to speak their mind. I would listen and take on board what they were saying, weigh it up, and if I disagreed I'd explain my feelings.

I always apologised if I got things wrong. If you do stuff you get stuff wrong! I found I was often having to say sorry.

I fought for all those things that meant something to me, that emanated from that ethos of fairness, such as mixed ability teaching, effort assessment (and not achievement), PSHE, a pastoral care and support system based on remedial action, support and relationship rather than punishment. I was delighted when this started coming through as restorative practice and SEAL. These are two of the best initiatives there had ever been. They mirror my own beliefs. They are transformative. Forget your teaching and learning – education is about relationship! Often these things are not universally popular. Headship is not about always making popular decisions. It is about making decisions that are right for the students. The students must always come first. When there were issues that were unpopular then I tried to discuss and explain rather than impose.

Management is also about relationship.

Gradually the ethos permeated everything that went on in the school. Over time the dissenters on the staff moved on and were replaced by staff whose appointment I oversaw. I appointed people who fitted it. My key criterion was not their ability to teach their subject, though of course that had to be a consideration, but if they were the types of personalities that fitted in with our ethos. I'd rather have a good teacher with the right attitude that a great teacher with the wrong attitude. We were building an institution that was a community. It was important that we were all pulling in the same direction.

Over a period of years the school became a happy, welcoming place to work in and be educated in. It was a fun place where the right kind of education could take place.

My philosophy was proving effective in raising examination results, as well as improving staff and student well-being and the development of the whole child. Our students were getting a reputation for being polite, articulate, welcoming, friendly and delightful to teach. They were bursting with creativity and self-esteem. They were not arrogant, selfish or aggressive but were self-assured and inquisitive. They were tolerant but critical of injustice.

They were proud of their school and ready to make a mark in the world.

They were not cowed, bullied or uncared for. They felt loved.

These were precisely the people I wanted in charge of the planet.

They fill me with pride and hope for the future.

They are outstanding.

Chapter 5 - The Purpose of Education

It always seems to me that this is where everyone gets confused. Everyone talks about education as if they are talking about the same thing. They are not.

Politicians rant about league tables and world standing without any understanding of what they are talking about.

Parents send their children apprehensively into the machine with a modicum of hope but no real understanding of what they are hoping for.

Students are consumed by the process without grasping what is actually happening to them.

The measurable outcomes are easy to assess and so are given greater importance. The aspects that are not measurable are sometimes acknowledged but usually taken for granted and brushed aside. You cannot measure happiness, empathy, responsibility and tolerance.

Industry cries out for more and better grist for the mill. We in education are always falling short. The economy requires more fodder. Students become numbers to be crunched, pegs to be slotted, and material to feed the machine of commerce.

Most importantly students are people; they should be happy, well adjusted, creative and inspiring citizens who care!

There needs to be a national debate.

There needs to be an international debate.

Everything stems from philosophy.

We have to stand back from it so that we can view the edifice of education objectively.

What is the purpose of education?

This is something that needs looking at from all sides. Out of this debate there must be some consensus and the application of intelligence. We can no longer allow education to be the football of political dogma and vested interest. It has to be based on sound philosophy and placed in the hands of educationalists who know what they are doing.

So what needs to be considered? Let us look at education in the widest possible light. By exposing the various philosophies we might explore them better. I do not necessarily agree all these objectives nor do I place them in any order. Indeed I abhor some of them. I merely moot them as considerations in order for us to debate the enormity of this subject. We cannot arrive at consensus without taking into account the full panoply of views. By looking at the monolithic construction that education has become from different angles we might begin to make sense of it.

Here are my views on what various interested parties view as being the fundamental purpose of education:

a. For enjoyment
b. To prepare students for jobs and careers in the modern world
c. To prepare students for life in the 21st century
d. To provide the basic needs for participating in a technological society – reading, writing, arithmetic and computer competency
e. To assume a place in society as a positive citizen – moral, sexual and political.
f. To stimulate imagination and creativity
g. To grade students so that future universities and employers can easily judge their competence
h. To create a hierarchy of status in society
i. To provide the skills, verbal and practical, that are required by employers, society and individuals
j. To broaden the mind and open it up to further understanding
k. To create wonder and awe.
l. To understand science and technological advances
m. To understand history and learn from it so that we do not make the same mistakes
n. To absorb knowledge so that it can be processed internally and synergistically used to arrive at new understanding
o. To explore feelings so that emotions can be understood and mastered

p. To explore love, sex and relationships so that adults and children can have better experiences

q. To promote the sheer love of a subject

r. To stimulate intelligence and an inquisitive mind

s. To satisfy the love of learning

t. To stimulate the love of reading where-in all human experience, the highest thoughts and aspirations, and our dreams are contained

u. To foster an appreciation of the arts as the highest, most civilised expression of humanity

v. To investigate morality so that we might build a better, fairer society

w. To foster tolerance so that we never experience racism, sexism, religious intolerance, homophobia, war, persecution or slavery again in human history

x. To socialise people so that they are able to enjoy the company of others from all strata and types of society

y. To teach teamwork and cooperation, so essential to human achievement

z. To enable the enjoyment of sport and play in all its varieties

aa. To teach about health and fitness so that we can lead vital pleasurable lives

bb. To foster an appreciation of the pleasures of life – literature, food, wine, theatre, opera, music, drama and good company

cc. To care for the environment so that future generations can enjoy the planet

dd. To consider all the issues that threaten life on this planet: overpopulation, pollution, war, species annihilation, overcrowding, poverty, terrorism, and so on – so that we might find solutions

ee. To consider political systems and analyse their effectiveness so that we might produce better systems.

ff. To objectively look at party politics and understand what different political factions stand for so that we might all be better equipped to function in a true democracy.

gg. To investigate capitalism and the world of big business to better understand how the world is organised and run

hh. To promote empathy, responsibility, tolerance, respect and care

ii. To build self-esteem

jj. To foster alert, lively minds who are optimistic and ready to step forward to push back the frontiers with imagination, creativity and exuberance

I am sure there are others to add to this list. Perhaps you could tick the ones you agree with?

There are some that I believe have no place in education. I do not believe that religion should be allowed anywhere near young vulnerable minds. There is no room for outmoded, primitive superstition in schools. It should be outlawed.

As for religious schools and the brainwashing of young children I view these as child abuse.

Too many minds are stultified by poor education techniques, their imaginations sacrificed on the altar of rote learning for league tables, and their enjoyment strangled.

The cleverest boy in my childhood secondary school was a genius. He passed every exam with a clear grade A. He was also a joyless, timid, and boring individual without spark or passion and was unemployable except to stoke the icy furnaces of academia or the depths of library archives. Heaven help us if we churn out such vacuous products of stifling education systems. He was an utter failure.

So that list and more make up the purpose of education. People have differing views. I know what I believe is important and I have heard what varying politicians believe.

It's time we discussed it openly and fully.

Let the debate begin ……………….. please!!

Chapter 6 – PSHE and drugs

I was a young teacher in my second year of teaching. The current Headteacher Mr Walton had decided that the field should be out of bounds. The wet weather had created such muddy conditions that the classrooms and corridors were becoming caked with mud. He informed the staff that anyone walking on the grass would be caned. He was hoping this deterrent would solve the problem.

He hadn't reckoned with Terry. He was a young student from the new comprehensive intake who had been a problem from the start and was no respecter of rules. Indeed it appeared that Terry regarded rules as a challenge. He earned the respect of his fellow students by flouting rules with blatant disdain.

Terry was the perennial thorn in the side of the school. He was loud, aggressive, rude and surly. He disrupted lessons, picked fights and openly defied everyone and everything.

I was walking down the corridor when I was asked by the Head to assist with the apprehension of young Terry. He had been brought to the Head for flagrantly walking on the grass and when he had ascertained his fate he had promptly got up and run away. This was not playing the game. The Head was used to Grammar School boys. They took their punishment like a man. They didn't run away!

We went hunting for Terry.

Soon Terry was found. But Terry refused to come quietly and what followed is indelibly imprinted in my mind.

Two burly male teachers marched Terry down the corridor to the Head's study. Terry was screaming and struggling. When he started kicking out at the two staff two other male staff grabbed his ankles and lifted him off the ground. He was carried headfirst, screaming and writhing along the corridor and he was manhandled into the study. I followed in the wake.

By this time the Head had become angry. His authority had been challenged. What originally was one stripe was now six. He intended to make an example of Terry.

The four male staff had to drag Terry to the desk and physically restrain him by all four limbs; each taking an ankle or wrist and tugging so that Terry was pinned across the desk like a frog awaiting dissection. All the while Terry continued to shriek and struggle to his utmost. He certainly had a florid vocabulary for a thirteen year old.

The Head retreated to the other side of the room and then ran, jumped in the air and brought the cane swishing through the air with all the force he could muster.

Terry screamed and went taut in some great spasm. Then he resumed his struggles in a futile desperate attempt to free himself from the four staff.

The Head repeated this five more times.

At the end of it they let Terry loose and he stood in the doorway with knotted fists and purple face swearing at the six of us.

Some say that caning does no harm. That it is a deterrent. The blood running down Terry's legs from the split skin on his bum was not the harm. In my opinion the hatred and loathing in his mind were the injuries that would leave the everlasting scars. They wouldn't heal.

As for deterrence – it was the same string of surly, defiant individuals who were paraded for beatings every week.

I'd never heard of PSE as it was then called. I was a biology teacher.

In the normal course of my lessons I came to the section on reproduction and as a natural part of the lesson opened up various discussions on sex and rounded it off with a lesson on contraception and sexually transmitted disease.

The lads seemed to appreciate it. Some of the questions were obviously geared to attempting to cause me embarrassment but when I fielded them honestly they realised that I wasn't going to get phased by it. It was obvious to me that there was a huge level of ignorance and interest and a great need.

This was before the age of the internet, in a post-60s culture which still had vestiges of 1950s prim prudishness. Information and contraception were not easy to get hold of. Sex was not freely discussed. They were desperate for frank discussion and advice and very receptive.

I thought no more of it.

Mike my head of department, who wandered in and out of my lab while I was teaching, had noted that I was doing sex education with the lads.

'Does the Head know you're doing this?' He asked.

'No,' I replied slightly baffled. Why should the Head know? It was only sex education. Most schools in the country were doing it.

'I think you'd better check with him first.'

I went and checked. He said NO.

Introducing sex education was a major event. We had to get a majority of the staff in favour of such a controversial venture. He agreed to put it on the staff meeting agenda for discussion.

The staff meeting agenda went up and sure enough there it was at number 11.

We had our meeting and went through seven items.

'Ah well' I thought. 'It will be featured next time.'

The next staff meeting came round and it was now number 14. Seemingly lots of really important issues had come up and required urgent attention.

The following staff meeting had fifteen items but sex education was not one of them.

I fumed.

I drew up a list of staff and went round to discuss sex education with all of them one by one. I even included both deputies. By the end of a week I had the agreement of every member of staff with only two abstentions, both of whom were catholics who abstained on religious grounds.

I went back to the Head and presented him with the fait accompli. I softened it by explaining that it was obvious that there wasn't time to discuss it at staff meetings with all the pressing issues that had to be addressed. The crux of the matter was that the staff were almost unanimous.

He blustered.

It would need governors' approval. I would have to take my case to the governing body.

I produced a presentation and amazingly won the approval of the governing body.

At my next meeting with the Head I may have inadvertently had a slight air of triumph.

That was soon put to rest.

The governors were only the first obstacle; the whole idea had to be put to parents. It was obvious from his attitude that he felt confident the parents would disapprove.

Unfazed I drafted a letter to parents with a reply slip and had it sent out.

Miraculously there were no objections and most gave their approval.

I once again returned to the Head's study.

'You know, Chris,' he said thoughtfully, finally admitting defeat. 'These lads are red blooded Englishmen. You can't tell me that they can watch films of young girls masturbating without being affected.'

I sat there staring at him.

It was obvious that he had not read any of my information and had his own idea of what was involved in sex education. In his mind sex education equated with pornography. His mind had gone down the line that I would be showing pornographic films to the boys.

It had taken me a year and a half to get approval. I realised, in that moment, that a little bit more verbal explanation might have saved a lot of effort.

PSE (or PSHE, PSHCE, SPACE – whatever you want to call it) is the most important subject in the curriculum. It is not a subject at all. It is life.

PSHE should never be a subject that leads to an examination; that would demean it and prevent the freewheeling', far-ranging potential that each lesson should have.

PSHE should always be taught in a room that is conducive to creating close relationship with students in an environment that promotes discussion and interaction.

PSHE is the most difficult subject to 'teach' and can only be successfully taught by teachers with the right sensitivities, skills and attitude. It is as specialist a subject as astrophysics. The vast majority of staff are entirely unsuited to teach PSHE.

As the most important subject in the curriculum it should be given pride of place. Time-tablers should start by putting the PSHE lessons in first, in prime times, early morning, and in suitable rooms. Then they can move on to the lesser subjects such as maths, music, French, science, English and the rest.

PSHE specialist staff should be carefully identified and fully trained.

If there are no suitable staff an urgent recruitment should take place.

Why do I think it is so important when most schools give it such short shrift and even students do not value it?

Most subjects deal with information and skills pertaining to specific interests and careers. PSHE deals with life and death. It is fundamental to how people live their lives, form relationships, involve themselves with the big issues and develop the skills, qualities and sensibilities to lead a fulfilled, productive life. It is real.

As a PSHE teacher I have dealt with health, cancer, death, heart disease, bereavement, relationships, divorce, work, reality, reasons for living, depression, suicide, purpose of life, spirituality, climatic issues, love, fascism, politics, diet, human behaviour, war, nuclear disaster, pollution, extinction, intelligence, cruelty, drugs, alcohol, smoking, friendships, parenthood, contraception, STDs, bear-baiting, racism, abortions, sexism, revision, mortgages, salaries and expenses, managing anger, pornography, female pornography, psychology and the reasons we humans do all the weird, vicious and wonderful things we do.

My lessons were based on tolerance, respect, empathy, responsibility, awe and wonder.

PSHE deals with the reality of life and helps people find their way to a meaningful existence, find harmony and balance and explore why we do the things we do in the hope we can do better.

PSHE helps mend broken people.

We are all damaged by life.

Many of our young people are scarred from bereavement, abuse, abandonment, divorce and horrid experiences. PSHE lets them know that they are not alone and helps guide them through the difficult stuff. It gives them succour and support.

Sadly I have witnessed PSHE taught by idiots who do not understand what they are doing.

I have seen it time-tabled for last lesson Friday. I have seen it reduced to the 'worksheets of death'. I have seen it reduced to a series of instructions. I have seen it time-tabled in laboratories. I have seen it 'bought in' with a series of dire outside 'experts' who have no relationship with the students.

PSHE should be illuminating.

It is the heart of the school.

As a PSHE teacher you don't know what is going to happen. You fly by the seat of your pants. You get kids in a circle to introduce a topic. It can veer off in any direction – from raising a family to aging and dying – from revision to the meaning of life – from why we developed religion to infinity and parallel universes. People talk about their emotions, desires and feelings and open themselves up. A PSHE teacher shares of their own experience; they give of themselves.

A PSHE teacher has no hidden agenda. Their job is not to stop people having sex, taking drugs, smoking or drinking. A PSHE teachers helps students explore the issues and arrive at their own personal decisions. A PSHE teacher plays devil's advocate, raises things to consider, and allows investigation of all sides of an argument. They take no sides, have no points of view and are there to expertly facilitate exploration.

By 'teaching' PSHE you learn much about yourself and your own views and learn so much more from the students.

Other teachers have often said that they teach these elements in their subject areas.

That might be true.

They teach these elements – PSHE 'explores' them.

I'd been teaching more and more sexual, health and social issues in the course of my biology teaching and was pushing for a separate PSE subject to be included on the curriculum.

The pressure came from outside. In the late 1970s the government was pushing it.

A new PSE programme was introduced and I got to teach the sex and health modules. Another member of staff, who had no real interest or knowledge, was placed in charge on a high promotion scale. Ho hum.

As a Headteacher my principle job was to ensure that the heart of the school was sound. PSHE was the heart of the school. It fitted with SEAL, restorative practice, Student Voice and a healthy pastoral support system to deliver care and remedial action.

To deliver these extraordinarily important areas you needed extraordinary people. We were lucky. I had found a unique person to deliver PSHE, champion SEAL, Student Voice and restorative practice. Rebecca's energy pervaded the school and the relationships with students were beyond anything I had ever personally seen. She was a whirlwind of risk taking energy. The only downside was that her huge success and popularity with students sparked jealousy among other staff. They resented her appeal. I think she made them feel inept. She is destined to become the most inspiring Headteacher there will ever be.

The caring aspects of education were always priority number one. The curriculum and teaching and learning were way down the list. If you had the ethos of the school functioning maximally the attainment would automatically follow.

As a Head I continued to teach PSHE, I appointed highly capable staff to teach the strands I could not cover and I refused to allow any old tutor to get involved. They were invariably not merely useless, they were often destructive. PSHE requires specialist staff.

I introduced circle time, following a lot of pressure from two very enthusiastic staff in Ali and Kathy, and I personally oversaw rooming. PSHE had to be in the right environment. I saw to it that it was.

All too often I have seen schools pay lip service to PSHE. They bung any old teacher in who happens to be free. They produce mind-numbing worksheets, outside speakers who have no relationship with the kids, watch DVDs and do the whole thing in halls or inappropriate classrooms.

PSHE withers.

A school without a brilliant PSHE programme is heartless. Their ethos is a meaningless set of words. Their curriculum lacks a soul.

There are two areas of PSHE that need to be developed more: spirituality and politics. I remain disgusted by the way educational institutions are allowed to teach religion in a partisan manner that verges on indoctrination. In my view religion should be looked at and discussed dispassionately with as much credence to atheism and antitheism as religion. Ironically the USA does it the other way round. They ban religion from being taught in state schools but study politics. That seems healthier to me. However I believe PSHE offers a neutral ground to discuss and explore without fear of indoctrination. As for politics I am equally appalled. Very little political education goes on in schools. Yet for me it is one of the most fundamental things. How can you have a democracy without a full understanding of politics? How can people vote if they are ignorant about the different political parties? Why are we so surprised at voter apathy when we keep people so ignorant? PSHE should be a vehicle to understand and discuss the underlying philosophies of political parties. This can be done, in much the same way as religion, without partisan views being introduced.

Most people now accept the need in schools to cover aspects such as sex, drugs, health, environment and careers. There are still sensational headlines from time to time as prudish reactionaries try to impose their mainly fundamental religious views.

I have stood for a liberal, open view. This is the modern world. We can open up a new world without the hidebound austerities of past generations. I have no wish to live in a joyless mediaeval society orchestrated by indoctrinated morons. This is the twenty first century.

The main reason that fundamentalists have an austere vision is the promiscuous society with its numerous casualties. There is no doubt that sex, drugs and rock 'n' roll have taken a huge toll and that many people find themselves caught up in a mindless lifestyle based on gratuitous hedonism. I am as concerned as anyone. As a society we have to find a way of guiding our young people towards a meaningful life and the way to avoid the pitfalls that go with sex, drugs and alcohol. I have lost good friends to that thoughtless lifestyle. However if the general population had access to the youngsters full of life, idealism and altruism as I have they'd probably be a lot more hopeful.

I firmly believe our youngsters will go on to solve these social problems. The way to do it is through good education. The way to solve drug, alcohol and sexual problems is through excellent PSHE, not restrictive prohibition.

If I had my way I would pour money into PSHE and training brilliant PSHE staff. This would impact on the future more than anything else.

As a society I would make drugs legal and increase drug education and support for drug users. The war on drugs has not only failed. It has back-fired and fuelled the interest in drugs. It has succeeded in putting money into the pockets of criminal gangs in the same way that prohibition in the USA created the rise of gangsters such as Al Capone.

Take the funding away from organised crime. Take the allure of drugs away from the young and educate everyone properly.

When I was at school I had a few friends who started experimenting with drugs. Jeff was one of them.

He started off drinking cough medicine. At that time it contained morphine. He would drink five bottles at a time and get out of his head. He moved on to cannabis and then acid.

Like Syd Barrett the acid 'fried' his brain. The big debate is whether it triggered some underlying mental illness or even if the need to take the drugs was induced by the illness.

It is obvious to me that much more objective research is needed.

We need real scientific study and less government propaganda. Kids do not believe the propaganda. They think it is all manufactured lies. They want truth.

The last time I saw Jeff he was highly disturbed. He thought machines were planted all around him, in trees, walls and people surveying his every move. His eyes were shiny and empty like those proverbial black holes.

Jeff jumped in front of a train shortly after.

I remember Jeff as a gentle, intelligent and highly creative young man. He should have gone on to be a brilliant talented photographer.

Jeff is like so many others whose life was blighted by drugs or alcohol. That has to be addressed. Prohibition is not the answer.

PSHE is not about telling people what to do. You do not go into a lesson trying to get students to stop doing things. You go in to get them to think and discuss issues, explore issues and come to their own view.

I know saying NO is counterproductive.

If I were to go into a lesson and tell them that I had a hugely powerful motorbike outside. It was 500,000 CC and would do 0 to 500 MPH in 2 seconds. Nobody who had ever ridden it had survived because it was so powerful – would anyone like to try it out? The hands would go up.

'I'll have a go, sir!!'

'Please me!!'

It's human nature. The adventurous and inquisitive see it as a challenge. There are the kids who think they are immortal, who are sure they could handle it. The more danger - the more kudos.

Teenagers are also acutely aware of the hypocrisy. It is no use adults saying that kids shouldn't take drugs while their parents are off down the pub pouring one of the most dangerous drugs of all down their throats. They know about the huge number of people using dope, cocaine and heroin.

They don't believe the propaganda.

I always found it more effective to encourage students to think about the effect drugs were having on their friends. It was powerful for them to recognise the slump in educational performance, the mental changes and mood swings, the demotivation and behaviour changes. They could see these clearly and note the affect this had on lives and careers. That was far more effective.

It is time to bring in better research, information and education. Our society is saturated with alcohol and dug abuse. Prohibition has failed.

One of my heads of year came to see me. He'd been told by a student that one of the gentlemen in our care was selling cannabis behind the sports hall.

I told him to investigate. He checked out with a few other lads and built up a picture of what was going on. The boy had been dealing for a while. On this particular day he had brought in a lot of dope in £5 deals. He'd sold one lot to a lad at the bus stop. He'd sold five other lots behind the sports hall. It had all been done quite openly in front of a number of our more innocent boys who were quite shocked. The head of year had the times and names.

The lad concerned was brought in and I questioned him. I told him what we'd found out embellishing it with a list of times and names. We had a good picture of the sequence of events and were confident we'd have the full picture before long.

The lad seemed quite relaxed about the whole thing and agreed that our information was correct. He admitted to selling £5 deals to all the boys we knew about and offered a few more names.

'Have you got any cannabis on you?' I asked.

'Yes,' he chirped, pulling a couple of big chunks of cannabis out of his top pocket and handing it over.

I organised the head of year to round up the boys involved and extract the cannabis.

Soon there was a pile of blocks of very black, oily and extremely potent smelling cannabis on my desk.

We noted the names of the boys concerned along with full details.

The boy who had been sold his cannabis at the bus stop claimed he'd popped it home and put it under his bed. I rang his mother who, with utter disbelief, rummaged under his bed and retrieved the lump of cannabis.

One boy, having heard of the round up, had twigged to what was going on and flung his cannabis over the fence on to the common ground.

'That's a shame,' I mused. 'I was hoping we might be able to sort all this out internally in school. Now you've done that we've got a bit of a dilemma.'

He looked at me in anguish.

'We've got a situation where there are dangerous drugs thrown on to a public area. A young child could find that dope. We can't have that. The only thing to do is to call in the drug squad and get the sniffer dogs out there. They'll find it.'

The boy went ashen.

'The only other thing I can think of,' I added. 'What if you were to go and have a search where you think you might have thrown it. If you bring it to me in the next half hour I might be able to deal with this internally.'

The boy went off in a hurry.

I was then called for an emergency lesson cover and found myself looking after a class. They had been set some work so I was merely child minding. I was very concerned that the boy might come back with the dope and find me missing so I positioned myself in the doorway where I could intercept him when he came back.

A member of staff came along and saw me standing there looking a bit expectant.

'What are you up to?' He asked.

'I'm just waiting for a lad to bring me some cannabis,' I replied nonchalantly.

'Oh yeah,' he laughed.

Just then the boy came rushing up.

'I've got that cannabis you were after, sir.' He shoved a big lump of cannabis in my hand.

The teacher stared at me open-mouthed.

By the end of the day I had a desk that was groaning under the weight of cannabis. I had over twenty big chunks. Members of staff were coming in to marvel at it. Between the head of year and myself we had pulled in quite a haul.

It was late and I locked it in my room feeling more than a little satisfied with the way the day had gone. We had got to the bottom of the whole thing, found all the boys involved and retrieved all the cannabis. A good job done.

The next day I opened the door to my room and the smell was overpowering. Despite the fact that the dope was all wrapped in Clingfilm the stuff was so potent that you could get high just breathing the air.

That day we had a police officer in for our Operation Lifestyle assembly. I took them aside and showed them the heap of cannabis.

'I thought I'd better seize the opportunity and pass this over to you,' I remarked in a matter-of-fact manner.

She was amazed.

I passed on all the details that I had typed up. She had a list of names and times.

'I want to deal with this in school,' I informed her.

'I don't know if that will be possible,' she informed me. 'I'll see what I can do. I think we'll have to follow it up with regard to the dealer.'

I shrugged with a grimace.

'I'd prefer to handle it myself.'

'I don't think that will be possible.'

She took all the cannabis off in a big bag, with each of the separate deals carefully placed in separate plastic bags along with details of the boy they had been retrieved from.

As far as I was concerned that was sewn up. I'd passed it over and it was all largely out of my hands.

I intended to bring their parents in, talk through expectations and punishments, and work out how we dealt with it.

Every school has drugs. It goes with youth culture. The main thing we tried to do was to keep it out of school and stop kids from smoking it before lessons. I'd seen the effect of that in USA schools. It was disastrous as far as education was concerned.

We dealt with drugs in PSHE but what kids got up to outside of school was largely the responsibility of them and their family.

To have picked up so many students and so much cannabis sent a clear warning out there. It was bound to have a beneficial effect – word soon gets around.

The students involved had been suspended. I sent out the letters summoning parents and students in and adding a caveat that this could result in permanent exclusion. I actually had no intention of going for permanent exclusion.

Half the boys in the school could have been kicked out if we tested for dope, it was that rife in youth culture at the time. I wanted to make a statement. We did not tolerate it in school.

I phoned and discussed it with the chair of governors. We were in agreement. You didn't hang someone for a bit of dope. To kick them out might have ruined their lives. Everyone deserved a second chance.

We felt pleased with the way it had gone.

The phone rang and the secretary told me she had the Chief Constable on the line. I told her to put him through. I was expecting to receive a bit of praise for the efficient way we'd dealt with it. My head of year had been really on the ball.

'Hello,' I said chirpily.

'I am ringing up to inform you that you have broken the law in two areas,' this cold voice intimated sternly. 'You have laid yourself open to prosecution.'

'Oh really,' I said rapidly changing my tune. My head was buzzing. What the hell was he talking about? 'And how have I done that?'

'Firstly you have infringed the rights of the boys concerned,' he pronounced pompously. 'You had no right to interview them without their parents or an adult being present. That is illegal under European Human Rights legislation.'

'Oh yeah,' I replied feeling myself getting angry. 'And the second?'

'You put yourself in possession of a considerable amount of illegal substances, sufficient to be charged as a dealer.'

I was gob-smacked. I knew that I had, as a Headteacher, the legal right to interview kids in my care. He was talking crap. As to possessing cannabis that I'd confiscated from the boys - that was simply absurd.

I was furious.

I felt that I should explain the law to him but I was not going to argue with the man.

'I tell you what,' I said in a measured tone. 'Do me a favour, why don't you. Go ahead and prosecute me. I'll have you plastered over every newspaper in the country. I'd love it!'

He hung up.

A couple of days later a police officer, in on the Operation Lifestyle project, nervously asked to see me.

'I've been asked to pass on a message from the Chief Constable,' she ventured with a degree of temerity. 'He wanted me to pass on that he was sorry he was a little heavy handed.'

'Well tell him he can ffffing come in an apologise himself!' I told her angrily.

She looked shocked.

I never heard anything more.

In my early years on the senior team I was selected to be part of County's PSHE Team. We were trained to go round from school to school training their staff. I enjoyed it.

On my first day of training the forty of us were welcomed and given a psychometric test. In the afternoon they placed me and one other in a room while the rest went off to do some training.

We were given no task and we sat around and talked.

'Why have we been separated off?' I asked suspiciously.

He chuckled.

'I bet you came out as a shaper on your test,' he stated.

'Yes,' I replied. 'I came out as a shaper/plant.'

He nodded. 'And an enthusiast?'

'Yep,' I replied, still not cottoning on.

'That's why we're here,' he stated. 'They don't want us interfering with this bit. We'd try and take control.'

It was a bit of an eye-opener. Every team needs a range of types and skills. Shapers can be bloody minded.

The best training we had was a great exercise that really summed up the way we human beings interact with each other.

It concerned a magical land far far away. A wizard came into the land with a big bag. When he met anyone he put his hand in his bag and gave them a little furry creature. As soon as they held it and stroked the animal it sent a great feeling of pleasure and happiness flooding through them. The wizard had an endless supply and soon everyone was carrying a bag around full of 'warm fuzzies' and passing them around to everyone they met. The kingdom became a beautiful place full of happy people.

The wizard left and another wizard appeared. He too had a bag but inside his bag were cold spiky little creatures. Everyone he met he gave one of these creatures to. The 'icy pricklies' ate 'warm fuzzies' and sent a feeling of fear and hatred through the person. Soon the kingdom was transformed into gloom and misery.

So what do we all pass on to others that we meet?

I wanted a school that ran on 'warm fuzzies'. 'icy pricklies' were banned. Whatever bad stuff had happened to you outside you left it at the school gates. I accentuated the positive. I tried to get everyone to recognise all the good qualities in each other. I wanted the kingdom inside to be warm and nurturing.

I think I achieved that.

Chapter 7 –Managing people

It was early on in my second year of teaching and Friday afternoon with my favourite group. I was teaching A Level Biology with the Upper Sixth. They were intelligent, friendly and engaging. It was a good way to end the week. I could relax.

That was the day my week nearly ended for ever.

We were in the biology lab for a practical session doing some standard food tests – all predictable and fairly boring.

I was drawing the results table on the old chalk board and turned round to instruct the class on how and when to fill in their results when I found the room almost empty. There was just one boy standing in the centre of the lab with a boiling tube full of liquid that was bubbling away. That would not have been too strange if it had not been for the fact that he wasn't heating it at the time.

'What are you doing Mr Johnson?' I asked puzzled by what I was seeing.

'Nothing sir,' he replied innocently.

I noticed a head peering round the door and another peeping over the back bench.

'He's making nitro-glycerine,' the half visible face informed me.

I felt a bit of a shiver run through me and squinted at the bubbling boiling tube.

'What have you got in there?' I asked sternly, striding over to the lad with the bubbling boiling tube.

'Nothing sir,' he replied again.

'He's put glycerine in with conc. sulphuric and conc. nitric,' my informant offered before ducking back down.

I weighed this up as I headed for that boiling tube.

The lab was lined with reagent bottles. The boy had mixed a big boiling tube of glycerine, concentrated sulphuric and concentrated nitric acid. Now I was no chemist but I knew that the concentrated sulphuric acid removed hydroxyl groups that could be replaced by nitrate groups from the nitric acid. From the extent of bubbling that was going on in the boiling tube a reaction was definitely occurring. It seemed quite probable to me that nitro-glycerine was a distinct possibility. If nitro-glycerine was formed it was highly unstable. Indeed the heat of reaction was quite certain to trigger an explosion. A boiling tube of nitro was quite likely to take out the whole lab. I did not think hiding behind a bench or round a doorway was going to afford much protection.

I walked briskly over and poured the contents of the test tube down the sink washing it away with copious amounts of water and rinsing the test tube out.

It probably wouldn't have made nitro-glycerine but I wasn't taking any chances.

The rest of the class started coming out of hiding.

What punishment do you give to a boy who could have blasted your lab to bits and killed everyone? - Perhaps a detention?

I settled for a lengthy discussion and an apology. He was a pleasant, enthusiastic lad with a good inquisitive mind, if a little silly. He'd been showing off and being daft. The fact that it could have been catastrophic was not really understood.

It was fully understood by the end of my conversation. What might have occurred was explained very graphically.

What should, and could, have happened to him as a result of doing this was also explained. It probably would have resulted in his expulsion if I had followed procedure.

What good would that have done? His A levels, his university, his career, my relationship with the class? The repercussions were enormous.

By the end of our discussion he had learnt a lesson. I was confident nothing of similar ilk would happen ever again. What more was to be gained?

Managing people is hard.

There are lots of complicated issues around people. No two are the same. Many people are working flat out doing a brilliant job. Some are coasting doing a good job. There are always a few who are working themselves silly but doing all the wrong things, driving themselves into the ground and being ineffective. Then there are the lazy ones and skivers who need a nudge or a kick, the ones who are working hard but not doing it in the way you would like and the small number who are useless or deliberately antagonistic.

As a Head you have deputies and middle managers with a system of line management that is organised to manage these issues. You can direct them to manage staff or student behaviour.

You cannot rely on them.

The first thing a Head needs is a good source of reliable information. There is no substitute for first hand intelligence. Getting out and about, talking to all staff and in particular the students, not only gives you a picture of what is going on but also a good understanding of the people concerned, their worries, concerns, the issues they are up against, their personalities, relationships with other staff and students, how hard they are working, their effectiveness and how things can be addressed.

With a staff of a hundred and twenty it is not possible to deal effectively with all of them. It is important to know exactly what is going on though.

This is no different to a head of year managing their tutors but needing to form a personal relationship with all 130 students in their charge.

A Head needs a network of views. The information coming in from this network gives you an overview of what is and is not working smoothly, what needs addressing urgently and what needs nudging. This network should come from all levels of the organisation. It keeps you informed.

It is essential that nobody else, including your most trusted deputies, know the sources of your information. It is often the case that your line managers are playing politics, keeping things to themselves, not wanting bad news to filter through to you for fear that it might make them look bad for allowing problems to develop in their areas, or simply retaining information to use later to their own advantage. Line managers need keeping on their toes. When you come out with information it is for them to guess as to where you got it from. Knowing stuff before your line managers is always a good idea. It makes them think you know exactly what is going on. It gives them an impetus to prevent things happening. They know you will find out what is happening and there is no point in trying to gloss over things. It also means they have an incentive to tell you before you find out for yourself. You finding out their muck-ups simply makes them even worse.

It is good to keep them on their toes.

It's all a game.

This is where touring, good relationships built up over a long time, and an open email, open door policy come in handy. It is quite amazing what snippets come out in casual conversation, as a single line email or behind a closed door.

This gives you the edge. You have to be aware of what is going on and have your finger on the pulse.

You also have to know your staff well.

It is pointless using the wrong tactics towards the wrong individuals. You have to tailor your strategies to the individuals concerned. Deploying the wrong tactics is not only ineffective, it is can be harmful. Using a heavy handed approach on some people can create life-long enemies who will hold grudges and become stubbornly entrenched in opposition to everything you are trying to do. They will then ferment bad feeling and be a focus for disaffection. One has to hone ones arsenal. It is all intuitive.

Flattery, praise, recognition, concern, logic, argument, dressing down, punishment and threats are part of the armoury.

This makes it sound cold and dispassionate, calculating and devious. Whilst there is an element of that it is not quite as bad as it sounds. The need to get people on side requires a degree of manipulation. That is the politics of the job. You work with staff the same way that you work with students in the classroom. Your tactics come out of sincere belief in what you are doing and care for everyone in your care. There is no dishonesty in the relationships. You just instinctively know the best way to get the best out of your staff and get them to go along with your policies. I genuinely liked almost all the staff I worked with, including the ones who were troublesome and had to be disciplined. In fact some of the rogues were the most interesting of all. Everyone has their reasons. Most of what you do is instinctive, intuitive and part of your everyday interaction. None the less it does not do any harm to review your tactics to make yourself more effective.

As a Head you have a vision for the school enshrined in your stated ethos. The object of your exercise is to ensure that this vision is communicated repeatedly to everyone with clarity and passion. You constantly harp on about it.

Your next task is to ensure that everyone on the team, in their own way, is buying in to your vision.

Those who are not buying in need coaxing, re-educating, telling or getting rid of. This is why you hold training sessions, meetings and apply your management skills.

Most important is that the students are educated in the way you want them educated, treated how you want them treated and valued and respected in the way you want them respected and valued.

Nothing else matters.

The problem is that people don't always agree with their managers, feel strongly that they know better than those above them, can be awkward, emotional, lazy, argumentative or plain bloody disruptive.

They have to be brought on board.

The greatest weapon, if weapon I can call it, is praise. Every one of us has a seat of insecurity inside us. Everyone, no matter how old, tough and experienced likes to be told they are doing a good job. Simply by going around praising the things people are doing well inspires them to do more of the same even better. You don't even have to mention the things you are not so keen on. They rapidly learn what they are being praised for and work accordingly. They work to please.

Children, teachers, grounds-men, office staff and Head teachers are all the same. We are animals. We love to please. Praise fills us with a warm glow. It makes us feel good. In my opinion you can't get too much praise and recognition. It's how you train dogs, tigers and elephants. Indeed every animal on earth responds to reward. Negative reinforcement, in the form of punishment or admonition, is nowhere near as effective.

There is nothing more infuriating than working your socks off and nobody notices, or, even worse, the boss takes it for granted, or worse still - claims it as his or hers. That is guaranteed to create resentment and it has happened to me on more than one occasion.

So rule number one – tour smile, praise, listen. By focussing and rewarding the good things the focus shifts. By downplaying the not so good things those bad things become fewer.

You set the tone.

People pick up on the small things.

To reinforce the positive it is important to set up a system of rewards and recognition for staff to make them feel valued.

One idea I was working on was a termly reward, a box of chocs, for the member of staff who was doing one of my pet things best i.e. The prize for the member of staff who had the most positive relationship with students this term is ……….. I held back on this as I thought that it could create jealousy and resentment. But it would be a public recognition of something I held dear and the focus could be changed termly. It might have been worth a spin.

You can't beat the boost a little note and a chocolate placed in a pigeon-hole can make, or a silly email, a phone call, a beaming smile, word of praise, a personal special visit. They are as important as the policies themselves.

For those whose efforts were ineffective there was always the maxim 'Don't work harder – work smarter' according to the wisdom of Mr Jones who was frequently heard to repeat the phrase at every opportunity. It made sense though rarely seemed to alter people's behaviour. Some people were doomed to repeat the mistakes of their methodology and were impervious to suggestion.

It works exactly the same with students. Your personal smiles, comments and general announcements and assemblies make them feel loved and valued.

This is the oil that makes the machine operate smoothly.

This was the part of the job that I loved and gave me most reward. There was nothing contrived or insincere about it. It was the element that came naturally.

The harder part was how to deal with the more difficult elements, those who were openly antagonistic or malfunctioning, and who appeared impermeable to praise and recognition. These recalcitrant individuals had to be addressed. Some of these awkward people and attitudes were languishing in positions of your own making. As a Head you have to make decisions and some people get knocked back. They blame you of course, never themselves. The usual reason they get knocked back is either they have an inflated opinion of their own worth and are simply not up to the job, or they have a modus operandi that does not mesh with the ethos you are promoting and they don't seem to get it. However, this is not how they see it.

The first line of attack is to review your own activity as regards the awkward squad. Do you see them as often as everyone else? There is a human tendency to focus on people you get on with and avoid people you find difficult. The staff teaching near your office might be visited more, just in the course of passing, while those in the far-flung extremes of the empire might require a major expedition and that is harder when time is of the essence.

Perhaps a deliberate programme of increased casual visits, quiet words, added praise, can bring them round?

Sometimes it works.

Whatever you do in way of positive reinforcement, praise and recognition will never be enough to solve all your problems. Sometimes you have to resort to other means.

The strategy of directly summoning someone to your office to instigate a quiet chat about 'concerns' is a good starter - 'It has come to my attention that you seem to be shouting at students a lot? Is there a problem I should know about?'

It at least notifies them that you are unhappy with how they are operating.

This can be reinforced with a review of alternative strategies that you would approve of.

Sometimes this works.

Regardless of everything you try there will be the moment where, for either a gross misdemeanour or a series of failures to adhere to policy, someone has to be really carpeted. For me this usually starts with the summons. They are invited in and the door shut. They are asked to sit. I never sat behind my desk. I usually went for the low comfortable seating so that we were face to face, on the same level, close and intimate. I did not want barriers or elevated seating. I wanted this to be up close and personal. I wanted to show I was on their level with no gimmicks.

I would make eye contact and hold it. 'I am extremely unhappy ………'

I'd let them explain.

I'd then tell them in no uncertain terms what they had done wrong and what I wanted them to do about it. There had to be no ambiguity. I then told them what I was going to do about it.

I always found these experiences emotionally unpleasant. I never enjoyed doing it, though I never ducked it or delegated. Rarely did I lose my temper though on two occasions I regret to say that I did. These were both regrettable and should not have happened.

They were probably the result of my own stress levels. I usually tried to remain calm, logical and clear.

However there is a time for anger and losing your temper. It is, in my experience, justified if you have been treated extremely badly and someone deserves it. It should be spontaneous and public. It does no harm for people to see that very occasionally you are capable of being extremely angry and believe in things deeply enough to react that way. They need to know you are human and also need to occasionally feel your power. As a regular feature it is completely out of order. That would be bullying and there is never any excuse for bullying particularly in a Headteacher.

Only twice did I reach the point of having to follow down an official disciplinary route. To have to resort to such a thing is, in my book, a sign of defeat. It shows your other methods have failed.

A Head tries their hardest to get poorly performing staff in line. I have drawn up a chart, listed the problem staff, identified their character traits, identified the behaviour or attitude I wanted to modify and drawn up a set of strategies to rectify the problem.

Sometimes it works and occasionally it does not.

For some people, I suspect, there is little chance of remedial success. They are incapable of change.

They have to be jettisoned.

For me the answer to most person-management was the smile, understanding, a good listen, a bit of give and take, a dose of praise and a dollop of good firm advice.

It usually worked.

Then we were all pulling together and everyone felt valued and good.

It's amazing what a smile can do.

Chapter 8 – Relationships

For me the philosophy I applied during my tenure as a Headteacher came right out of my experience as a student. There were lessons to be learnt from how I was treated and taught as a child and youth and the things I had witnessed.

Simon was in my class at school. He lived in a council house on the estate but Simon put on airs and graces. He and his family had pretensions.

Simon, who in my memory was the spitting image of Rimmer in Red Dwarf, always came to school immaculately groomed, his crinkly fair hair brylcreamed into place. He had a supercilious attitude that got up people's nose. He adopted a sophisticated voice that sounded a bit put on.

Simon, like Rimmer, annoyed people and became the focus of bullying.

Every class has a pecking order. Boys vie for position by being hard, showing off, cracking jokes, developing attitude, being athletic, being violent, being big and tough. It is very primitive.

Simon was considered soft, puny, annoying and a pretentious pain in the arse. He had few, if any, redeeming faults.

Simon was rooted to the bottom of the pecking order.

This was good news for all those swimming in the benthos of the Form's lower levels. The heat was off them. They could keep their heads down and let Simon take the brunt.

Simon was laughed at, pushed around and abused. He was the butt of nasty quips and put-downs. It seemed as if no-one in authority cared a jot about this. Boys will be boys. Fighting was normal. Simon got picked on; Simon got in fights – so what?

One day word got round that one of the hardos in the year was going to have a fight with Simon and flatten him. This was all going to kick off after school on the top playing field.

It was all very electrifying. The whole school was in a state of extreme excitement. There was a touch of mass hysteria.

The only person who amazingly had got no inkling of what was planned was Simon. He remained oblivious. To this day I cannot conceive how he could have remained so unaware of what was kicking off. It seemed to be the only topic of conversation around the school. Simon must have gone through the day in a complete bubble.

Simon always walked home through the back entrance, on a path past the adjoining junior school on the right with our school playing fields on the left.

When the bell went the whole school rushed out to gather on the top field to wait for the main event. There were literally hundreds of us.

Simon rambled off home in a dream.

There was a short cut-through to the field and it was only then that Simon must have got a sense that something was up. He must have heard the crowd gathered on the other side of the cut-through and somehow realised it was to do with him. He turned round and tried to dodge back into school to avoid them.

Unfortunately for Simon this eventuality had been foreseen and arrangements made. The path was blocked by four sneering sidekicks and Simon was pushed and herded down the cut-through out into the open field the other side.

A great roar went up when he appeared and everyone surged round like a pack of excited dogs.

Soon there was a circle in the centre of which was the hard kid and Simon. Simon tried to bolt through the crowd and escape but they pushed him back. There were far too many people for that. They were too densely packed.

There was a great roar of excitement, with chanting and jeers.

The struggle seemed to go right out of Simon as if, realising there was no possible escape; he resigned himself to his fate. He turned round to face the other lad and stood there limply with his hands down by his side.

The other lad was grinning at him with his fists up.

'Come on then you faggot,' he gestured, playing to the crowd.

He stepped forward and punched Simon in the face.

A great roar went up. They must have heard it in the school.

Simon stood there and looked back dolefully so the lad hit him again. Blood trickled from Simon's nose but he just stood there.

The lad goaded him and pushed him but got no response.

Someone shoved Simon forward into the boy. They wanted action. The crowd were shouting at Simon to fight back.

The lad hit Simon hard but still there was no response. He shoved him and hit him again.

Simon just stood there defencelessly and took it. He stared straight at the kid with his arms dangling and did nothing.

This was not quite the fight we had been expecting and it certainly wasn't what the lad wanted. He'd wanted to provoke a fight, knock a flailing Simon around a bit, floor him and walk off a hero.

This was not quite going to plan.

Simon had blood dipping from his nose and mouth and still just stood there. It was evident that there was no white knight from the school who was going to charge to his rescue. There was no help to be had.

The crowd had quietened down and become a bit apprehensive.

The kid sensed his moment of glory was passing and decided to get it over with quickly.

He stepped forward and started whacking Simon in the face as hard as he could with a flurry of blows. He wanted Simon to go down so that he could walk away the victor and still retain a little of that glory.

However this didn't work out either.

Simon refused to go down. The punches smacked into his face and he reeled and jerked but remained standing defiantly facing the lad and took those blows.

The crowd had changed. This wasn't the exciting spectacle they'd been expecting. It was nasty. It was getting revolting and everyone wanted it to stop.

Some called out for Simon to fight back. Some called out for the lad to stop. Some instructed Simon to go down.

The lad desperately tried to knock Simon down. He threw everything at him. He was getting frantic now as he could sense the sympathy of the crowd had turned. He had no exit strategy.

Simon's face was rapidly becoming a swollen, bloody, bruised mess and still the punches thudded in and still Simon neither fought back nor went down.

There was something really sickening about it by now. It was making everyone ashamed to be there witnessing it.

It is incredible how quickly the mood of a crowd can change. The lad felt it. There was no glory to be had here. It made him feel cheated and angry.

He tried a couple more shots and then stood back, a little confused, raising his fists and declaring himself the winner while Simon stood there swaying with his swollen wrecked face streaming with blood, tears and snot.

That's all I remember except to this day I am utterly ashamed that I got caught up in it and went along, all excited like everyone else, to see Simon get beat up. Not one of us told a teacher. Not one of us warned Simon. Not one of us tried to stop it.

That's human beings for you.

We can be so cruel and heartless.

At the heart of everything are relationships.

Young men form strong bonds with their friends that feel so much more important than bonds with their family. They are breaking away from home and forming their hunting groups. In primitive times these bonds had to be so strong you'd trust your friend with your life. It took a team working together to bring down a kill or defeat a large wild cat. We still have those instincts.

That's what our sports are all about.

Alongside this was the rivalry of getting a mate - the classroom pecking order with those at the top of the pack putting out their pheromone attractants.

The girls too played similar games, tarting themselves up to be more desirable, Looking to attract the top males, bitching and in-fighting between themselves.

We haven't been around long as a species.

We haven't evolved much.

Civilisation is a thin veneer.

Scratch the surface and you unlock a seething mess of primitive behaviour all boiling away at a subconscious level.

We've not got too far away from the bear-baiting pits, the dog fights and cock fights that used to be prevalent as entertainment in Shakespearian times.

Schools and young people are particularly prone. Teenage years are confusing times. The brain is being rewired. The hormones are kicking in.

Yet young people are capable of the most loyal, kind, altruistic actions. It doesn't take much to bring out the compassion and for things to go the other way. That is what we have to tap in to.

Good friends of ours, Kathy and Toby, were running an enormous farm in Zambia for CDC. In one summer break we went out to impose upon them and take the opportunity to look round at the amazing things they were doing out there with housing, roads, water supply and hospitals.

Tobes took us to meet the doctor and see the hospital. It was a bit of a shock.

The doctor was a really nice guy. He worked from dawn until late at night seven days a week. He started out at five in the morning to deliver supplies to the AIDS orphans in the surrounding villages. He hadn't been paid for months.

The hospital was dingy with stained mattresses, no sheets and lots of sick people lying around without a great deal of care or medicine. Everything was very do-it-yourself.

Outside a lady was cooking some tiny finches she had caught. They were for lunch. The hospital couldn't provide food or nursing. Relatives had to come in and do that and the relatives were usually paupers.

It was desperate.

Back at Tobe's house there was a knock on the door. I opened it to find a small, scraggy kid standing there. He looked to be about nine or ten. I later learnt that he was fourteen but was a little undernourished.

He stared resolutely at the ground.

'Please sir,' he said without raising his eyes. 'I heard you are a teacher. I wondered if you could help me with my writing?'

Teachers are so revered pupils do not look them in the eye. They are the passport to a different life.

English was probably his fourth language out of seven but Meshack was fluent.

I agreed and sat him down to talk to him about his life and what he wanted to do.

He started to tell me about wanting to escape the poverty of the countryside and gain qualifications so that he could be a clerk in the big city of Lusaka. It was his dream.

He went to school but had no money and although the education was free he had to have a uniform with shoes. He worked all summer with his uncle fishing on the lake and selling fish so that he could buy the uniform and shoes.

The school was over twenty miles away and he walked there through the bush. He wrapped his uniform in cloth and carried it so that it did not get messy and he tied his shoes round his neck so they did not get worn. He wanted to look smart for school. At the end of the week he walked back.

I asked him to go away and write up his story.

In an hour he was back with three pages of writing. I'm no English teacher but I corrected his spelling and grammar and talked through how he might develop the story further.

He rushed off and was back again in an hour clutching four sheets of rewritten pages.

I began to realise that this would go on and on for as long as I allowed it to.

His thirst for education would never be slaked.

I got him to hone his story into a good account and then set him off writing about his other experiences.

He produced tales of encounters with lions, bandits raiding his village shooting someone dead and stealing their food, and life with his mother and sister in the village.

When I returned to England I was full of emotion. I wanted to do something to help that hospital and put my mind to raising money.

I talked at assembly, read Meschack's stories and launched a money raising scheme. I asked the boys to give an hour of their time to do some paid work for their parents, a neighbour or relative and donate the money to the hospital.

My audience were the teenagers people are wary of. They turned out to be compassionate stars.

They had listened and were filled with that same desire to do something.

I kept a total running on the side of the stage with a big thermometer.

I printed out the names, amounts raised and what they had done to raise the money and stuck them up on the wall of the corridor going into assembly.

It became a full time job. Money started pouring in. Boys were washing cars, gardening, shopping, baking and selling cakes, holding sales of unwanted toys, donating pocket money, doing housework, decorating, holding sponsored silences and organising a series of events. The range and enthusiasm was astounding. The response when I updated them on the totals was incredible.

One boy came in with over a hundred pounds he had raised by himself doing shopping for pensioners, gardening and running errands. He'd become a one man delivery service.

There were 750 boys in the school and within weeks we had raised over £6500. It was with a great deal of pride that I sent the cheque off to the hospital.

The thermometer had had to be redrawn with a different scale and target. The corridors were lined with sponsorship sheets.

I knew what a huge impact that would have on the lives of those African orphans and patients. What was even more important was to experience the kindness and altruism of our students. They really cared and were prepared to put their hearts and muscles into helping other people in a far off country.

I was so proud of them.

That's the other side to the Simon story.

Teaching is not just about knowing your subject, planning your lessons well and organising your timetable.

Teaching is all about relationship and personality. You have to find a way of expressing yourself. Teaching is like being on stage. You pick the elements of your personality that you need to project and you exaggerate them. Whatever you do you have to be true to yourself.

That is why you can never create a one-size-fits-all policy for teaching. The three part lesson is great but it is also a strait-jacket for those teachers whose personality is different. We need to have the latitude to fly. It is the eccentric, wild teachers who inspire us; not the hide-bound one who follow every rule.

Teaching comes from the heart not the head. We need that flair, imagination and variety.

Teaching is about relationship.

Managing is also all about relationship. You have to lead and manage your team. You can do it by numbers or you can do it your own way.

I made up my rules as I went along.

Leadership and management are both crucial to Headship.

Leadership is all about getting people to believe in you and follow.

Management is about planning out what needs doing to get to where you're going.

I was asked about leadership and management at my headship interview. I used a military analogy.

If you're a leader you have the ability to get people to believe in you, gather up arms and follow you to hell and back.

A leader points to the hill in the distance and shouts 'Forward!' Everyone gathers their loins and charges off after him without a clue as to where they're going on how they will get there.

A manager paws over the map, sorts out the distance and directions, works out how to get across the river and round the swamp and plans out the provisions needed and where they are going to billet. The trouble is that they are managers and do not inspire others and so they cannot get anyone to follow them.

Each without the other is a disaster.

If the mighty leader has not got a clear goal and passion to get there nothing will work. If he does not posses the management skills to sort out how to deal with the obstacles we'd never get there despite all the passion in the world.

If the Head is just a manager then the school would simply get bogged down in intricate practicalities.

If the Head is just a leader they will go charging off towards unattainable goals until everyone drops with exhaustion.

The ideal Head has both leadership and management skills but in order to do anything well they need to work with people and that is all about relationship.

Strong leaders can be the biggest disasters of all. You can name loads of them:- Pol Pot, Hitler, Stalin, Mao. How come so many leaders are psychopathic sociopaths? - Because psychopathic sociopaths appear strong, black and white and believable; they seem to have the answers. The trouble is they have got to the top by being devious and not caring about anyone they hurt. They are ruthless and dispassionate. So how come we vote for them? – Because they are strong and clear! In primitive times it was good to have leaders who were decisive and ruthless. We haven't evolved much. The question we need to ask is; how come so many of our Headteachers and Industry leaders are also power-mad sociopaths?

When Cameron became ill the whole school rallied round. Cameron had cancer.

You could have bottled the determined camaraderie. The boys were right there for him. The cards and emails rained down.

Cameron went in for operations and then chemo. His hair fell out and he was wheelchair bound.

As soon as he was strong enough he was back in school being wheeled round the playground like Ben Hur in his chariot at the coliseum. Cameron was brilliant! He was laughing and cracking jokes. His friends were so pleased to see him. There was nothing they wouldn't do for him.

You could always tell when Cameron was in because there was a great crowd gathered round him all laughing and hooting like it was party-time. In the centre Cameron was more rowdy than all of them put together.

When Cameron died there were tears everywhere but there was also a resolute determination. Cameron might be gone but there was no way they were going to let go. Cameron would always be part of them and part of the school. They set up a football match in his memory and bought a cup. Every year they would contest it and remember him.

They played the first match and raised the cup up high. You could see in their faces the defiance. Cameron was there. They'd never let him go.

That's the positive strength of a community. That's what comes out of a PSHE programme, a positive pastoral system, Student Voice and restorative practice. That's what happens when you empower boys and put them in contact with their emotions. They are beautiful.

No amount of GCSE passes or Ofsted success can equal that.

When you are a Head you lead the school. You are responsible for the education of all the staff, all 120 of them; the students, now and in the future, thousands of them; the buildings and the implementation of all the education changes.

Your decisions affect the lives of large numbers of people.

If your decisions cause a drop in exam results, deterioration in behaviour, or affect the reputation of the school, the future of all students might be affected. Student numbers might drop, and staff jobs could be lost.

It is a huge responsibility.

When the students, staff, parents and visitors see you they need to see a leader, trust in your vision and be prepared to follow. They need to trust that you have the skills and qualities to get them to where they need to be.

This is a relationship that has to be based on mutual respect.

You stand on that stage and you have to totally be the part. There are no half measures. There can be no human frailty on that stage. You have to perform. You represent the hopes and dreams of the whole community. They have to believe in you.

As a teacher you sometimes find that whatever you do fails to work. Relationship with a class just breaks down and you can never get it right.

That happened with me and the infamous 2W.

The irony with this is that I probably have 2W to thank for getting me the job in the first place. There is no other explanation I can think of as to why a very traditional boys' grammar school should chose to appoint a long-haired rebel like me. It was obvious at interview that I did not espouse the values they stood for. I made no bones about it. I did not approve. I did not fit in. I would do my damnedest to change it. Still they appointed me.

The school had been forced to change the year before from a grammar to a comprehensive school. Suddenly they had a totally different type of student on their hands and they were floundering. What was obvious to me in hindsight was that they were getting hell from the new comprehensive kids. They hadn't been there for a year yet but none of the staff really understood how to get to grips with them and the comprehensive students were running rings round everyone. They saw me as the token comprehensive teacher. I was to be the Galahad riding to the rescue.

By the time I got to them 2W were lost. They were convinced they were unwanted and that nothing at the place was worth bothering with. They were right. When I first met them they informed me that 'Yes – we're the thickos!' Their raison d'etre was to cause as much mayhem as possible. They did not respond to my politeness and respect. This soft approach was fresh meat to hungry lions.

I did all my fun lessons and they deliberately wrecked every one of them.

It got to the point where I began to dread Wednesday afternoons when I taught them. When period four was over I breathed a sigh of relief and relaxed. By the end of the weekend they were back at the forefront of my mind. I'd wake Monday morning with a churning in my gut that gradually built until Wednesday came back around.

It probably would have gone from bad to worse except for one terrible afternoon.

For some reason they were completely hypered up and out of control. Perhaps it was a windy day. I already had to shout and storm even at the beginning of the lesson and they would incompliantly grin back at me in brazen defiance.

I would turn my back to write something on the blackboard and those four on the back bench were banging their fists on the bench and laughing. When I turned back they'd stop and grin at me goadingly. I ranted and warned them ineffectively. They grinned. I turned back and they exuberantly resumed the banging.

That was the moment I lost it.

It had never happened in my life before and it has never happened since.

I had a complete moment of red mist.

Without consciously being at all aware I vaulted over my bench, and then the next three benches, like some crazed steeple-chaser and confronted the two miscreants trying to wind me up. I shouted into their faces in some spittle wracked frenzy. They had shocked expressions on their faces like you see in cartoons in the cheapest of comics. They had not realised what I was capable of.

The red mist cleared and I became aware of where I was. The two boys were frozen in disbelief. I looked back round and it was like an elephant had rampaged down the centre of the laboratory. Furniture and books had been shunted violently to each side as I had stormed through. It was as if time had stood still as they gaped back up at me from within the debris. The class sat there and nobody twitched a muscle.

I pulled myself back together, mustered all my calm and dignity and walked back to the front.

It was a signal. All around the lab boys rearranged the furniture and stools.

There was a stunned silence.

I turned to face them and they returned my stare. I could see a new respect in their eyes. They now knew what I could do.

They straightened the lab up and sat there watching to see what I was going to do next.

I went back to my place and resumed the lesson as if nothing had happened. They worked like beavers.

I don't recommend this tactic. Not only could you give yourself a hernia but you could easily terminate your entire career if you happened to knock one of the boys on the way. But then I also doubt that you'd find yourself in such dire circumstances. We have much better support systems in place. These days systems would kick in and the miscreants be escorted away – not that I have witnessed classes ever being as difficult as that in modern times. Schools are better organised and students are much better behaved.

When two of our staff, Mary and Sarah, both had mothers with breast cancer they decided to do something positive and raise money for cancer research.

They went to the school assembly and movingly told the boys what they were doing and why. They talked about their mothers and every boy sat there rapt. The empathy was total.

They asked the boys to support Cancer Research in the 'Wear something Pink' campaign.

Nobody was sure what would happen. Boys and pink don't naturally go together. It doesn't quite fit with the macho image!

The next day the school was awash with pink. It brought tears into your eyes to feel the intense support the boys were offering.

They donated thousands.

This was a boys' school and their emotions were on display. It felt so good. I have rarely been more proud.

Chapter 9 – The Curriculum

In America I was teaching a class about blood groups. We were doing the standard practical lesson using Eldon Cards. It was always a crowd pleaser. The method is to prick yourself with a sterile lancet and place a drop of blood on each of the four squares on an Eldon card. The blood reacts with antigens and agglutinates. From the pattern of agglutination you can tell what blood group you were.

Kids were extremely excited at the prospect of sticking lancet in their thumbs and producing blood. Indeed it was so common for students to faint at the prospect that I always insisted they sat down even during the explanation. There was an average of two faints per class.

However this was not the chief attraction or principle cause of the excitement.

The chief attraction was watching the teacher repeatedly stab themselves with a lancet to prove to everyone that it was painless.

They all knew it was far from painless.

'See,' I'd explain, cleaning the area with alcohol before blithely jabbing the lancet into my thumb and squeezing out a bead of prime teacher blood. 'It's easy and painless.' I'd smile in the hopes that they were thoroughly reassured.

''I didn't see that,' someone would chirp up. 'Could you show us again?'

By the end of the lesson your thumb was red, swollen and throbbing from repeated jabs.

On this occasion I'd brought the class together, demonstrated the jab and extracted the crimson bead. At this point the class was usually rapt and gleeful. They loved the whole idea of teachers inflicting pain on themselves. However this time they were not so rapt. They all seemed to be focussed on something behind me.

I looked round and there was Reuben, one of the gang leaders, standing behind me grinning from ear to ear. He was holding a huge flick knife in one hand and had sliced his thumb open so that blood was dripping freely on to a slide that another student was holding underneath. The slide was itself brimming and dripping to add to a puddle on the floor.

'Hey Goodwin,' Reuben grinned. 'I got enough blood for everyone.'

I was given the job of managing the curriculum by Barry the Head at the time. He'd promoted me to senior teacher. I was already in charge of the pastoral system, school activities, attendance, assessment, biology, PSHE, equal opportunities, and GNVQ. There was a bit of a question as to whether I could juggle all those balls and keep sane, or whether it was appropriate for me to be doing all this at that pay-scale. I was doing at least two deputy heads jobs plus a couple of head of departments. They were certainly getting value for money. But Hey – I was a man with a mission. I was after proving all my ideas worked. I was Mr Agent for Change. There weren't enough hours in the day. I worked round the clock to two in the morning six days a week. When you're enjoying yourself it is not work. Being taken for granted rankled a bit though. I used to have long moans about it with my counterpart Ann in our sister school. She was in the same situation. But we were both driven and could see the value and impact of what we were doing.

The formal curriculum was easy to address. I had to manage the heads of department. The curriculum was addressed by a team that consisted of six member head of faculty team. They were quite a powerful group, used to being chaired by the Head and rather reactionary. My major problem seemed to be that they thought I might be creating too much work for them. They did not like change. They wanted to keep things just as they were, ticking along nicely thank you very much. They also thought I was some jumped up senior teacher, not even a deputy head, I lacked the authority. What I was suggesting was too radical.

Their tactic was to go behind my back to the Head. He then said yea or nay.

I was not happy with this. I went to see the Head and told him that either I did it or I didn't. If he wanted me in charge I did it my way. If they bleated to him he kept out of it and referred them back to me.

He reluctantly agreed.

At my next meeting I told them in no uncertain terms that I was running the team. I was happy to discuss and compromise but they had to deal with me.

They formed a delegation to the Head. He sent them away.

I promptly disbanded the heads of faculty group. The Head was very uptight about my tactics but he let me do it.

I put together a new curriculum team which expanded the team of six into a team of twelve.

For some reason they did not like this but I made them eat it. Sometimes you have to stand tough and sometimes you have to take full control. There is no way you can move to a consensus, democratic manner of operation without ever exerting power. That's the nature of life. You have to prove yourself.

Things settled and we began addressing issues such as assessment in order to unify practice and make it more effective. There was a balancing act between keeping individuality and the excitement of experimentation and having a unified approach. We got there through endless discussion.

I wanted them to unify their departments by working on a departmental handbook which could be put together through joint agreement. I knew the process would bring out all sorts of discussion over ethos, purpose of education and teaching methodology. It gave me the means to say what I wanted it to address, which included such things as: school ethos, active teaching, skill development, racism, sexism, gender bias, equal opportunities, purpose of education, etc. I wanted to get their heads out of the mundane nuts and bolts of delivering the syllabus and teaching and learning.

The crucial thing was the way it was done and why.

There were bigger issues than mere subject delivery.

They really did not like this. It looked like a lot of work. They could not see the point of it.

They had hardly begun to reluctantly address this when I hit them with the need to produce detailed five year planning. Once again I furnished them with the headings I wanted addressing.

They went berserk.

I persisted.

I had identified 40 development areas. I was producing a plan for the whole school that interlinked and identified the development areas, interlinked them and fed them into department development. I wanted cohesive planning.

I know that sounds horrendous and one huge bureaucratic exercise but that is not what it was. It was a vehicle to promote change and get the school to address those issues that needed addressing universally. If we worked together we were much more effective.

As far as I was concerned we had to change and change fast. I needed to build momentum.

Once we got going we would be alright. The change would begin to perpetuate itself.

I produced the whole interlinking plan for the 40 areas on my computer.

I needed a room to display the hard copy. It would take up a whole wall. I needed a curriculum room.

There was no curriculum room.

I made a fuss with the Head.

I introduced a curriculum link team of ambitious non-heads of department, one from each subject area, who would promote change in their departments, report back to the link team, and discuss the various developments.

The heads of department were furious. They thought it was usurping their power.

I was having fun.

I had an assistant. We devised a weekly newsletter relating progress. It was called CDI – curriculum development initiative. I had a logo designed for it. We wanted to get some competition into the changes by reporting departmental achievements. I kept the pressure on by attending departmental meetings and talking through the imperatives, checking on progress.

I identified an area in an old abandoned room next to the staffroom that I could use. I informed the Head that if I couldn't have a room I'd build my own.

He was bemused but he agreed and allowed me to order basic materials. I don't think he actually believed I would or could do it.

Timber, plasterboard, nails and paint arrived. Over Easter holidays I went in and built a room within the abandoned area. I put up stud walls and painted them. By the time we came back I had my 5 year plan for 40 development areas displayed, along with the sections of handbooks and planning that were beginning to creep in. The newsletters were also on the walls.

In the staffroom I put up a display on the high wall above the notice-board. It was a huge dark cloud that I'd painted on card.

There were 40 balloons brightly painted on card with the initials of the 40 development areas on them. They were all in a line along the bottom.

I had a big bright yellow smiley sun with long rays painted on card. I hid that behind the cloud.

Every night, when they'd all gone home I fetched the ladder out and began moving things. The balloons with areas that had developed were raised up a little according to my assessment of how well they were doing. I then moved the cloud a little to the side so that more of the sun's rays peeped out. Gradually, over days, the sun began to pop out from behind the cloud.

It was daft but fun.

At first they all found it intriguing. What was it all about? Then they cottoned on.

Some members of staff complained to the Head. This was intruding into their area. They came in there to relax. They didn't want to be bombarded with work when they were trying to relax.

The Head listened to them and made me take it down. It was done publicly at a morning briefing. He had not even had the decency to tell me he was going to instruct me in advance. It was extremely humiliating.

I got over it.

It had done its job. It had raised awareness.

One thing was certain – all the staff knew that no one was working harder than me. No one cared more than me. No one had more passion.

The school had its first Ofsted. They loved my stuff. All my areas were deemed outstanding.

As the results were still poor we only gained Satisfactory but the heads of department knew that without the handbooks and planning they would have been crucified.

We had laid the foundations to go forward.

These were the same drives I took into Headship. No one worked harder or had more passion. You have to believe in what you are doing. You have to fight to get your vision up and running.

While I was doing the easy formal curriculum I had simultaneously started work on the more important informal curriculum.

What were the subliminal messages we were putting out to students by the way we taught them? What were we saying by the way we organised the school?

I went back to my ethos.

By this time I had, through many long discussions, pushed the ethos and vision through senior management and out into the school at large. It was discussed all over, fed into handbooks and planning and informed how we worked.

I wanted to make the informal curriculum overt. I wanted to bring it out into the open and harness it. I wanted to ensure that it was, in their own inimitable ways, being addressed properly in all areas of pastoral and curriculum.

Was it fair?

Was it open? Did everyone have a say?

Was it caring? Did we include, support and care for everyone?

Was it promoting equality? Did it address sexism? - racism? - environmental issues? - people's rights? - animal rights?

Was the curriculum being delivered in active ways that enabled skill and quality development?

What new exciting teaching styles were being deployed? Was experimentation being encouraged?

I was having so much fun it was carrying me along. I was getting things moving. You could feel the momentum.

The importance I gave to things was causing them to be addressed.

By sharing the exciting new teaching styles I was encouraging risk taking and experimentation.

I was giving the more dynamic a licence to go for it.

I got the Head to offer bursaries so that we could map out how things like equal opportunities, multiculturalism and spirituality were being addressed across the curriculum. We began a dialogue on what needed improving and where the gaps might be.

The departments were being forced to address issues and interconnect with other departments. The questions kept coming up: was racism being addressed in a way that gelled together between the departments? Were gender and racial stereotypes still appearing in books and displays? Could we positively address Multicultural issues?

When you walked round the school you could see more thought going into displays, you could see lesson planning taking on board the issues.

The momentum was building and all over the school people were taking ownership.

The 'hidden' or 'informal' curriculum was the important thing. This was the real message the school put out. If we could harness that so teachers were more conscious of the impact of their techniques, words and teaching styles we could be really effective.

We had to drum in the mantra: - open, caring, friendly, equality, responsibility, respect, empathy, tolerance, and fun.

The first aim of every department handbook was to have fun. Education must be active and enjoyable.

By the time of our next Ofsted inspection I had become a deputy head and we were deemed an 'Outstanding School'. Once again every one of my own responsibilities was considered outstanding. That gave me added clout.

The revolution was bearing fruit.

An ethos does not come about by accident. It is the product of a great deal of thought, planning and enthusiasm. Nothing happens by chance.

It is the little things that count.

Smile!

You are always welcome in my lesson even if sometimes your behaviour isn't!

Chapter 10 – Inspections

Nowadays a few teachers are lazy, a few are stuck in their ways, a few are vicious and cruel, a few are incompetent but the vast majority are brilliant, dedicated, hard-working caring individuals who always give of their best.

In my class at secondary school Charlie was overweight. He hated PE and couldn't do it.

Mr K our PE teacher had set up a rota for us. He'd organised all the apparatus and we did a circuit. It was great fun. The idea was that you rushed round as many circuits as you could do in the half hour. There were benches to walk along, ropes to climb, beams to do a hand over hand, wall-bars to climb, horses to jump, ropes to skip, steps to step.

Most of us loved it.

For Charlie it was a nightmare.

Mr K stood in the middle and bellowed instructions and encouragement.

This usually took the form of shouting at someone to hurry it up.

His attention was drawn to the beam where a queue had formed and he went over to investigate.

He discovered Charlie was the cause. One or two of the class bullies had decided to take the piss. Charlie wobbled and shook like jelly. Try as he may he could not jump high enough to get a grip on the beam let alone swing hand over hand along its length. Charlie's way of dealing with this was the same for nearly all the apparatus: he'd have a perfunctory few attempts and then move on.

What had amused the class bullies was the sight of Charlie trying to jump up and landing amid a series of wobbles as if an earthquake was running through his body. His fat rose and fell and rippled before settling back into its usual contours. It was normally hidden from sight inside his expansive uniform but the skimpy PE t-shirt and shorts afforded no camouflage.

The pulsations of Charlie's flesh were highly amusing to the assembled boys. The class Mafiosi wanted to exploit it. Rather than allowing Charlie to try a couple of times, fail, and move on, they were insisting he did it again. Charlie was refusing.

'What's going on here?' Mr K enquired sizing up the situation with a grin.

'Get up there boy and get on with it. You're causing a log-jam.'

Charlie jumped for the beam. His fingers scrabbled at it but could not get a purchase and he fell down to the sound of much amusement. The rest of the class were homing in on it by now. We were all gathered round chortling and calling out. This was good class entertainment.

Mr K swiped him round the arse with the cane. 'Get up there boy.'

Charlie jumped again with the same result. You could see his bottom lip trembling and tears in his eyes.

The class guffawed, pressing forward, gesturing, calling out and laughing with excitement.

Mr K whacked him harder.

Charlie tried again and again. It was whack. Jump. Whack. Jump. By this time Charlie was blubbering and there was blood on his shorts. His attempts had become more and more pathetic and it was obvious that there was no way in hell that he was going to be able to do it. It was simply beyond him.

Yet Mr K would not call it a day. His response was to hit Charlie harder and shout in his ear.

The excited class suddenly became sober and began to squirm. It was going all too far even for the bullies. The fun had gone out of it.

Whack! Blubber! Scramble. Fall. Whack!

We stood and watched as it went on and on.

Finally even Mr K had had enough and walked away in disgust.

What is in place to prevent any abuse of power?

What mechanisms are there to ensure that the staff and the senior team are doing their jobs, and that the students are getting the education they deserve?

In the early years of my education experience, as a child and as a young teacher, I witnessed the most appalling examples of so called education.

One teacher used to tape record his lessons, play them on a tinny old tape deck, put his feet up on the desk and go to sleep while the diligent students made notes.

In one class the RE teacher used to give out handouts for us to copy and then sit back in his chair and nod off. We would wait for him to be away with the nymphs and slip out of the room for half an hour then slip back in. When the bell woke him up he'd find us working away.

One PE teacher used to throw a ball out from the staff room, instruct the kids to play football on the top field while he watched the cricket or tennis in the staff room.

For biology A level the teacher used to dictate sections of the textbook to us.

One Head teacher used to wander in for briefing, wander back home, make a brief appearance before lunch and then off for a two hour dinner break.

It was also quite normal to see lessons that resembled a riot. On one occasion, as a fairly new teacher, I was out coaching tennis when I saw and heard uproar coming from a nearby classroom. I watched for a few moments and it looked like mayhem. It was obvious that the class was unsupervised and anarchy ruled. I went over and rushed in. The boys had actually started piling chairs and desks into a heap in the middle of the room, running and jumping about like red Indians in an old western film. I shouted, quietened them down and retrieved some semblance of order. It was only then that I noticed the teacher cowering behind his desk.

Most teachers were professional and tried their hardest but a few were lazy and incompetent and there was no easy way to weed them out. Whether the kids were short-changed or not the teachers walked off with the same pay packet. It did not matter if they worked every hour possible and strained every sinew and neuron or kicked back and did nothing – they were paid the same.

There is no doubt in my mind that the present day teacher is more professional, better trained, and hardworking than those of the past. These days a lesson is analysed from start to finish and judged on many different criteria. It has to cater for gender, race, academic range and learning type. There has to be a range of styles and techniques with built in rewards and recognition. A lesson is an all-singing all-dancing event. It can take days to prepare with multimedia inputs and interactive components, electronic whiteboards, computers and even the odd smattering of question and answers. A lesson is now often a work of art.

Perhaps one good reason why we have got to this advanced level is the much dreaded Ofsted inspections.

But not necessarily so as inspections are limited in what is observed and concluded. They are in danger of driving education into narrow pathways.

The school had a health and safety inspection. I went round the whole site with the inspector and recorded all the improvements he wanted me to make. Most of them were minor and concerned with signage.

At the end of the inspection I was standing in the top corridor, at the top of the stairs looking down towards the library, discussing incidents with the inspector.

In my then thirty five years at the school we had suffered two fatalities on the site. Both had involved cross-country. One boy had been hit by a car while crossing a road on a cross-country race. The other had collapsed at the end of a cross-country race. He had suffered a major rupture of his aorta that appeared to be caused by a systemic weakness that no one knew about. He had been a fit lad and nobody could have predicted any problem. There were no symptoms.

I also knew one boy who was knocked off his bike on the way into school.

Death is a hard thing to come to terms with. I have fond memories of brave boys who fought and died from cancer. All their deaths greatly affected the school.

One of my first tasks as Head was to tell the Sixth Form that one of their friends had committed suicide. I had to follow that with giving a eulogy at his funeral. It was not easy.

The situation I was bringing up with the health and safety inspector was that I had personally witnessed or been involved with two near fatal accidents.

The first of these had occurred on a Friday afternoon in my first term of teaching. It was last period in the day and I was in the staff room on my own having a cup of coffee and glancing through the newspaper. The bell had just gone.

There was a knock on the door.

I opened the door to find a young lower sixth student standing there.

'Excuse me sir,' he said pleasantly. 'I've just banged my head and need to sit down for a minute until my head has cleared.'

'Where did you hit it?' I asked, guiding him in and sitting him down. He vaguely indicated that it was nothing and motioned to the back of his head.

'I just gave it a bang, sir,' he reported quite chirpily. 'It's nothing much. It just left me a bit dizzy and I wanted to sit down quietly to clear my head.'

I checked his eyes. Dilation was fine and even. There were no obvious symptoms of anything wrong.

I watched him for a few minutes.

'Are you alright?'

'Fine, sir. It's beginning to clear. I've just got a ringing in my ears.'

I checked him again and everything still looked fine.

I watched him for another couple of minutes. There was nothing I could put my finger on but he did not look quite right.

'I'm going to get a member of staff to run you in for a check,' I said, getting up. I had no car.

'There's no need, sir,' he protested. 'I'll be fine in a minute.'

I went along to get someone to run him in anyway. I took their lesson and they took the boy in their car to the hospital.

On the way the boy collapsed.

He had sustained a three way fracture of the skull.

He had run along the corridor outside the library and swung on a big old central heating pipe that ran close to the ceiling. His feet had gone right up to the ceiling and then his hands had slipped off the pipe and he had fallen down on to the tiled floor. As he could not reach behind him to break his fall the back of his head had taken the full impact. It must have been quite a thud; not the simple bump on the head he had suggested.

The bleeding from the fracture was causing pressure to build up on the brain and it was in danger of collapsing which may have killed him.

When he arrived at the hospital they rushed him in for an emergency operation that saved his life. They said that if he had arrived ten minutes later he would have been dead.

It sent chills through me when I heard. I could easily have kept him in the staffroom until he collapsed. It would have been too late then. I still do not know what made me make the decision to get him to the hospital. There had obviously been some minor clues I had intuitively picked up on.

Fortunately he made a full recovery.

I surveyed the corridor with the Health and Safety officer.

'Do you see anything down there that I might need to address?' I asked him.

The Health and Safety officer made a few comments about crowding in the corridor.

'What about the pipe? I asked.

He could see nothing untoward.

I told him what had happened all those years before. He shook his head in disbelief.

I then directed his attention to the stairs.

A few years before, one lunch-time, I had been walking along the bottom corridor towards the front office at the end of a dinner-time duty.

As I approached the stairs a boy came flying out of the stairwell feet first parallel to the ceiling. He fell back to the ground and I saw the back of his head hit the edge of the bottom step with a sickening thud.

I stood paralysed for a moment. It brought flooding back the memories of the first accident. The similarities were obvious.

I ran up expecting to find him dead or at best unconscious. I felt sure no one could possibly have survived such a solid blow to the back of the head.

He was not unconscious. He groaned a bit and was already beginning to sit up. I rested him back down and gingerly began to check for injuries.

I called someone from the office to get an ambulance.

The strange thing was that he was bleeding from a great gash across his forehead yet I had clearly seen the back of his head striking the edge of the stony composition stairs. I was imagining a fractured skull. Perhaps it was so badly fractured that it had actually split the skin on his forehead?

We kept him still and comfortable until the ambulance arrived and took over.

Fortunately the boy was alright. He had X-rays and there was no fracture. He didn't even have concussion and just needed a few stitches to the wound on his forehead.

He too had run down the top corridor and then jumped a whole flight of stairs. When he'd tried, with the considerable momentum he had built up, to jump from the landing to the bottom corridor he had misjudged the ceiling. His brow had struck the edge created by the ceiling so that his momentum had propelled his body out level with the ceiling and he'd fallen down.

I had merely seen the end of the incident. It must have looked like a cartoon character accident; his head stopping still with the impact while his body went on. It explained why he'd got the gash on his forehead though.

I showed the health and safety officer the stairs but he couldn't find any improvements we could make.

Inspections don't always provide you with valuable information. You cannot legislate for every possible contingency. You cannot reduce risk to nil. It is all about a question of balance. If you make too many rules you get bogged down in pointless and ineffective bureaucracy.

On the whole I think Ofsted inspections are a necessary evil. They should be made regularly and come completely out of the blue. There should be less emphasis on the paperwork and results should not be used for political gain.

Inspecting a lesson is easy. It is not hard to do. You walk in a classroom and smell the relationship. An experienced inspector should be able to sort out what's going on in a matter of minutes.

It may then take a bit of delving to find out why things are going wrong.

The best way is to ask the students. They are invariably honest.

One Ofsted inspector stood with me looking at the interactions of the boys at break-time. There were lots of staff around talking and laughing with the boys. The atmosphere was lovely.

'You know,' the inspector remarked. 'Your boys are better behaved at break-time than students in many schools are in lessons.'

He'd picked up on the friendly atmosphere and great relationships between the students and staff.

I smiled.

The boys rarely let you down. They were a source of great pride.

I remember when I was on teaching practice way back at the beginning of my career. I had a quite lively year 8 class that my tutor wanted to carry out a formal assessment in. I was nervous as they were a little unruly and not the best class to be assessed on. On the day they were brilliant. They listened carefully, every time I asked a question lots of hands shot up, they carried out the practical with enthusiasm and diligence. It was a real transformation.

When my tutor was at the other end of the lab checking on the progress of a group of students one of the lads sidled up to me – 'Don't worry, sir,' he whispered. 'We'll see you alright.'

Chapter 11 – The Pastoral System

To understand and deal with incidents effectively you have to know the history and take that into account when you explore a way forward. You have to understand the people concerned. No two seemingly identical incidents are the same. They might require entirely different solutions.

Reuben 'El Gangster' Alvarez (the blood test guy) was the gangster of the class. He was a real-life gang leader and all of seventeen. He had the knife scars to prove it.

Reuben took me around the school district to explain the graffiti. It was all extremely stylised with lists of names drawn up in different colours and types of writing.

One set of names was the role of honour. They were the gang members who had fallen in the line of duty, defending their turf against rival gangs. The territory around the school was carved up into areas held by two gangs – the Crips and the Bloods.

'What are these?' I asked Reuben, referring to another line of names written in a different style.

'They're the dead,' Reuben explained with a grin.

These were the members of the other gang implicated in various crimes against Reuben's gang. They were on the death list. Every night Reuben's gang would hunt for them. They had machine guns. For them life was all about honour and respect.

As head of pastoral I had to deal with one lad repeatedly. He was always being surly, disruptive and aggressive.

'You been kicked out again, John?' I asked when I saw him standing outside the classroom.

'Yeah,' he replied scowling.

'What for this time?'

'I dunno.'

'I think we'd better go and talk about it,' I said, poking my head round the door and telling the teacher I'd deal with it. I led him back to my room and we had a chat.

He'd been rude and told the teacher to fuck off.

I asked him why and he told me he was in a bad mood.

'What caused that, John?' I asked.

'My parents had another big row last night,' he confessed. 'It pissed me off.'

'That's no reason to take it out on other people.'

'No. I guess not.'

We talked around things for a bit, about his recurring problems in class, his rudeness and aggression and the reason why he felt like that. The trigger seemed to always go back to trouble between his parents. They argued. He was afraid they were going to split up. It made him feel bad and he took it out on others.

'How long have your parents had these difficulties?' I asked.

'Since the house burnt down,' he replied.

It was a bit of a bombshell. He told me all about it. There'd been a big fire one night. They'd all got out alright but he'd sat watching while the house burnt down. It had been a bad fire and taken all their possessions, photos, treasured stuff. Worst of all his pet dog had been trapped upstairs and nobody could get to it. He'd had to sit and listen to it howling and screaming as it was burnt to death.

'I can't get it out of my head,' he told me. 'I keep getting flashbacks and nightmares.'

He had not told anyone. He couldn't talk about things to his parents because they kept arguing. He'd been bottling it up. In his head there was no purpose to anything. There was no security. Anything you loved could be taken away from you overnight.

It was very salutary for me.

Behind every bad behaviour was a reason. Find the reason and you stood a chance of addressing the behaviour. Merely punishing the behaviour would at best contain the problem.

Somehow we had to let our damaged kids confront and deal with their demons. Sometimes we had to get in expert help.

I saw the lad's parents and we had a talk. We organised some counselling and it seemed to help.

I inherited the pastoral team as a senior teacher. They had previously been managed by a deputy head so they, like the curriculum team before them, were a bit sceptical. It felt to them like a demotion.

There were a good bunch of heads of year and they were all greatly involved with their year groups and tutor teams, dedicated and hard working.

The problem as I saw it was that they did not work cohesively. They discussed policy in meetings and went off to put it into practice. I went round looking at what was going on. It was all good but all different. I knew that if I could get practice more coherent and consistent it would become more effective. They really cared about the kids and that was a good place to start.

I proposed that we concentrated on going back to basics, discussing policy, agreeing what to do and writing it down. We would accumulate the policy and procedure into a pastoral handbook.

We started from philosophy and the ethos.

At first they were very cynical but as we went along they began to see the worth of the project. By discussing philosophy and policy we drew closer. We could argue and compromise. They were extremely passionate. Once we had agreed we wrote it up and started to make the handbook. Then we were all singing from the same hymn sheet and things started to zing.

They had assumed that all of them thought the same way and were doing the same things. It came as a shock to find they were all doing different things.

What emerged was a collaboration of best practice. They were getting a buzz out of doing it. It was rewarding to see the handbook coming together. It was stimulating to be having lots of ideas and putting them into practice. Things started to work at a whole new level. The intensity was so much higher and more rewarding. Best of all it was more effective.

Alongside the handbook I introduced a new five year planning. There were lots of areas that needed improving and whole school issues that could be included or addressed through good practice. We had to produce a plan that was fully costed out, made achievable without driving us into the ground, and was prioritised over five years.

I also introduced a tutor developmental monitoring programme to ensure the tutors were focussed on what they were meant to be doing.

The test of a pastoral system is that it addresses the student needs. It is caring, works from the ethos, is preventative, rewarding and recognising.

The monitoring sheet was based on a pump priming monitor sheet that Phil one of our heads of year, who had previously been an engineer, had brought in. It worked.

I wanted something quick, easy to do and not time consuming. The important thing was to focus tutors on to relating to kids and supporting them. It achieved that.

We overhauled the reward and recognition systems, bringing in certificates and celebration assemblies.

We reviewed attendance and carried out a similar process with another raft of certificates and celebrations.

We focussed on counselling and were doing restorative practice before it had been invented.

Behaviour improved throughout the school. Attendance rose to best in county and stayed there.

When Ofsted came in they gave pastoral the thumbs up. It was the best practice they'd seen. They said the handbook, all three hundred and fifty pages, was the best they had ever reviewed and took it off with them. I later found out they had been using it in Devon as part of their training, holding it up as exemplary.

What they did not seem to fully realise was that it was not the actual handbook that was most important. The important aspect had been the unifying, stimulating effect of putting it together. It had gelled us into a team and raised the passions. The pastoral team became like family. I was having real battles with the curriculum team and coming to a pastoral meeting was like coming home. I could relax and feel I was among like-minded friends. We had our moments and rows but we trusted each other and were on the same wavelength.

After the handbook was completed it was never quite the same. A few new members came in and it lost the close camaraderie.

At the time I moved into Headship I was seriously considering the fresh impetus of a major change. I had drawn up plans for a move to vertical tutoring and a complete revamp of the team.

That was put on hold. A new pastoral leader came in and took charge.

One thing you have to do when you move on is to leave some things behind. The same when you delegate. Other people never do things the same way as yourself. You have to keep your distance, only offer advice if requested, and give them the chance to develop it their way. I have had that with biology, science, PSHE, curriculum, pastoral, assessment and equal opportunities. It is hard – so hard.

It's so difficult leaving your babies in other people's hands. But I have seen people who are afraid to delegate because they suspect someone else won't do it as well as themselves. They work themselves silly doing other people's jobs as well as their own. The end result is that their own job suffers; they wear themselves down into a state of exhaustion, and their new assistants become bored and are not allowed to rise into the role.

You have to let things go and not mourn the changes.

Resist interfering.

Chapter 12 - The whole child unwrapped from 'red tape'

I merely wanted to bring some humanity into teaching. I was there to help, guide and teach. I did not see the need to be an authoritarian figure. I myself had been taught by some mean, brutal bullies, straight out of the army and messed up by their experiences in the second world war, who really could not care less. I wanted to reach out and form pleasant positive relationships.

For me teaching was never about my subject. I loved biology. I was inspired by biology but teaching was about so much more. I wanted to reach out to young minds and open them up to become greater, more aware, more questioning, more alive. I wanted them to feel, empathise and care. I wanted them to be tolerant, respectful and concerned with the issues of human beings and life.

Don't get me wrong – I did not desire to make them clones of myself, or even be in agreement with my views and sentiments. I wanted them to be involved, vital and critical. I also wanted them to release their passion, turn them on and get them motoring.

In the present climate we have become stifled by bureaucracy, heavy handed health and safety and a fear of paedophilia that is completely out of all proportion.

We need records and system. We need planning. We need policies. It is when the detailed writing of all of these becomes so onerous that many of our top teaching practitioners are spending more time writing stuff than they are interacting with kids that something is wrong. Things have to be simplified.

When I started teaching I spent my lunch-times and free periods talking and playing with the students. I would be sitting around playing music and chess and engaging in discussion and debate. In the tennis season I would be out playing all the time. We'd play five a side football. We even had staff v student rugby matches.

All this has become impossible. Most staff are too pressured with marking, planning, meetings and paperwork they could no longer dream of relaxing with students. The playing of sport between students and staff has been largely outlawed. Some one somewhere must have been injured and sued. Yet these are the activities that were crucial in forming positive relationships. That loss is catastrophic.

Of course, I do not want any injuries on a school site. It is imperative that we have rules and these are stringently applied. It is when these rules are stifling, reductionary or overbearing that they become oppressive and impair good education.

The stupidity of insisting that staff should not be allowed to go around with a cup of tea unless it is in a lidded cup is a good example. It is silly.

In thirty six years of teaching I never saw anyone injured by scalding tea. There have been a few slips and slops but invariably tea is not hot enough to scald. Good common sense should prevail.

This is true of a number of other stupidities. We had workmen operating on our pavilion roof. They had put up scaffolding round three sides and were working at the front. The health and safety man visited and ordered them down. They were instructed not to proceed until they had scaffolding on all four sides. They explained that they intended to move the scaffold from the front round to the back when they came to doing that part. This was not good enough. Work was halted and more scaffold hired.

This held up work for a day and cost us an extra two thousand pounds.

Nuts.

We had work taking place on a new extension.

I went across to discuss certain practicalities with the foreman. They had laid the foundations and just started laying bricks. At no point on the site were bricks above two sets high – less than a foot.

The foreman came across the compound to talk to me and I stood just within the perimeter some twenty metres away from the building to talk to him.

We had just started talking when the Health and Safety officer blew his whistle to stop work and officiously ordered me out. Seemingly by stepping inside the compound without a hard hat I had broken the rules. He could have come across and pleasantly asked me to step a yard to the side but no – he had to make a scene about it. It seemed to be more about power than safety.

Absolutely nuts.

The current trend towards huge perimeter fencing designed to stop paedophiles gaining entry has turned our schools into prisons. This has a psychological impact on the inmates and it is not a good one.

As a Head I wanted my students to have open horizons, green fields and trees. It raises the spirits. Razor-wire and chain-fences overseen with security cameras like machine gun posts on Stalag 19 are not, in my opinion, good environments for healthy education.

I have never seen herds of wild paedophiles roaming outside these fences searching for gaps to get in to abuse students, neither have I ever seen queues of depraved machinegun clad psychopaths lining up to gun down my students. Sadly such individuals would more likely come in through the main gate and find a way of slipping through any security.

Likewise I am sceptical of all the silly security badges. I cannot see their worth. Are we meant to hold them up like a crucifix to ward off vampires? Do paedophiles or unwanted guests see establishments with badges and think 'Aaah, that's impregnable then' and simply go away? Or do they borrow a badge, make a badge, ignore the whole business and bypass the system or simply join the staff?

Does wearing a badge make anyone safe?

Most abuse is carried out in the home by relatives. The most effective weapon against paedophiles is for professionals to have a good relationship with students, be available and to listen, report and take action.

There are undoubtedly a number of paedophiles out there. But let us get things in proportion and develop effective systems and not knee-jerk bureaucracies that impinge on people's freedoms and good education. We know paedophiles gravitate towards professions where they gain access to young, vulnerable children. These include religious leaders, hospital workers, doctors, scout leaders, babysitters and school workers. We have to be vigilant and provide mechanisms so that the abused can report abuse within organisations quickly instead of relying on nonsensical so called security.

One only has to look at the mind-blowing activities of Jimmy Saville to see this. I wonder how many security fences, cameras, and numbered door pads he waltzed through? I wonder how many security badges he was issued with?

The major thing I wonder at is why there were no mechanisms, no environments of trust, no relationships sufficiently close that his hundreds of victims felt unable to report him so that he was able to continue his abuse for decades.

Have the fences, door codes, and security badges reduced the incidence of paedophilia? Where is the evidence?

Only by creating an environment in which children are loved, cared for and listened to, in which positive close relationships are nurtured can we prevent paedophilia. Children may disclose incidents but only if they feel trusted.

Staff can be trained to be vigilant and look for the signs in other staff and students.

The stifling of healthy relationships with adults and creation of a pedantic, over-zealous rule-driven obsession with minor health and safety rules creates an oppressive environment which is not conducive to the development of a healthy child.

We cannot completely remove risk from the world. We can only work to reduce it.

We had a frightened Down's syndrome student who had started at the school and was traumatised. He had never been among so many people in such a big place. He was overawed, upset and unable to cope. He was standing to the side of the assembly hall sobbing. His carer took him outside and was talking to him in an effort to comfort him. I went over and gave him a hug. He clung to me and slowly began to calm down. All he needed was a hug of reassurance.

Later his carer came in to see me.

'I was so pleased you gave him a hug,' she said.

'It's what he needed,' I replied.

'I didn't feel able to do it,' she said. 'The health and safety regulations mean I could lose my job.'

It is madness when human contact is legislated against. It is abuse that an upset child is left to cry for want of a cuddle. It is inhuman.

We are primates. Cuddles enable us to feel secure. Our fear of paedophilia should not prevent us from doing what is right. I do not want to be part of a world that is cold and inhuman. It is too big a price.

If we want to develop the whole child and instil the skills, values, qualities and feelings that make up a healthy adult you have to promote healthy interaction.

There is nothing wrong in this.

You have to move away from overbearing, authoritarian relationships to more informal 'normal' interaction.

Teachers are role models.

My first experience of lunch-time at the BGS was an eye-opener.

I walked into the dining room which was a prefabricated, corrugated asbestos roofed shed from the second world war.

The students sat on tables of eight supervised by a pair of sixth formers who served the food, sometimes rather unfairly, from metal dishes retrieved from the cook.

The staff all sat at a high table at the end of the dining hall, replete with table cloth, serviettes and posh cutlery and were served by students.

I chose to sit with the students which caused uproar with the older stuffy staff but was much appreciated by the students.

At that time the students were called by their surnames. I used their first names. They found this amusing.

The staff were all male apart from the cook, secretary and one lone teacher of French. We were addressed as Sir by the students. I introduced myself by my first name and surname. They were shocked. First names were top secret. Students spent ages researching to try to find what the initials actually stood for. I had spoilt the fun.

A number of students could not deal with this level of informality. They saw it as weakness. They tried it on. I had to take them aside and spell it out to them, it wasn't a weakness. Surprise, surprise - I was a human being too – get used to it.

Shortly after I joined I was approached by a group of students. It appeared that they were not allowed to play music in their form rooms without supervision. If they could get a member of staff to sit in with them they could call it a music club.

'You don't have to do anything sir,' they remonstrated. 'Just have to be there.'

'You can wear ear-plugs if you like,' one suggested.

'You could get on with some work,' another added.

'Please sir, you're our last hope.'

I readily agreed. I loved rock music, the louder the better, and I was a little out of touch with the current scene. I was hopeful they might fill me in on some great new bands.

In that I was disappointed.

This was 1976 but I soon found that the kids were playing stuff that I'd been into back in 1969/70. There was lots of Doors, Velvet Underground and Hendrix. I loved it but wondered where the new bands were.

'Don't you have any of your own stuff?' I asked. 'This is what I grew up with.'

'Naw, there's nothing much worth listening to,' was the reply.

I started bringing my own albums in and telling them about the bands I had seen. The numbers swelled and before I knew it we had a real music club.

This led to me organising the first school dances complete with live bands. Dances had been stopped 11 years before when a bunch of motorcyclists, described to me by the Head as 'Hells Angels', gate-crashed the event and had to be forcibly ejected. Though what the mythical Beverley branch of the 'Hells Angels' might have actually resembled was anybodies guess. They were probably a small group of youngsters who happened to have arrived on motorbikes. Over time the Chinese whispers had run their course and these had grown into a horde of huge razor-blade toting, chain festooned bikers, crazed on drugs and intent on pillage if not rape. There were more of them and all twice as big with every telling. To hold another dance would likely result in the school being raised to the ground and the staff staked out on the rugby pitched for systematic torture.

The fact that senior management and the stuffy brigade really did not want it to happen was an added spur.

By organising the events with supremely complicated staff supervision rotas and duty systems, with intricate rules, I was able to arrange three live bands and a disco.

It went down a storm.

If you don't hold the informal events, the wear what you like days, the discos and concerts, the football world cup viewings, the charity events, the sporting events and such like you can never create good relationships with teenagers.

Students have to see you as human beings – not teachers. They have to relate to you as human beings.

Education is about relationship. The whole child is too big to fit into a single classroom.

I opened my front door to a large group of excited Y11 students clutching a carrier bag, all with short spiked hair and skin-tight jeans. 'Overnight' they had gone from long-haired, flared trousers to super-punks complete with razor-blades and attitude. Everything was now 'Boring' and had 'No future'.

'Right you boring old git,' one of them announced. 'We've come to play you some real music.'

'Can we come in, sir,' another added.

We spent the evening playing Sex Pistols, Stranglers, Clash and Damned. There was a new age of rebellion, complete with anarchy symbols, nihilistic outlooks and sneering contempt for authority.

I loved it.

When I moved house these young rebels all came round to help decorate. They painted walls and ceilings with great gusto.

We drank tons of coffee, consumed cheese on toast, played lots of loud music, had a good natter and right laugh, and got the whole place done in no time at all.

My own young kids were well enamoured with them, bewitched by these older boys filling the house with their enthusiasm. The boys were likewise really sweet with my kids.

It turned out that these spiky haired rebels with mean attitude were a bunch of intelligent, super-friendly, eager to please, young men who later went on to become editors, solicitors, educators, doctors, vets, musicians and teachers.

It was obvious from the standard of work produced that none of them were destined to become decorators.

My music club went on excursions. This mainly took the form of me driving some of the keenest members to gigs I was already going to.

As we lived in Hull and nothing much ever came near to Hull or Beverley this usually entailed driving to Leeds or Sheffield.

One January, with snow thick on the ground, I was driving a bunch of Years eleven and twelve students to a Roy Harper gig in Leeds in my old beat-up Ford.

We hurtled down the motorway and found ourselves getting hotter and hotter. Coats were taken off, scarves discarded; jumpers pulled over heads, boots shed. The sweat was running off us and yet outside the temperature was below freezing.

I'd even turned the heater off and still the car kept getting hotter.

Just then a car pulled up alongside us and the panic stricken driver indicated to us to pull over and stop.

I did so.

He stopped a good couple of hundred metres ahead.

As soon as we came to a halt smoke and flames billowed out from under the bonnet.

The kids were out of the car in two seconds flat and standing with the driver of the over car watching.

I got out and opened the bonnet. It became obvious what had happened.

The air-filter had a big plastic cover. This had become loose and fallen on to the exhaust manifold. As the exhaust manifold had heated up it had melted and set fire to the plastic. This had then been blown back under the car.

From behind it had looked mighty impressive. The car was zooming along with flames searing out from underneath. This was augmented by burning, dripping plastic – a veritable firework display - all very impressive.

The driver had been convinced the whole thing was about to blow up.

The remains of the plastic were still burning fiercely even though no longer fanned by the wind of our progress.

I think the students all thought it was going to blow up. I was also worried; the car had fuel pipes and a petrol tank.

I looked around for something to put the flames out with and grabbed handfuls of snow and grass. I shoved these on top of the burning plastic. In so doing I brushed my hand on the red hot exhaust manifold and jerked it away with a yell banging my head on the bonnet which promptly came down on me.

The students told everyone at school that the bonnet came down and there was all this smoke and flames with two little legs poking out kicking for all they were worth.

It wasn't quite as dramatic as that.

I put the fire out, prised the remains of the plastic off the manifold and inspected the car. There was little damage. Some electric cables from the starter motor had been burnt out but that seemed all.

We bump started the car; all piled in and resumed our journey to another immaculate Roy Harper concert.

These are the things people remember about school. These are the incidents that forge relationships that go straight into the classroom and enable you to take the risk in which lessons can flourish and reach new heights. These are the things that allow students to grow and develop those qualities that we idealistically crave.

For the whole child to develop you have to put in more than the standard lesson. The teaching experience has to surmount the confines of a lesson. This requires mutual respect and trust. That comes about when you can relax and enjoy each others company.

When my lessons soared so did I. I have never been happier than teaching a group of young people and being taught by them in a completely relaxed environment where discipline and rules are figments of the imagination.

Some of my early students went on to become good friends (now in their 50s!) that I have kept up with through life.

Chapter 13 – Great lessons – great teaching

I had a poster up in my room which was a quote from one of my heroes Haim G. Ginott. It always sent shivers through me. He concluded that the teacher was the decisive factor who had the power to create misery or joy, to inspire or torture, heal or humiliate, escalate or de-escalate, humanise or dehumanise.

That is inspirational. It sums up everything I believe in. Haim said it so much better than me and I urge everyone to find a copy of the quote and put it up somewhere prominent in their classroom. That quote and the one about being a survivor of a concentration camp - they get to the heart of what I believe teaching should be.

The question everyone always comes back to is what makes outstanding teaching.

When I started teaching in 1975 nobody was talking about learning outcomes. There was no great over-riding doctrine. We were taught to teach at college in a perfunctory way. It was how to control classes, what experiments to do and some rudimentary lesson planning.

When it came to it you were left on your own in a classroom. There was no pastoral system to bring in the cavalry. You sunk or swum. You knew this from the start. You'd heard all the tales of teaching practice.

Once the door shut you existed in your own little world. Nobody checked on you or what you were up to. There were no rules or work schemes. Those all came later.

Nobody even much cared what we did in years 7-9. We did interesting experiments and investigations. All the hard work was done in years 10 and 11.

I sat down with my head of department Mike and put some ideas together for years 7-9 that looked interesting and laid the foundations for O level. Fortunately we thought very much along the same lines.

For year 10 and year 11 we had a syllabus. We put the topics in some semblance of order and tailored them to fit the number of lessons available.

My lesson planning consisted of a list I put up on the wall in the prep room. It had a hundred lessons on it. This read like photosynthesis 1, photosynthesis 2, photosynthesis 3, respiration 1 etc. That was it. There was nothing else written. As a teacher I knew I had to cover photosynthesis in 3 lessons. You kept it all in your mind.

I had similar lists for years 7-9 and the sixth form. The sixth form had four lessons a week – two were theory and two were practical. The sum total of my sixth form lesson planning was to borrow the A level notes off one of my friends Tobes who'd got a grade A. I figured that if he'd got a grade A they were good enough. I just had to dictate, explain and embellish with my own wisdom.

You'd cross the lessons off as you did them.

We had a technician, making other subject teachers deliriously jealous, who would get the apparatus out for experiments and wash them up.

Sometime, towards the end of a week, I'd sit down with the lab book and look at what was coming up and decide what experiments I was going to do and write down which apparatus I needed so that the technician could get it out. That's the nearest I got to formal planning.

Nothing was written down. What you did was in your head. I did not spend a lot of time even thinking about it. You got used to consulting the list as you went into the lab and trying to remember exactly what you had covered last week. On more than one occasion I used a question and answer session to orientate myself as to what I was doing.

Everything was by the seat of your pants but it was alive and exciting.

The lessons were organised around the chalkboard and experiments. You started the lesson with a quiet registration, handing out books with praise and then a question and answer to bring everyone up to speed. You'd introduce stuff, remind them of what we'd done and relate it in. Then it was experiments and you'd put results tables on the board. Give them a few notes and discuss conclusions.

It sounds formulaic and boring but it wasn't. It was fast paced and fun.

All the time you were trying to think of new and better ways of explaining things, exciting approaches, new experiments, or jokes you could add. The fact that it was spontaneous meant that your mind was switched on. You were constantly searching for improvements. You relied on your own knowledge and were always seeking that perfect, easy-going relationship.

Looking back I think that because I wasn't burnt out on a huge burden of planning, or chained into a relentlessly boring routine I was fresh and sparkly in the classroom. Lessons were dynamic, despite a lot of blackboard stuff and a fair bit of dictation, and full of humour. I was quick witted in my younger days; light on my feet, nimble of thought. I could produce a pun or witticism to fit any situation.

Teaching was fluid. You could digress or take as much time as you needed. If it was obvious they were not cottoning on you'd think of a different approach.

Teaching is relationship and I worked hard at that. I wanted my classroom full of fun and good harmonious relationships. That usually worked though there were still some very challenging and frustrating classes and individuals. My lab was always full and buzzing at breaks and lunch-time.

During lunch and free periods I was free to interact with students in clubs, I ran a biology club, a rock music club, a film club and an animal house, or went out to play tennis or football with the students. This different, more normal relationship fed straight back into the classroom.

I always believed that there should be no need for heavy handed discipline and distance between teacher and students. I was there to teach. They were here to learn. I tried to make it fun and exciting. I hoped they enjoyed it and were turned on. I could not understand why we had to have a gulf. It seemed to me that this stemmed out of a bad education system that kids rebelled against. Experience has taught me that it is a tad more complicated but good relationships are still essential to good teaching and learning. I wanted a free and easy relationship and usually I was allowed to have it.

That's why I love teaching.

On a hot sunny day I would sometimes take my class for a nature walk. There was a nature reserve across the road and common land to the side of the school. We'd have a pleasant walk looking at nature. I'd point out fungi, lichen, water voles, frogs, lizards and newts. Unbelievably some of them had ridiculously never noticed this wild-life even though they were all around us. I found this hard to understand. I had spent my youth wading in ponds, lifting up rocks and corrugated iron, collecting anything that moved. It was hard to understand that some didn't delight in it. I tried to show them a little of the wondrous world they lived in.

After a number of years my head of department and I started typing some of these lessons up and produced them into booklets that we could work around. We were very proud of these rudimentary efforts.

I produced a whole batch of homework sheets with little experiments they could carry out at home and a few exceedingly corny jokes. They became much sought after. The kids would avidly read them and groan.

So was this good, poor or even outstanding teaching? I don't know. I certainly came out of some lessons thinking we'd reached new heights, I'd explained things well, they'll been engaged and turned on by it, and we'd got along great. At those times life couldn't have been better. At other times I'd have a run in with students or lessons seemed dull and boring and I felt depressed.

Is it better now that everything is planned to the nth degree, analysed with built in variety catering for different learning styles, and structured to tick every box, with internet access and interactive sections? I don't know. For some teachers it is immensely improved; for others it is restricting.

I have observed some lessons that leave me gob-smacked in their scope and dynamism. I have seen others that slog away through the plan.

At the end of the day it comes down to the teacher, their personality, enthusiasm, attitude and humour and the relationship they strike up with the class.

That's why teachers pay is so important. If you don't pay enough you don't attract in quality staff! The kids get short-changed! We need to pay teachers well and attract those with dynamism and energy.

Teaching is a complex set of skills. It requires exceptional personalities. Only a limited number of people are good at it. We should care about our kids enough to attract in the best. Those kids are our future.

On a biology field course the 6th form students were studying ecology and being taught by a young enthusiastic ecologist. She was very good and passionate about nature but the students were overawed by the new surroundings of the Field Centre and were being very quiet and unresponsive.

I was watching and could see she was struggling to get a response.

The student nick-name for me was 'Bod'. I was never sure where that came from, Mark Ruston, an ex-student, recently told me it came from this cartoon character called Bod who was a bald Buddhist monk. It was student irony. They called me Bod because I was so hairy, but I was fond of telling everyone who asked that it stood for 'Brilliant, Out-the-Ordinary, Devastating'.

I tore off a tiny scrap of paper from my notepad and scrawled '1 Bod point' on it with a picture of a cartoon spider. The next time one of the students answered a question I passed the scrap over to them.

They were bemused.

As the lesson went on, and I passed round 'Bod points' with various insects, they began to catch on. Soon it became a competition to get the most 'Bod points'. The lesson was transformed. The concentration levels went up. The mood lifted. Hands were shooting up.

It is incredible how a simple thing can make such a difference - the more informal and quirky the better.

I tried typing up the 'Bod points' and cutting them out with scissors. They worked but not so well. Students like to feel special. They like to feel that it's personal. They do not like to feel they are subject to some formal process you have devised and will use with everyone. It does not make them feel important. The scruffy bits of paper worked best!

Perhaps it is a good idea to reflect back on the teaching I was exposed to as a boy. The majority of it was terrible.

We had teachers who made you copy endlessly from textbooks or blackboards, who dictated boringly, or droned on for hours. It was all one great memory test.

One English teacher had trouble controlling the class. She discovered that we all loved the poem 'The Jumblies' and allow us to endlessly recite it excitedly every lesson. That's all I can remember of her lessons. The class all went to sea in a sieve!

My Latin teacher Tatters (Mr Tatloe) used to translate Pliny to us. We were given a Latin text and had to write the translation down in our exercise books. He held our attention by sitting on the back of a wooden classroom chair, holding the book in one hand and absently pulling at the elasticised wristband of his wristwatch. He got right into it and used to tilt his chair so that he teetered on two legs. I can't remember much about Pliny but I can remember watching intently, waiting for the inevitable when the tilt would go too far, he'd lose balance and crash to the ground. It strangely never happened.

The only other thing I can remember about his lessons was when one day my friend Billy hid in the cupboard behind the blackboard. Throughout the lesson he kept pushing the blackboard open and peeping out. Tatters was lost in his translation, never cottoned on to the reasons for the laughter and did not catch Billy.

Our A level biology teacher, used to pointlessly read sections out of the uniquely turgid textbook Grove and Newell for us to copy down verbatim. I could not see the point.

On the other side of the coin there were teachers who seemed to really care about us and seemed to enjoy their subjects. They managed to communicate this to us.

Mr Brand tried to create a relaxed easy going atmosphere. We did maths with radios playing the latest pop music.

Mr and Mrs Shoedbrooke were the epitome of friendliness and were well respected.

But when it came to active teaching and holding a classes attention it was Mr Bell the chemist who held sway.

He adored bangs.

Every lesson you arrived to the banging of his tin can terrors.

Mr Bell took a variety of empty tin cans of varying sizes, made a hole in the top and a hole in the bottom, filled them with gas and set fire to the hole in the top. The gas would burn with a big yellow flame. It was replaced with air drawn in through the hole in the bottom. When the gas and air mixture inside reached the right proportions it would explode blowing the lid of the tin off which hit the ceiling and clattered off onto the floor.

Every lesson we'd troop in to find a half dozen tins with flames already lit. They'd explode in succession and prompt an exciting start to the lesson.

We all loved explosions.

Mr Bell's classes were never short of explosions, smells or drama. They brought chemistry to life.

My friends and I had great fun making our own bombs. We'd take to bits penny bangers, or better still Chinese crackers, and extract the gunpowder. We'd use this to make bigger bangs. We converted an old length of metal tubing into a cannon to fire ball bearings up until it dramatically ruptured.

In the sixth form we had lessons on gun-cotton and tri-iodo-toluene, which was a paste that dried into a contact explosive.

We made tons of the stuff and had great fun smearing small bits on blackboard rollers or under stools in the lab. It would dry and when the blackboard was moved up there would be an accompanying series of minor crackles and bangs, likewise when a stool was moved or sat on.

It was great fun.

As with all things we were not satisfied with small crackles and began using bigger and bigger dollops. Stools would go off with a big bang.

It all came to a head after we'd put a big dollop on the floor. The unsuspecting laboratory technician, while carrying a glass trough of apparatus, trod on it. It went off with a big bang and he dropped the apparatus which smashed everywhere.

We were called in to the head of science and told in no uncertain terms that we had to stop.

I still remember those lessons more than any others.

What makes good teaching is when a teacher allows their passions and interests to flood over the students and carry them along on the tsunami they create. It's when the minds are engaged, stimulated and inspired. It's when lessons soar.

Forget the structure.

I've seen it done in a hundred different ways.

I've see the new teacher, as a geekie wimp, come in unable to control a class and go away to work on it. They came back with a set of resources so inspiring that the kids were carried away with them. I've seen charismatic teachers hold classes transfixed with wonder as their personality and imagination transmitted itself to the students.

While a student teacher on teaching practice I saw the best example of student control ever. It was atrocious weather and all thoughts of taking groups outside for games had to be abandoned. The head of PE decided to take the hundred boys in the main hall for an indoor hockey lesson.

He told us that it was OK, he'd handle it, we could just watch. He'd end with a competition and we could ref the matches.

He bought in dustbins of hockey sticks and hockey balls. Each lad took a stick and a ball. He brought them all together and explained what he was going to do. They listened intently.

For the next twenty minutes he had them practising passing, stopping and dribbling around the hall. The hall would be a bewildering mass of excited boys dribbling round each other at speed. He'd blow his whistle and it would instantly stop. He'd instruct them to reverse sticks and it was off again accompanied by a cacophony of noise. He'd blow and it would halt. He'd arrange pairs for passing.

It ran like clockwork.

Then he called all hundred in, arranged them into teams, organised the dividing of the hall into pitches and set about organising a competition.

The games were played. There were quarter finals, semi-finals and a final. Right on time the final ended, a team was crowned winner, and every boy ran off, red faced and glowing with satisfaction, to get changed putting their sticks and balls back in the right bins.

Within a minute the whole hall was cleared and empty with everything in its place as if nothing had happened. The organisation and control exerted in the course of this impromptu lesson, with no planning or preparation was astounding. One hundred boys had thoroughly enjoyed themselves, developed their skills and run themselves into the ground.

As a young teacher looking to get started it was salutary. I felt like a novice guitarist watching Sergovia or Hendrix. It made you feel like giving up. Yet it also made you realise how good things could get. They loved him and respected him and that had been the cement that had held it together. You didn't get response like that out of fear or intricate planning. That came out of carefully building relationships over time coupled with experience.

It finally seems that teacher training has got its act together as the standard of new teachers has become scary in its brilliance.

Certainly I think the increase in pay and prestige has attracted a higher quality of student into teaching.

I have had the privilege of visiting lesson after lesson of outstanding genius. This transformation has been assisted by the development of the interactive whiteboard and computers.

Long gone are the days of textbooks and talk and chalk. The whole world has been opened up. You can now interact with a class the other side of the world in real time. The old ways, with exercise books and endless writing, are as dead as the dodo, as dead as chalk-boards.

There is no excuse for boring teaching now.

I've seen young teachers providing such brilliance, interchanging activities, bringing in interaction, giving individual praise and guidance, showing short videos, providing all manner of different learning experiences tailored to different learning styles, interspersed with active group-work and research off the web. Juggling ten balls would be easier and they do it all with such passion, enthusiasm and effortless skill. I knew I was the old dinosaur who'd had his day. I felt that it was time for me to bow out.

If I was starting out in science I'd just give them the apparatus and set them off exploring and investigating. I'd facilitate it. I'd have them recording the setting up of apparatus on their phones and filming what happened. I'd have them recording it in tables they access on the web, and writing up their conclusions on line.

Lessons would be totally active.

All results and conclusions would be downloaded onto my computer and I'd mark and give feedback electronically.

I'd look for fun, excitement and discovery.

It's a different world.

I just wish the politicians would move into the real world where the internet and phone rule; where everything is done by text or twitter; where nobody needs to remember a thing and the sort of overblown, memory based examination system is completely and utterly irrelevant.

Mr Politician, just watch the skills possessed by young people as they adeptly thumb their way through a keypad, multitask on electronic devices, and intuitively find their way through the novel developments of cyberspace and its gadgetry. The future is in good hands. They don't need your memory tests and essays. We're a million miles beyond essays.

My advice to politicians - Your old world has rapidly faded so get out of the new one if you can't lend a hand! – To paraphrase Bob Dylan.

Chapter 14 – Knowing your students

Terry Bolton was in my class when I was at school. He was the class tough guy. He earned his status from being ultra hard. Terry put his fist through the window in the door, slicing his hand badly in the process and laughing about it. Terry put Mr Sole through the glass fronted bookcase.

He was 'a bit of a lad' with his sneer and hair that was long enough to curl up at the back.

To make an example of Terry they decided to cane him before the whole school.

We all sat in our rows.

Terry was called out. He swaggered up the aisle on to the stage and smiled sneeringly at them. They bent him over the table. He put his hands up both sides of the table gripping it firmly.

Terry looked sideways at all of us sitting there and winked.

The Head strode purposefully over to the other side of the stage and flexed his long bendy cane then ran across the stage leapt and brought the cane down on Terry's buttocks in as vicious a swipe as he could muster. All his strength went into it.

The whack resounded round the school hall. Terry did not flinch or register the blow.

The Head repeated this for the remaining five blows before dismissing Terry.

Terry stood up slowly, turned and grinned at us. He sauntered down the steps and up the aisle to his place and sat down.

We were amazed.

You were excused being seated if you were caned. The swipe of the cane broke the skin in a line across your buttocks. It instantly swelled into a ridge of a solid welt. This welt gradually softened over the next days, starting purple and fading to brown then orange.

When you were caned, as I was a number of times, it was liquid agony. Everyone gave an involuntary squeal. Your eyes watered and the blood trickled down your legs. It was agony. You could not possibly sit on a chair. It hurt too much.

I don't know how it made other people feel but it filled me with anger and hatred. It never worked as a deterrent on me or my friends.

We watched Terry take it without as much as a flinch. It was awe inspiring.

He left the hall a hero.

It is important to know your students. What works with one student does not work with another. People have different natures.

Some people can be punished and put it aside and move on, others hold a grudge for life.

The important thing in education is to punish the behaviour and not the child.

I always affirmed that my students were equally welcome in my lessons if sometimes their behaviour wasn't. I meant it.

I always had affection for some of the biggest rogues. They at least had a bit of a spark about them.

Life is pure chance.

You cannot help where you are born and what circumstances you are born into. You are at the mercy of your genes. Children are like paper blown in the winds of adult intrigue.

If your parents divorce, argue or abuse each other there is little you can do. I have taught boys who go home to neglect, physical and sexual abuse, violence, drug abuse and alcoholism. This informs their conduct. It has to be taken into account when dealing with students. It affects their concentration, their ability to work as well as their behaviour.

This is precisely why a rigid traffic lights system of pastoral care cannot possibly work. The same crime does not always warrant the same punishment. Not only is there severity and context to take into account, there is also background.

A child stealing from the canteen may be stealing to sell to others for profit, out of greed, for the thrill of it or because he is hungry and hasn't eaten all day. I've known them all.

The key factor in pastoral care is to know your students and apply fairness and justice.

This is where restorative practice comes in.

Relationship is built up over time. It is the result of all those greetings in the corridor, the pleasant words, little chats, praise, advice and admonishments. It is the product of the way you talk to people and treat them.

There is no excuse for rudeness, lack of politeness or brusqueness if you want to run a friendly school. The art is to be firm and jolly without being soft.

When the big crimes arise it is the sum total of all the interactions that set the tone. That is pastoral care.

If children are treated with coldness or are bullied or ignored they build up resentment. That is human nature. Nobody likes being talked down to or treated meanly. It creates distance.

Fairness and justice; warmth and friendliness, those are the basis of a pleasant community. They do not come about by chance. They have to be worked at every day. A Head sets the tone for the school.

Cold, distant Heads run cold mechanical schools.

Warm, jolly Heads are part of a pleasant community at peace with itself.

We have often had students who had been placed in care. They were often a cause of great worry.

One lad we had come to us from a foster home. He had been taken by Social Services from both his parents and then his grandparents.

He was caught threatening boys in the dinner queue, taking money off them and generally bullying.

It seemed that his reputation in the village was similar. He was terrorising the neighbourhood. The violence was not merely threats. He was not averse to using his fists, head and the boot. There was also rumour of sexual shenanigans with some of the local girls and even the boys. This was not of the normal nature. Seemingly there was a knife involved and a lot of humiliation and perversity. Nothing was proven as no-one would talk. They were too terrified. For a thirteen year old this was a real litany of crimes.

I read the report from Social Services. The boy had been abused as a child by his own parents. They were both heroin abusers and his mother was on the game to earn the money. She brought men back to the family home. It sounded like a scene out of the film 'Trainspotting'.

He and his young brother had witnessed everything. They knew more about drug use and sex than the entire adult population at school. They had seen it first hand and probably experienced a lot of it.

He and his brother had been forced to fend for themselves.

Social Services had stepped in and removed them, and about time, you might say. They placed them with the grandparents.

One would have thought that this was a happy ending, but no. The grandparents were long term heroin abusers and repeated the same pattern of abuse. It was out of the frying pan into the fire.

The boys were removed and placed in a foster home at a distance from their home environment.

It does not take a genius to work out what these boys desperately needed was a stable, caring environment coupled with some expert counselling. The psychological damage must have been immense. They needed help.

Our school was thought to be a secure environment to assist that process of healing.

I was agreeable.

Something had to be done.

Our heads of year and tutors were really caring people.

We took him on.

I sat and talked to the boy. He had passed through a large number of homes and schools. He had, in a relatively short period of time, completely lost faith in the system. Nothing lasted.

'You need to settle down,' I suggested. 'There are a lot of people who care for you here.'

'What's the point,' he said morosely. 'I won't be here long.'

You could see that he was reluctant to allow himself to settle. If he formed attachments he'd only get hurt.

'That's not true,' I argued. 'If you settle down and stop causing trouble you'll be able to stay. Don't you like it here?'

'It's alright I suppose,' he grudgingly admitted. He had his own personal tutor whom he got on with very well. There were many signs that he was actually enjoying it here. He spent a lot of time in our special needs area. He felt safe there. The staff were friendly and accepted him in. There was hope.

'It doesn't matter if I like it or not. It doesn't matter if I try or not. They'll still take me away,' the boy added belligerently.

I didn't think this was true.

The next week his social worker came in. She told us they were moving him from his foster home. There were issues.

He had to be moved.

The decision had been made. His things had been collected and already moved to his new home.

'Does he know?' I asked.

'No,' the social worker replied. 'It's best that they don't know.'

'So he didn't even get a chance to say goodbye?'

'It's best to have a clean break,' she explained. 'It saves having a scene.'

It did not seem like a good idea to me. Psychologically it looked like a disaster. This did not look like stability.

'How many changes of foster parents has he had?' I enquired innocently.

'We're trying to get him settled in a permanent home,' the social worker replied defensively.

'So how many?'

'Well there's been a lot of upheaval. It was all done in a rush. There have been a lot of things to sort out behind the scenes. He was placed in temporary care. We had to set up his schooling.'

'What he needs is stability,' I asserted.

'We know,' she replied. 'That's what we're trying for.'

I watched out of my window as he was led off into the car by the social worker.

Later I heard about the terrible case in Doncaster where two brothers had attacked and tortured two boys. They had tried to kill them dropping a ceramic sink on one of their victim's head.

It wasn't him but it could have been.

I couldn't help thinking of what he was going to be like when he was in his twenties. I don't think I would like to meet him in a pub or down some dark alley and yet if we had that opportunity to work with him for long enough, show him that care and love, he would have probably turned out OK. I hope he got it wherever he ended up.

Schools are not just about exam results.

One training session that had a big impact on me was a course I went on about multicultural education. I was bringing in an anti-racism policy. We were going to assess all our teaching materials for positive representation and removal of stereotyping. The Head thought I'd benefit from a training course.

The main speaker worked in a London school and related the experience of one young Asian student.

The young girl had moved into the area and arrived at the school bright and cheerful from a stable professional family.

At first everything was fine. The girl settled in quickly and was doing good work. She was achieving at a high level and teachers realised that she had a lot of potential.

It all started going wrong in her third term. Her work tailed off. Her performance went down and there was a long period of absence.

The school tried repeatedly to contact home with no luck. Nobody responded.

They tried talking to the girl but she clammed up.

A teacher went round to the address.

The teacher reported that the house looked empty, boarded up and burnt out.

They tried talking to the girl again and persuaded her to allow someone to accompany her home and talk to her parents. She was very nervous about doing so.

When they arrived at the house it was as described, all boarded up and burnt out. The girl knocked on the door and someone came down and let them in. The family lived upstairs.

It took a while for the family to open up. Apparently they had been under racist attack from the National Front. A gang of youths started regularly harassing the family.

The mother escorted the daughter to school but was attacked in the park with a cricket bat on the way to school. She was hospitalised with a broken arm. Nobody was ever prosecuted. This was the reason the girl had been absent from school.

Worse was to follow.

The gang took to congregating outside their house every night after midnight. They would shout racist abuse for a couple of hours.

The police had been contacted and sent a police car. They had parked and watched the behaviour for a while and then left.

The harassment intensified as the youths became bolder. They started throwing stones at the windows and threatening the family.

The family had to board the windows up. The girl was finding it hard to sleep. The abuse and stoning went on regularly through the night.

The police did nothing about it.

The culmination of this phase was when the house was set on fire. According to the family petrol was poured through the letter box and set alight.

The family escaped but the downstairs was gutted.

The council accused the family of deliberately setting fire to the property in order to get themselves re-housed. The police still did not seem to do anything. The family were still being terrorised by the gang who turned up every night and hurled bricks at the boarded up windows. They lived in a state of terror. It was no wonder the girl's education had gone to pot. She was getting no sleep, had nowhere to work as the whole family was crammed into two bedrooms, and she was petrified.

The school thought this all sounded far-fetched and exaggerated. A teacher volunteered to stay over at the house and verified that there were attacks on the house from the gang.

The school contacted the police and remonstrated about the situation and still nothing happened.

Behind every problem at school there is likely to be a bigger problem outside of school.

You have to know your students.

In order to create a fair, just and friendly society it is essential that all agencies should work together holistically.

I believe there have been big strides since the days I went on that multicultural training course. I would like to think that racism has been stamped out of public institutions. The National Front and British Movement have lost a lot of their power base and are largely derided by the population as the fascists they are. However, the holistic approach to dealing with children has a long way to go.

There is a great deal of work needed to interlink education with social services, the police, and local authority care. It requires an input from psychology and a big chunk of funding.

Our students are too precious. On a cynical financial level it costs us too much in the long run to treat them so badly and let them down. It would pay to do the job properly in the first place, provide the stability, provide the care, and psychological treatment.

Damaged adults hate, mug, rape and destroy.

Chapter 15 – Open doors and open minds

When I was the pastoral deputy I seemed to spend my life mopping up problems round the school. Much of my day was spent collecting boys who had been put out of classes for disrupting lessons.

You might suggest that this was not a good use of my time. You would be wrong.

A fair number of these problems were not the fault of the student; they were caused by the teacher – either intentionally or inadvertently. By going into the classroom to find out what had happened I was able to ascertain the cause.

At the end of the lesson I could process the event with the teacher concerned, express my views, offer suggestions and hopefully bring the miscreant in to talk through the situation, smooth things out and ensure it didn't happen again. On rare occasions this meant informing the teacher that they had handled the situation badly and that the student was not guilty as charged.

One thing you learn about pastoral work is that things are rarely as they might appear. When you dig around you will find out all kinds of things that pertain to the incident. You also learn is that there is never a black and white situation. Every single incident is different and the degree of culpability diverse. This is why setting misdemeanours and punishments in black and white tables is misguided. You cannot say the punishment for punching another boy is two days exclusion. You have to look into the incident and decide.

Consider two boys with the same offence of punching another boy.

Incident 1 – the boy was in class, lashed out and caught another boy in the mouth causing bleeding.

Incident 2 – a boy waited in the playground and attacked another boy hitting him in the mouth and causing bleeding.

In incident 1 it turns out that the boy was deliberately being wound up by the other boy. This had gone on for three days with the boy calling out racial insults, insulting his brother and finally telling everyone that the boy's mother was a whore. The boy had reached breaking point and lashed out. He was wrong and he was punished with a detention. He should have reported it. But it was not a direct punch, it was on the spur of the moment and he was severely provoked. The two boys were brought together. The incident talked through and they shook hands and made up.

In incident 2 the boy had been bullying the other student for over a year. He regularly hit him, called him names and intimidated him. He enjoyed it. On the day in question he had deliberately waited with a group of his friends to attack the boy. When he had turned the corner he'd grabbed him and punched him hard in the mouth knocking him to the ground. He'd then gone off laughing with his friends. I put him out for 5 days, called his parents in and placed all of his 'friends' in detention. I brought everyone together and talked it all through with all repercussions discussed.

You don't manage to resolve everything but you solve a lot. One size never fits all.

The problem is that many staff actually like things black and white. It makes life easier for them. Everything is quick, cut and dried. They have not got the time to go through the process. They believe that having a clear, black and white policy is best. I think they are wrong.

But I digress.

By picking the boys up from the classroom and walking back to my office together we had an opportunity to talk. I asked questions and listened. They told me what had happened, why it had happened and who was to blame. Invariably I found the boys open and honest. If they were guilty they held their hands up and admitted it. On some occasions they felt aggrieved that they had been picked on or that it was mistaken identity. It usually was as they had described.

I did not take sides.

I did not judge.

I listened.

When I had ascertained what had gone on I set about investigating further, calling in witnesses, until I had the full picture. Then I made my judgements and brought the parties together to resolve the issues. If the student was in the right I represented them. I did not automatically take the teacher's side.

Often when I have asked the guilty party what punishment they deserved they came out with a much harsher punishment than I would have awarded.

I gained a reputation for being fair, for listening and being approachable.

My door was always open. Students could come in and tell me their concerns; I would listen and try to help.

This was a practice I continued as a Headteacher. Any student, or member of staff, could come and knock on my door. I would welcome them in and listen. They would tell me what was troubling them. I would try to help.

If you have an open door you will find out what's going on, people will come and see you and problems can be dealt before they become entrenched and out of control.

If you have an open mind and listen you have a chance of finding the truth of the matter.

If you prejudge before you have all the facts you will invariably get it wrong and nothing will be resolved. Little things become big things. I say nip the little things in the bud.

Never take sides.

Never prejudge.

On rare occasions teachers can sometimes be vindictive, conniving or incompetent. They are human. They are not infallible. If they have had a bad day and been wound up by a class they might put the blame on someone they don't like. We all make mistakes. Sometimes the answer is not to take something at face value and simply punish the student without investigating but to delve into the incident and find out what really happened. Occasionally the student is innocent and it is the member of staff who is wrong.

Pastoral work is slow, time consuming, requires good relationships, a lot of listening, restorative practice, fairness and appropriate sanctions. If matters are resolved well there will be no recurrence. Get it right often enough and the school becomes a calm peaceful place full of happy students. Run it like a tick list with punishments and you end up with an establishment full of seething resentment, frustration and violence with lots of disaffected students.

Another aspect of having an open door policy is that you get to find out things because boys trust you.

One particular student seemed to have gone off the rails completely. From being quite an outward going individual he had become aggressive and surly. He was constantly in trouble and often excluded. The teaching staff were finding him rude, violent and unteachable. He was completely turned off and heading for a lengthy exclusion.

I used to deliberately seek him out at lunch-time for a chat. I did this in as casual a manner as possible. I was always cheery and friendly. He was usually his surly self.

Then one day he came to my office and started to talk. He cried and splurged it all out. His family had split up; Dad had gone off with another woman and did not want anything to do with him. He was consumed with resentment, anger and incredibly hurt and did not know how to deal with all those emotions.

I don't know if I really helped but he got through to the end of his schooling and at least we knew the reason why he was behaving the way he was and could get him some help.

I always say there are no naughty boys. All behaviour has a reason. Our job is to mend the damaged boys.

Chapter 16 – Managing Change

Nobody likes change. People like things just the way they are and have always been. Change is threatening and takes us out of our comfort zone; change means work and having to learn how do everything differently. It can be perceived as criticism.

There have been times when I thought I could get nothing right. Whatever I said would be met with resentment. I sometimes thought that even if I was to go into the staffroom and announce an extra weeks holiday they would all be up in arms. 'How were they expected to get all the teaching done with a week less?' If I were to go in and tell everyone they had a £1000 extra each week they would be anxious. 'How could the school afford it? It would only lead to redundancy!'

I was used as an agent of change by all my previous Headteachers and I was notorious for bringing in change.

I am a firm believer in constantly trying out new things and having a regime of improvement.

When something is newly introduced there is energy. It then becomes jaded. To keep the momentum of change going forward it has to be managed properly and introduced at the right rate.

Whenever I brought in change this is what I did:

- I planned carefully
- I produced detailed, costed plans to satisfy the logical minds
- I shared these plans, talked them through and listened to the arguments
- I looked for compromises and made concessions where possible
- I processed it openly at staff meetings
- I weighed up the advantages and disadvantages and discussed them
- If it was clear that it was not a good idea I abandoned it
- If I was convinced that it was good for the school I brought it in

In most instances the ructions diminished as people adjusted and most of the changes were later viewed as being necessary and beneficial.

During my first year of Headship when I had to address that major funding crisis of just short of a half million pounds I had to ride a storm of dissent.

Part of the way I had solved the crisis was to initiate a diversion of money from a projected building project into a general refurbishment project.

It was an ambitious refurbishment that created a lot of change.

The downside was that I had to move a large number of departmental faculties from one area to another.

I drew up a plan and floated it. It was widely resisted. Faculties did not want to move. The staff thought I was exaggerating the financial crisis. They thought this was some sort of management ploy.

I held staff meetings and went through the finances. I described the strategies I was using to deal with the crisis. They remained suspicious. They thought this new management transparency was merely a ploy.

I had no choice. If I didn't do it then I could not deal with the finances and the result would be horrendous. It would have certainly led to redundancies and increased workload with effects on morale, results and Ofsted.

I had no option. I forced it through. The maths department was the biggest change. I moved them out of the Main block and into the Sixth Form area.

There was fury about that from the sixth form who were now roomed around the school. I was happy with them being round the school though. I wanted sixth formers on every corridor having a civilising effect on students in the lower school. I wanted the lower school kids to aspire to being cool sixth formers.

There was incandescence from the maths department. I pointed out that they were effectively getting the best rooms in the whole school. It did not appease them at all. They were being forced to move from where they had always been. They came out with a string of arguments. We ended up measuring the width of entrances and stairs! I listened but they did not convince me. I knew we had to do it.

On the day of the move the corridors teemed with staff and students sullenly carrying paraphernalia from one area to another. You could have cut the air it was so full of pheromones. I liken it to the partition of India.

In a short while everyone realised that all the arrangements were working and it wasn't such a catastrophe. After a few months there wasn't anyone who would have wanted to go back.

Change is traumatic but if it is well thought through, there is good logistical planning and a good consultation process, it can be extremely beneficial.

Chapter 17 – Work ethic and Effort

Many teachers, particularly from areas of the curriculum which are extremely logical, such as physics and maths, find it incredibly hard to judge effort. They do not like making judgements about how hard a student works. They find it much easier to judge on test results or correct answers.

Ten sums correct – ten out of ten – excellent.

Eight sums right – eight out of ten – good. Etc.

The problem with this is that it does not reward or encourage effort. The brightest will have breezed through in no time at all. They will waltz away with all the prizes and accolades. Others might have sweated over problems for ages and achieved a measly four or five.

It is human nature to give up trying if you struggle.

Education is about encouraging all students to continue making effort and pushing the boundaries. Only through sustained effort can you reach your potential. A person's reach should always be longer than their grasp.

All of my students were equally important. To discourage most in the interests of a small elite is reprehensible. We have to find a way. That way must include assessing how much effort a student has put in and rewarding that effort.

Teachers from areas of the curriculum, such as English and art, where they have to continually make value judgements as part of their assessments find effort scores easier.

If a teacher is unable to make a judgement about the effort put in then I always told them that the answer is to ask the students.

In my experience students are usually objective when assessing their own effort. Most students are scrupulously honest.

A good teacher will know their students and be able to tell if a student is trying to pull the wool over their eyes. Simple discussion and soft questioning will settle these problems.

Marking for attainment is simply wrong!

Marking for effort is right!

There is no discussion!

At the end of a PSHE lesson on revision a student hung back to talk to me.

'Sir,' he said. 'I listened to everything you said. It all made sense.'

I nodded with satisfaction.

'But I'm not doing it,' he continued reasonably but emphatically.

I raised my eyebrows.

'If I did as you suggested,' he continued. 'Drew up a revision timetable, carried out the revision programme and put in the two hours a day there is no doubt it would raise my grades.'

I frowned. That was the point. What was the problem?

'I know I'm not very bright,' he explained candidly. 'At the moment,' he went on in a thoughtful manner. 'I am doing very little and I'm on a G/F grade in most subjects. It's not great. But I've got sorted that I will leave school; go to college and do a bricklaying course. They've accepted me. The thing is sir......'

He was extremely respectful and had obviously weighed it all up very thoroughly.

'If I were to do as you suggest and pull out every stop I know I could improve my grades by two or three in most subjects.'

I nodded my head. I still had not completely cottoned on to where this was going.

'So what good would that have done me?' he asked rhetorically. 'I work my arse off for three months and leave school with Ds and Es at best. It doesn't get me anywhere else.'

I had to admit he had a point. The magic 'C' grade pass meant that anything below that was almost considered a fail. To have a 'D' or an 'F' in a range of subjects did not make a huge difference and he had no chance of getting Cs.

When I was teaching Science we had the new Salter's scheme come in. We had been used to teaching discrete modules. We taught eleven lessons on a topic and then tested the students and moved on to the next topic. The lessons were all teacher led and fact based. Salter's took a different approach. There were lots of skills based topics, role plays and investigations.

This upset a lot of people who thought the knowledge content was being watered down. It also created problems because this methodology took longer and they could not see how to fit the content in.

It opened up the perennial debate about standards. I still fervently contend that you cannot compare two disparate systems from worlds that are totally different. If I was to bring a student, with a head full of knowledge, into the modern world with all its computers, wikipedia, I-phones and internet, they would flounder just as much as a student from now trying to get their heads round lengthy essays. The world is different. The needs are different. The skills are different. There can be no real comparison.

I spent a lot of time thinking about this. I came up with a pupil based scheme. I broke a biology module up into three units each consisting of three lessons. I graded all the work on a one to ten scale for difficulty and presented a variety of exercises. Students could carry out an investigation, an experiment, look up some information, produce a project, devise a presentation, make observations etc. I made it so they could choose and work on their own or in small groups. I provided the apparatus and facilitated the activities. I collected in work and marked it. The students recorded their progress on a table I put up in the laboratory. I did the first lesson as a teacher led introduction and then set them loose to select what they did for two lessons. I brought them back in for the fourth lesson for another teacher led lesson and then set them loose to choose their own activities again. At the end of the module I gave them a test.

The results were astounding.

Firstly the lab was a hive of activity with a great buzz of electricity. There were no individuals opting out. They all were energised.

Secondly the amount of work being carried out was far greater than usual. Students were coming back at lunch and break to continue with projects.

Thirdly the standard of work produced was brilliant.

Fourthly the enjoyment levels went through the roof.

Fifthly there were students attempting levels of work that they normally would have found too hard. These were usually the sort of things kept as extension work for the high flyers.

Sixthly the end of module tests revealed a seismic shift in the order in the class. Some students who had previously straddled the summit with monotony, as if their place at the top was somehow ordained, had dropped lower down. They would have to fight if they wanted their positions on the pinnacle back. Some students who were normally much lower in the class order of attainment were now striding out to achieve at a much higher level. The overall achievement was greatly increased.

Student facilitation was a huge motivator.

As a biology teacher, early in my career, I had discovered I had brilliant success with lower school students. I would take on a class and over a short period have them working harder and harder with great relish. Our relationship was really positive. I could tell they looked forward to coming to my lessons. We fed off each others enthusiasm and we all loved it.

I had become increasingly aware that as these same students moved into years 10 and 11 we lost that enthusiasm and rapport. It wasn't that the lessons were bad; they merely lacked the zip and mutual satisfaction. They were still usually a delight to teach. We got the results, the lessons were enjoyable to a level but something was missing.

I had put this down to puberty. The boys were bigger, more aggressive, more sexually charged and going through major hormonal changes which provoked not only great changes in their bodies for them to get used to but also a rewiring of their brains to contend with. Most of the boys were going through their insular, sullen phase where the whole world was conspiring against them.

One day, for no obvious reason, I started to ponder if that might not be the reason our relationship was not as good. Perhaps it was something I was doing differently?

I analysed everything I did. The work was harder and more pressured but I used the same techniques and manner. It just did not work as well.

The only real difference I could see was that in the lower school I taught the boys once a week and in year 10 and 11 I taught them twice a week.

I looked at the way I operated. At the beginning of every lower school lesson I would begin by handing the books back. I say handing back but what I really did was having a bit of fun with aerodynamics. I would stand at the front and toss the books back to the individuals. I'd put a spin on it so the exercise book spun through the air in an arc at an angle that took them out and then in and brought it into the boys hands. It was fun. I was a good aim and the kid loved it. Occasionally I would mess up and they'd all jeer. As I called each boys name I would call him by a pet name usually based round a mispronunciation of his name, always careful to avoid derogatory connotations, and I would find a positive comment to make about his work and sometimes add a little comment on how to improve. Invariably the first thing the boys did was to check their mark and read the short comment I'd written. I always marked generously to encourage. I always used effort scores and never attainment. They always vied to get top marks. They had the right to come up and challenge me if they thought I'd got it wrong. If they did I'd listen and if I was convinced I'd change their score.

In the upper school I only marked the books once a week as lessons were only a couple of days apart, which meant that I did not start each lesson returning books.

I wondered if this is what made a difference.

I determined that I would try it out. I would somehow mark the books so that I would start each lesson with a personal bit of praise.

It was like turning a tap back on.

The pleasure and intensity of relationship was back and firing on all cylinders.

It's the little things that count.

It's the personal touch.

It's the recognition and reward for the effort put in.

They do not give a damn about diagnostic marking and detailed instruction on how to improve. A simple piece of personal praise will suffice.

Chapter 18 – Those that can't do!

There's the old maxim – 'Those that can, do – those that can't teach.'

That might have been true at one time when teaching meant writing notes on a blackboard for bored kids to copy down, memorise and regurgitate. In this day there is nothing further than the truth. To get out there every day, stand in front of a class, command respect, deliver a lesson brimming with interest, with awareness of different levels of understanding, different learning styles, taking into account SEN and learning difficulties, incorporating investigation, group work, audio-visual and putting on a performance that is captivating and inspiring is probably the most difficult job of all.

I have seen so many glib outsiders think they can glide in and deliver to a class of discerning students and I've watched them fall flat on their face. It's all about relationship, delivery, pace, interesting material, and personal skills the like of which the average punter can only guess at. It looks so easy but it's the hardest thing in the world. When you're standing up there before a group of thirty youngsters you have to perform. They expect high standards. They are the most critical bunch you will ever encounter. They are knowledgeable and astute. They will find you out.

Teaching day in and day out is akin to giving a performance on stage for a whole day, every day. The energy required in substantial.

On top of the teaching you have to deal with outside agencies. There are the police, education welfare, social services, health, Ofsted, parenting groups, charities and a host of others. You have to liaise and interact. There are many multi-agency meetings. A child might be involved with a number of them at the same time. They have to be coordinated.

The art of organising a classroom to reduce behavioural problems and enhance learning is an art in itself. It does not just happen. A teacher establishes well thought through protocols. After a while they do it instinctively. The expectations for entering a classroom, getting out books and materials, levels of quiet, behaviour and attention are all carefully planned for and achieved through insistence and skill.

For those who do not know these are the Seven Learning Styles:

1. **Visual**: The student prefers using pictures, images, and spatial understanding.

2. **Aural:** The student prefers using sound and music.

3. **Verbal:** The student prefers using words, both in speech and writing.

4. **Kinaesthetic:** The student prefers using their body, hands and sense of touch.

5. **Logical:** The student prefers using logic, reasoning and systems.

6. **Social:** The student prefers to learn in groups or with other people.

7. **Intrapersonal:** The student prefers to work alone and use self-study.

A teacher builds in opportunities for the class to experience all seven so that every student can access the lesson. Teaching has become much more scientific and advanced with our understanding of the psychology of learning. 1950s teachers would be amazed!

Chapter 19 – The government and politics, worst experiences

I was really moved when our Headteacher in America read us a statement using the words of Haim Ginott, the concentration camp survivor. He started every year with those words.

I make no apologies for referring to them again. I referred to Haim in the foreword but there are never too many opportunities to reinforce the message: Haim is someone who is a hero of mine.

We have to teach humanity to our children. We cannot be cold, dispassionate and objective. We have to take sides. I am on the side of the idealists.

I do not think the world gets better through people teaching their children to hate, to be intolerant or to despise.

Education has to teach people to care, tolerate and love. Only out of that will we begin to address the huge problems that face the world, problems of overpopulation, despoiling of the planet, violence and war.

This piece by Haim Ginott is not only moving but it summarises how I feel about education.

This is more of an imperative than teaching knowledge or skills.

What is the point of doing anything if it does not make things better?

Education is our only hope for a better world!

My message to our government, and all governments, is to keep the hell out of education!

We do not need your constant reorganising of the goalposts, your insane targets, your messing around with the exam system and curriculum.

Get politics out of education!

Set up a board of educationalists and allow the professionals to sort it out for the good of the students and the good of society at large.

Stop draining our energy with your constant new ludicrous schemes.

Give us stability and the funding to do the job and keep the hell out of things you don't understand!

We are sick to the teeth with political dogma!

One government idea is to bring more ex-soldiers into the classroom to promote discipline.

As a victim of traumatised soldiers deployed in classrooms I am exceedingly sceptical. Army discipline and procedure is hardly the type of nurturing relationship I'd like to see in a classroom.

My maths teacher, Mr W, was an ex-soldier. He ran his classroom on fear.

On my first lesson in his set he strode into the class like a colossus.

'There's a stench in here,' he bellowed. 'Open the windows.'

He was a twenty stone Welsh ex-rugby forward. He was in his fifties and not a nice man.

A gale of winter chill blew through the classroom turning it into an ice-box.

The room was quiet as a morgue.

He began writing equations on the board for us to copy and solve.

I dutifully clicked my biro on.

He stopped in his tracks, spun on his heels and demanded – 'Who clicked that biro?'

Tentatively I put my hand up.

He strode over, grabbed my ear twisted it and lifted me out of my seat. The pain was excruciating. It felt like my ear was being torn from my head.

He proceeded to smack me round the face. 'You don't – smack – click biros – smack – in my lesson – smack.'

He flung me back into my chair.

My ear was throbbing in agony. It felt like something had been torn.

Mr W strode back and proceeded to chalk on the board. He filled all three boards with equations.

The room was like a tomb.

'Right,' he announced. 'Copy that down and solve them.' He glared round at us. 'If there's anyone here who doesn't understand these equations speak now. For if I find out later you don't understand you're for it!'

One boy had once dared to put his hand up and had received a clout round the ear that had knocked him out of his seat. 'Well boy

– you haven't been listening!!' Mr W bellowed. Nobody had ever dared speak again.

He sat behind his desk and scowled at us as we scribbled.

I floundered. I found out that hardly anyone had understood. At the end of the lesson we'd all go to Richard a fellow pupil. He was the only one who understood. He explained it and everyone copied it down. Heaven help anyone who got it wrong.

Mr W was seen as one of the best. He always got hundred percent pass rates.

I hated maths.

Mr W was a traumatised bully. He destroyed maths for me. I hated him and I hated maths forever.

My worst moment in teaching came when I was on duty. I had been teaching for about ten years and felt very secure and settled.

I was clutching my cup of coffee and touring around the back of the school. It was a nice sunny day and everything was quiet. These were the halcyon days when you basked in the atmosphere around you. Kids were polite and the sun's heat felt good on your skin. All was right with the world.

I noticed a quite scruffy man walking towards me across the back field. He looked like one of the gypsies who kept some horses out on the field at the back of the school.

He was wearing a crumpled dark suit with a shirt undone at the collar and a flat cap. As I got closer I decided he was definitely one of the gypsies.

I walked out to intercept him. We encouraged visitors to check in at the front office. He seemed to be striding across quite purposefully and looking very agitated and determined.

'Good morning,' I said in way of greeting. 'Can I help?'

'I need to see someone about my horses,' the man replied. We began to walk back towards the school buildings. A few students had begun to hang around to see what was going on.

'Is there a problem?'

'You could say that,' he replied angrily. 'Some of your boys have been chucking bricks at my horses and jabbing them in the eyes with sticks.'

This news was horrifying.

As we walked slowly back towards the school he began to tell me what had been going on. I was putting a picture together in my head. The horses were tethered. Apparently some of our boys had been going out to them at lunch-time. There were gaps in the back hedge where they could get through into the field. It had started with them trying to ride them but when the horses had objected the boys started throwing things at them.

I could see that this was really serious. There had been some cruel and nasty injuries inflicted on the tethered animals. They couldn't escape and the boys had thrown half-bricks and pointed sticks at their heads causing some bad wounds. One had nearly lost an eye.

The whole idea of our boys doing something as mean as this was very upsetting. I hate cruelty to animals. It was my intention to take the guy directly round to the Head so that he could tell him what had happened.

We had now got back to the buildings and were going along the drive at the side of the school. A group of over twenty students had begun to crowd round us.

I told them to go away and they retreated. I thought nothing more of it.

We walked alongside the school deep in conversation. I could see he was very upset by what had happened and I was assuring him that we would find out who had done it and punish them.

By now the crowd around us had built up to over fifty students.

'Gyppo!' Someone yelled out.

I turned round to see who had called out but all I could see was grinning faces.

I glowered at them and told them all to clear off right away. They retreated a bit.

By now it was apparent that students were piling out of the classrooms and we were getting rapidly surrounded by a big crowd.

We were finding ourselves at the centre of a big crowd. It was like what happened when there was a fight.

'Fuck off Gyppo!' someone shouted.

There was a real feeling of menace. The crowd had become a mob. It seemed to have happened in an instant. They were pushing in around us, shouting out, and generally getting excited.

Kids were still pouring out of classrooms and the density of the mob was growing by the second.

I shouted and bellowed at them but it seems that when a mob reaches a certain size it is immune. The ones at the front, pressing in on us, could not move back if they wanted to because of the crowd density behind.

'Gyppo! Gyppo!' the chant was going round. Every time I turned to see who was doing it the shouting quietened down from that area but intensified somewhere else. It was like a game but it wasn't a game. It had become really sinister.

We'd only got halfway along the school. We still had a way to go.

The mob was really excited. There was a real sense of violence. I was getting frightened and I knew them all. The man was really scared. He was not a big man and suddenly found himself the victim of a raucous mob.

I was furious. I grabbed the man and began pushing through the mob towards the side door. I had to fight my way through pushing my way though the densely packed mob.

'Gyppo! Gyppo! Fuck off GYPPO!!' There were fists raised and students jumping up and down, pushing and shoving.

Somehow we had fought our way to the door without any major injury. I got him inside.

We caught our breath and calmed ourselves down before we went to the Head. We were both shaking.

I talked to my sixth form biology group later that afternoon. I explained to them how frightening it had been. The man had rightly come in to report cruelty to his horse and had been abused by a mob. I could not believe how quickly it had sprung out of nowhere. I also could not believe how a bunch of pleasant, intelligent, caring students could have become such a violent mob in no time at all.

The prejudice and intolerance obviously ran deep. All it took was a minor exposure and it came bubbling to the surface.

My biology group listened to me.

One of them said that I should talk to the school about it. He was sure that if everyone heard what had taken place they'd all feel ashamed.

I hoped so.

I took his advice and talked to the school.

This incident highlighted the need for more PSHE and not more of the army type discipline favoured by the government.

The only politics in schools should be the unbiased education of our children in the basics of politics so that they can fully participate in the political system as informed citizens.

Schools should not be influenced by political dogma. It is scandalous the way we are instructed on high to do things in a certain way and then castigated for doing it how we'd been told. It is scandalous the way we are made to jump through hoops and huge sums of money are wasted as one gimmick is forced through on the heels of another. Who on earth remembers 'records of achievement' and the massive training and pressure to adapt all our teaching materials and methods?

It is scandalous the way exams are decried and chucked out for political motives; how their replacements are brought in too quickly, poorly thought through and poorly funded because some politician or other wants to make their mark in the short time they are in office.

Education should not be subject to the vagaries and whims of politicians.

Chapter 20 – The Tick-Box culture

When I started in teaching I became NUT Rep in my first year. I rapidly went on to be voted as staff representative on the governing body three times in a row. I finally stood down when I went into senior management.

After one governors' meeting the chair of governors grabbed me by the throat in the corridor and accused me of deliberately stirring up trouble.

I was not stirring up trouble. I was merely strident in arguing for fairness and justice. Nothing more.

The staff liked someone who was prepared to speak and stand up to senior management. Most of them would not say a word. They would keep their heads below the parapet and grumble, moan and drag their heels. They would remain miserable and demotivated without voicing their opinions.

I felt that if you believed in something with a passion you should stand up and fight for it even if everyone else disagreed. I always believed in democracy but that did not ever stop me voicing my opinion or putting my argument forward as strongly as possible. That's what real democracy should be.

Most people thought that speaking out made you unpopular with management and unlikely to be promoted.

I was never hampered by wishing to get promoted but in any case I know that being strong and outspoken is not necessarily a problem when it comes to promotion.

That same chair of governors later apologised to me and oversaw my promotion to deputy head.

Education is something worthy of idealism and passion. If you don't passionately care about the future of our society and the lives of our children what the hell can you be passionate about?

Management always knew where I stood.

I did not get to be Head by following all the rules and regulations blindly, by ticking boxes and methodically doing what was laid down by politicians. I got there by doing what was right; what I fundamentally believed in and doing it my way. The list and the tick box are the death of flair and invention.

I paid lip-service to them.

My first PE lesson as a child at my new secondary school was a lesson in understanding the politics of inevitability.

Mr K was a gymnast. He'd impressive everyone by doing the crucifix on the rings in the gym. To hold it for a few seconds was excruciating. Mr K held it for minutes. He had muscles on his muscles.

Mr K was another ex-military recruit to teaching. He ran lessons like a drill session in the army.

He wore white track suit bottoms and a white singlet whatever the weather. He was tough.

Our first lesson was in the sportshall. We were eleven years old in our first week at big school.

He lined us up on the side of the basket-ball court.

He stood in front of us like a giant. He had a chair with a cane.

'Right boys. This is my chopper.' He held out the cane and smacked it into his palm. 'And this is my chopping block.' He pointed to the chair. 'Step out of line and you'll meet the two of them.'

We quaked.

'Now I want you to run round the outside of the gym. Step inside the lines and I'll give you a clout. Last one round gets a clout.'

We sprinted off, being ultra-careful to stay outside the lines; no one wanted to be last. We were desperate to comply.

For half an hour he stood at the side whacking us as we ran past. Someone always had to be last. Someone was always doing something wrong. It was indiscriminate. He seemed to be enjoying it.

By the end of the lesson most of us had blood streaking our thighs.

Mr K was tough, mean and nasty. He treated children like scum. The man was a sadist. He should never have been allowed near children. His teaching method was child abuse.

We loved PE. We hated Mr K.

I work by intuition. Under my previous two Headteachers I was often given the task of showing candidates for jobs round the school.

I would go off with a bunch of nervous, likely lads and lasses and show them the sights of the site. We'd meet staff and students and I'd watch and listen. By the time we got back I had them placed in order.

The interview team would go through their extensive interview processes, panels, lesson observations and tasks and invariably reach the same conclusion as me.

I could always walk into a lesson and sense the air. I could tell in a minute if it was good, poor or outstanding. I did not need a tick-list to judge it. It was obvious. I could learn more with a quick tour round the school and a breezy drop-in at a dozen lessons than a detailed formal observation of one. I knew all my staff, their strengths, weaknesses and abilities. I did not need to record it.

The trouble with tick lists is that they tick only the things you can see and judge.

The things you can see and judge are not as important as the other things that are going on.

The other things can only be sensed. They are not tangible. They cannot be quantified and ticked off on lists.

There are no tick boxes for caring, friendliness, humour, honesty, empathy, respect, niceness or pleasantness. But those were some of the qualities I'd prefer in my teaching staff; they were the qualities I'd like my children's teachers to have.

Tick boxes give too much importance to the wrong things. They exist merely to justify the decisions being made so that they cannot be contested. They are an attempt to make the subjective decisions objective.
That cannot be achieved.

I go with my gut feeling any day; whether that is how good a lesson is or whether to employ a candidate.

Tick boxes are mechanical. The people who are successful are usually those who tick the boxes; not always those with flair. It you live by tick boxes you die by them. You end up with a soulless staff and boring kids.

Politicians try their hardest to get us to do it. It should be resisted!

Chapter 21 – Assemblies

By law British schools have to have a religious assembly, predominantly Christian, for all students every day. The idea being that religion is the basis of all good morality and that our students can only be civilised when dosed with religion.

As an atheist I find this repugnant and insulting. I am a highly moral man and I do not have a religion. My morality comes from my humanity and not some ambiguous doctrine handed down by a small desert dwelling tribe thousands of years ago. My morality is based on good psychology and experience. It is well thought through and enshrined in documents such as the United Nations charter of Human Rights. I do not need to back it up with some religious doctrine.

We live in a secular society. Most of our students do not have religious views.

I believe teaching religion in schools is wrong. It is an attempt at indoctrination that should be resisted. Children do not have the mental ability to distinguish between fact and fiction. They are gullible and open to being brain-washed by religious people. Psychologically this is extremely damaging.

For the State to insist that we treat all our students in this way is outrageous.

I prefer the American model. Children should be left until their mental processes have developed before being exposed to religion. Then they would be free to make up their mind.

Having said that, I am not opposed to assemblies. It is just that mine wouldn't be, and weren't religious. I think there is great value in bringing the school together to share in experiences. It nurtures that sense of community.

I had a range of different types of assembly - assemblies to share good news, to give out information, to share moral and inspirational stories and to celebrate success. They were positive affirming events that brought people together, reflected the values of the school ethos and the philosophy that unites the community.

I've heard lots of great assemblies including one on rock climbing by Mark Parish where he explained how he had to cut someone's finger off to free them. That was good but the best assembly I ever experienced was delivered by Lester Jones. He was one for telling stories with a moral message.

The bones of this one went like this:

Lester was walking along the beach one morning following a big storm. The waves had uprooted and washed up thousands of starfish. These starfish were now stranded and in danger of being baked by the hot sun.

Lester began gathering them up and throwing them back into the sea.

A man watched what he was doing and came up to him to ask why he was bothering. There were tens of thousands of starfish and throwing some back was hardly going to make much difference.

'It makes a difference to this one,' Lester replied throwing another one back into the sea.

It was a little more detailed and delivered with panache by Mr. Jones. I fail to capture the impact but it sure impacted on me. I loved it.

That is what all good assemblies should be about: - a clear moral message that inspires; not an indoctrinating religious sermon!

Chapter 22 - Time management

There is nearly always too much to do and too little time to fit it in. That means you have to prioritise.

I made lists and used a kind of triage. There were the essentials hat had to be addressed straight away; even if you didn't want to do them. They had imminent deadlines. There were the important things that needed doing soon and then there were the less important that could wait until I got round to fitting them in. Some of those never got done.

I also developed a daily routine that was made up of various things that I considered essentials:

• I tried to get in before anyone else. I usually failed. There were always a few early birds. But most staff saw me working in my room as they came up the drive. I demanded a lot of them. I wanted them to see that I worked at least as hard as they did. Nobody ever accused me of being lazy.

• I'd start the day by checking emails to see if there was anything crucial that needed dealing with immediately.

• On duty days I would walk up to the Top Shop and have a chat to the Lolly-Pop man. I'd ask him how he was and how the kids had been. He'd give me a view of the week from his perspective. I'd make a point of cheerfully greeting every boy and member of staff I passed and saying hello to the mothers and fathers taking their small children to school. This was the most important thing. I was handing out 'warm fuzzies'.

• I then positioned myself in the corridor and made a point of warmly greeting everyone that passed. The handing out of 'warm fuzzies' set the tone for the school. It said exactly what sort of place I wanted it to be. Their reticence had faded away and they began to smile back and respond. I'd try and intersperse little personal touches like asking after people. It was great when they started responding warmly.

• Then it was morning briefing. I started the week. The rest of the week was done by members of the Senior Team. I wanted them all to have prominence. I made a point of never missing a briefing. If I expected staff to be there I had to give it the same importance. I always found briefings nerve racking. I don't know why. I hope nobody noticed.

- I'd go back to my room get a cup of tea and produce the bulletin for the secretary to put out.
- For the remainder of the day I would work at my computer or on the phone with my door open. If a member of staff or student dropped in I would stop and give them priority. I wanted them to know they were more important than anything else. Some days I had a non-stop stream. That was OK. At three thirty it would dry up and I'd have three or four hours to catch up.
- Every break-time I would wander the corridors and speak to the boys spreading 'warm fuzzies' and keeping things quiet. On duty days I patrolled the same as everyone else.
- I made a point to try to tour round the school and drop in on staff to say hello, spread 'warm fuzzies' and ask how they were. I tried to make a special point on going to the far flung places and also meeting with staff I did not particularly get on with. I wasn't always as successful at getting round as I would have liked. It is so important.
- I tried to do regular lesson observations – most on an informal basis. I wanted to get a feel of the school.
- I talked to any boys who had been sent out of lesson and found out why, offered advice, told them to apologise and make up with the member of staff.
- At lunch-time I went to the school canteen and ate a healthy meal – usually a bowl of vegetable soup. I was aware that I was setting an example. I would make a point of talking to the students, wandering around and making pleasantries. I would always share a joke with the kitchen staff and sit with whoever was in. I always found that the best way to keep things calm was to have a quiet presence. Ofsted always picked up on this.
- My work was made up of planning, policy making, replying to emails, opening and replying to post, dealing with outside agencies, parents, government initiatives, internal documentation and staffing matters.
- I wrote the termly school bulletin. It usually ran to thirty pages and was a view of what had been going on in the school. I wrote it because I wanted control of it. I knew it had five audiences.

It was read by staff, students, parents, governors and outsiders such as Ofsted Inspectors. I knew that the spin was important. I'd taken a leaf from Goebbels. If I said it was like this then that's what it was like. I reported all the positive stuff. I gave out as many 'warm fuzzies' as possible. I recognised all the great contributions. I saw it as my chance to blow my own trumpet and tell everyone how great the students and staff were and what a brilliant school it was. I wanted to do that myself because I knew it inside out, knew how I wanted to say it and knew how to get the informal warmth into it. My wife Liz was a wonder. I always bounced it off her first and she amended it wonderfully. It wasn't hard to do because it was a snapshot of the school. It couldn't help but be positive. I didn't have to make anything up.

• I signed every one of the huge number of certificates we produced termly. Students were given certificates for good attendance and good effort. There were hundreds. If they were prepared to come in when they weren't feeling too good or were prepared to put in the effort then the least I could do was to sign a certificate.

• When everyone had gone I'd get down to a few hours work and then get off to the school gym. I had got into the habit of doing 90 minutes on the treadmill with weights and the cross-trainer. A lot of my work was sedentary. The training helped me control my weight and reduced some of the stress. I'd get home around 9.00 pm if there wasn't a parents evening, concert or event. There was usually one a week.

Sometimes it all got on top of me. A member of staff would wind me up. Some union opposition would get really nasty. A parent or student would kick off. A major issue would arise. It felt like the last straw. You were working flat out and that last thing often got out of proportion.

I often found myself lying awake all night trying to find my way round some issue or other, usually a major financial problem, and end up going in the next day exhausted and bad tempered. I ended up shouting at a couple of members of staff but there were points when you were close to cracking up and yet you were in charge. You had to stand up there and look unperturbed. You had to get on the stage and perform.

In thirty six years of teaching I only had nine days off sick. As a Head I never had a day off. It was important staff saw that I went in when I was feeling crap.

Everything I did was an example to others. I modelled the behaviour I expected from others. If I could be pleasant, open, caring and friendly then so could everyone else. If I didn't do it then why should they?

I wanted a school to be proud of. I wanted it to be warm and friendly. I did not want to hear any shouting or rudeness. I did not want violence or aggression. I wanted it free of bullying.

It was no good asking for that if I behaved differently to what I was asking others to do.

Chapter 23 – Banding, Streaming and Comprehensive Education

I have already mentioned the first lesson I ever taught at BGS with 2W. After a year in the school with its strict streaming they had all written themselves off. That is something that lasts for life.

But it is not merely the effect on the B band failures it is the effect on the A band as well. I witnessed so many A banders who became lazy and arrogant. They never reached their potential.

I wanted all my students to be successful. All of them were equally important. All of them deserved to feel good about themselves.

In life you get to work and interact with many people with a wide range of ability. They all deserve respect. They all have different qualities. Intelligence is one small factor in a personality.

BGS had been forced to go comprehensive and had one year's experience of comprehensive kids. Staff were used to the rarefied atmosphere of bright boys who were creamed off from all around and were bussed in from all over the area. The grammar system used to take the top 8% of boys based on an IQ test known as the 11+. 92% of boys were sent into the Technical Colleges or Secondary Moderns. They didn't have the brains so they had to be good with their hands. It always amused me to hear parents talk about the grammar system and how much better it was. In most cases their son would not have got in. He would have been consigned to the Secondary Moderns. I wonder how pleased they would have been with it then?

When comprehensive education began at BGS the kids were streamed into two distinct groups. There were four classes; two larger classes who were basically A stream and would followed a grammar education and two smaller classes that were B stream and followed some watered down version. Some bright spark had the idea of naming the classes with letters. The A stream were called N & S and the two B Stream were called X & W. Somehow the connotations went over everyone's head. At least they were not A,B,X and W.

2W had been in the school for one year. It was long enough. They'd picked up the impression that they were not wanted, not valued, and were only there under duress. They were not expected to achieve. They told me: 'We're the thickos.' That was how they saw themselves.

That is the worst indictment of a system I have ever heard.

It is basically human psychology. If someone is labelled as a failure they will feel a failure. If someone is not valued they will feel worthless. If someone is not expected to achieve they will not bother to try.

I remember a talk I had with a previous Head about a very prestigious grammar school which will be nameless. They creamed off the top 6% of boys from a large catchment area in a Northern city. They then streamed these kids into five classes. They ranged from the super-bright to the very bright. The top class were destined for the top of the top. They left with inflated egos and clutches of Grade As heading for Oxbridge as a staging post to high office. The bottom class were disaffected and barely scraped a pass.

Any one of those lads from that bottom class would have been among the highest achievers from my school. They would have felt valued, worked hard and left with their A grades and a bright future.

I believe in the comprehensive system. I believe that it is the best system possible. It is also the hardest to teach but none-the-less the most fulfilling.

To make it work you have to really value every single child. It's not about intelligence. There is much more to a human being than intelligence. It is not about achievement either. It is about effort. It is about valuing and rewarding effort. It is not about the outcome.

Once you start valuing kids for their results you have lost it. They must be valued for who they are and the effort they put in.

Once you stream them or band them you create failure. That's as bad as the 11+.

It all comes down to finance. Mixed ability teaching is not impossible but it is extremely hard. With good support, great lesson planning and use of resources the bottom end can be extended.

Everybody wants to do well. How can we soften the frustration of those who find that no matter how hard they try they can't do it as well as the others?

For those people who say: 'That's life. They've got to learn one day. They need to learn what life is about. There are winners and losers. It's a hard lesson.' I say you are absolutely wrong. I wanted my school to counter that heartlessness. I wanted to foster empathy, compassion and respect. Superior arrogance is wrong. I say we do not have to have winners and losers. That is just the way the old establishment operated. They were wrong. There are better ways of doing things. All my students were winners.

I remember one lad with great admiration. I ran a human biology course as a mixed ability class for both streams. It was a big lively group with a wide range of ability. Everyone thought it would be a disaster. It was a great success.

This one boy was from the B stream. I'd checked his test results. He was 79 on the scale. 100 was average. 79 was quite low. In order to achieve an exam pass you were supposed to be over a 100.

This lad sat at the front and concentrated really hard. He was totally focussed and putting everything in. I can still remember his serious face and wrinkled forehead. No one was trying harder.

At the end of each lesson he was invariably there at my desk.

'Please sir, I didn't quite understand this.'

I sat down with him and went through it until he'd got it straight. He went home and worked at it.

He got enough passes at GCSE to get into the 6th form. He got an A in human biology. He did the same in A level and got three passes. He should not have been up to doing A level.

He went to college and although he dropped out at the end of the second year he found a good interesting job.

You don't get much greater success than that.

Chapter 24 – my early years

I went into teaching through ennui.

I had experienced a wondrous three years as a student during the late sixties. It was my hedonistic years of Rock 'n' Roll in London. Three gigs each week, a wild social life, loads of reading and being madly in love, was the backdrop to having to go to a few lectures here and there. I shared a room in the East End with a mad genius and we had fun and put the world to rights.

After that it was all downhill. I had to get a job. I worked at my old college as a lab tech doing a part-time M.Phil.

I figured that when I had reached the end of my tether I had another year of freedom up my sleeve; I could go back to college for a year and do a post graduate certificate of education - PGCE.

That came after three years. I had a big row with my supervisor who wanted me to do another year before submitting my Master's degree. I told him to stick it, in slightly stronger words, and walked out.

Hull University accepted me on to their course and I found my year in mid seventies Hull far removed from my three years in sixties London. Ho hum.

At the end of the year I drifted into applying for teaching posts. I was offered the first one I applied to. It was at Beverley Grammar School. In some ways it was considered the best job on offer and my tutor, with whom I had major confrontations over his hypocritical teaching methods, was amazed. Unbeknown to him there were things he did not know. BGS had been forced to change to a comprehensive school and it was struggling. They had realised they needed young comprehensive teachers. I was it.

What my fellow students could not understand was why I had accepted the job in the first place. The school seemed the opposite of what all my ideals stood for. It was.

I liked it because it was a challenge. I knew exactly where I stood.

I was reminded of the car stickers I had seen in America. There were two types: America- love it or leave it!! Or America – love it or change it!!

I knew which side I was on.

I started at the school as a young idealistic teacher. I had a very jaundiced view of education. My own experience had been stultifying, claustrophobic and the epitome of how not to teach. I wanted something better.

I could not see why there had to be this standard teacher/student relationship. The whole premise was wrong. Teaching should be about relationship, enjoyment, and helping kids expand their horizons, experience awe and wonder, investigate, experiment and reach their potential. This adventure should be a partnership. Why the distance? Why the arrogance?

I was staff rep on the governors and NUT rep: I was on the bottom rung of the school hierarchy but I was the most influential member of staff.

The school changed. It moved from being a violent, macho establishment into a more pleasant, welcoming establishment.

I had a vision that came out of my experience of education. I knew how I wanted it to be and I fought for it tenaciously. I loved doing that. I was the thorn in management's side. I was the champion of the disaffected.

To top it all when we had inspections I was held up as an exemplar of good practice.

You could say that being pinned to the wall by the chair of governor's suggested that I hadn't endeared myself to the hierarchy. I can't say that did me any harm though.

I am a driven man. I am an idealist. I truly believe that we can build a better world. I have spent my life fighting for my vision and my beliefs.

I believe that education is a relationship, a partnership and should be enjoyable and fulfilling for all. Out of that came the concepts of fairness and equality. When I got into management I formulated these ideals into the open, caring, friendly ethos that took the school to the peak of its success. These were not just words. These were real ways of operating. My door was always open. Nothing was off the agenda. I would explain the reasons for all policies and open them to scrutiny and discussion. I worked democratically. It meant introducing a vibrant student council that permeated the whole school and was involved in appointments, promotions and decision making. If I could not gain support it did not happen. Our policies were all based on caring for every student and every member of staff. This means giving staff extra support and leave when necessary, introducing support systems, getting teaching right, so that it was dynamic, based on investigation and experimentation. It meant treating students with respect.

I got my vision operational. I was lucky. I saw it reach fruition and work. It was extremely fulfilling. It was a career well spent.

Chapter 25 – Outside interests

I have a huge passion for education but it is not the whole of my life.

When I was a young man I looked at my Dad and his life and I was not impressed. From my perspective his life was empty. All he had was work.

I wanted so much more than that. I was determined to do something with my life. I wanted a creative outlet that I could look back on and feel fulfilled. I wanted to experience as much of the world as I possibly could.

We have one life. When you shut your eyes for the last time it is over. There is nothing after that. I believe your life is made up of seconds and you have to make the most of each and every one of those fleeting moments. It is soon gone.

I am an antitheist. I think the idea of a god is naïve wishful thinking. The human concept of an after-life is psychologically laughable. I believe that religion has prevented billions of people from living life to the full. I won't make that mistake. I want to drain every drop out of it.

My major pleasures, outside of sex and the wonders of my family, are reading, rock music, travelling, arguing with friends, sharing a meal and a glass of wine, and writing. I happily fill my days with that.

I filled myself up with wonderful experience and then shared it all in the classroom.

If you've got nothing in your life outside the classroom you've got nothing to give in it.

I wanted students to wring every drop of enjoyment and fulfilment out of their lives. My job was to help them do that.

That is the purpose of education.

Chapter 26 – Dealing with bullying

As a child I rapidly gravitated towards the back of the classroom where I decided I might attract less attention.

During one maths lesson I discovered I had made an error when doing a sum. I had taken to doing things in pencil so that I could correct mistakes. Unfortunately I had forgotten my rubber. I knew the boy behind had a rubber and turned round to borrow it. Silently I picked it up and mouthed 'can I borrow this?' holding it up.

He nodded.

I turned back to address the mistake on my book when a wooden blackboard rubber hit me right between the eyes and knocked me flying out of my seat.

Mr W had seen me turn round and flung the wooden blackboard rubber at me. His years of rugby must have given him unerring aim. He got me dead centre in the middle of the forehead.

I was unconscious for ten minutes while he continued with the lesson. Nobody was allowed near me.

When I came round I was obviously concussed. I did not know where I was or what I was doing. My best mate had to guide me round the school for the rest of the day. I was in a complete haze.

A huge lump had shot up on my forehead. It was so large I could actually see it.

When I got home my Mum was appalled but my Dad just said I must have deserved it.

Nothing happened. They never even went in to complain.

Within any classroom there is a pecking order. Boys compete with each other to be top dog. It is biological. The top dog produces different pheromones that makes them more attractive to females.

The hierarchy is established through aggression, humour, physical prowess, looks, fashion and verbal dexterity. The relationships are constantly reinforced. Those of similar status vie with each other for position and those at the bottom are the butt of everyone's put-downs. That is the game.

It can manifest itself in schools as bad behaviour, attention seeking and showing off in the classroom. This is often hard to deal with. Punishments are water off a duck's back and often seen as a badge of honour. It is amazing how an attitude can change when you take them out of the classroom, deprive them of an audience, and deal with them as an individual.

The other manifestation is bullying. This can take the form of verbal, physical or internet bullying.

Bullying occurs everywhere. There is no institution without it. It has to be dealt with.

The first way is to provide good mechanisms for prevention and reporting:

- A high profile 'Bully Box' for anonymous complaints that is regularly emptied and all inputs processed fully
- Explaining clearly what constitutes bullying and what action will be taken
- Working throughout the school to raise sensibilities, promote empathy and the need to respect all people
- Celebrating difference and promoting responsible behaviour
- Having poster campaigns and assemblies
- Having a zero tolerance of all negative attitudes towards minority groups
- Using 'Student Voice' to set a tone
- Opening avenues of communication involving parents, students, all teaching and non-teaching staff, form tutors and heads of year
- Having clear well publicised procedures for reporting bullying (putting letters in the box, telling friends, parents, tutors, teachers, head of year, deputy or Head
- Instilling the facts in all staff, students, and parents that it is serious and even lesser examples need talking seriously and dealing with. Ensuring they give it priority over everything else
- Dealing with small examples so that they do not grow into bigger problems
- Processing all bullying incidents through restorative practice. Gathering all the people involved together. Talking the whole thing through. Agreeing culpability and degree of culpability and getting all involved to agree the punishment for their actions
- Checking with students through anonymous surveys.

- Being constantly vigilant

No school completely eradicates bullying but I am proud that my school had extremely low levels. Students reported feeling comfortable and said that the school was friendly and supported those students who were geekie, different or odd. Those individuals felt secure. Racism, homophobia, sexism and negative attitudes towards other minorities were at an all time low.

That is quite an achievement and one of my greatest.

A previous Head Mike Day told me a heart-warming story. During the eighties he worked hard to counteract the high level of violence, endemic bullying and the elitist system that produced these things.

He did away with streaming and set up mechanisms to deal with all the problems.

He had been there a year and transformed the school. An anonymous note was pushed under his door thanking him for what he had done. The lad wrote that for the first time in his life he felt safe walking around the school.

Chapter 27 – Grammar Schools and selection

I am my best argument against grammar schools and selection.

My last measured IQ, recorded at Hull University in 1974, was 159. That is good enough to put me comfortably in the top two of any year group in BGS.

Yet I managed to fail my eleven plus exam.

I was not picked up during my years at my 'bilateral school' (an early example of a comprehensive).

I am the classic result of self-prophesy. I was labelled thick. I developed no confidence or self-esteem. I put my energies into other things; namely girls, rebellion and loud rock music.

I could at least be the one with the longest hair and most outrageous views.

I scraped 7 O levels – all low grades.

I scraped 3 A levels – a D and two Es.

I scraped a 3rd class honours degree from a polytechnic.

I could make endless excuses for all my various lack of success. There were plenty. But the main fact was that I was not engaged with education and various educational establishments allowed me to remain unengaged. My Headteacher called me an enigma but rarely did anyone recognise that I might have skills, talents or abilities.

On one occasion I was hitch-hiking and had a lift with the chief education officer of Surrey. He quizzed me about my education and determined that I had O and A levels and was doing a degree but had failed my 11+.

He was bemused by this and made the comment that I should not have been able to study A levels if I failed the 11+. I should have followed a technical route.

He was talking to someone who is notoriously cack-handed when it comes to any practical work. I was soon removed from woodwork, metalwork and technical drawing yet I was considered unsuitable for academic routes. It demonstrates the muddled thinking that is applied to education.

Every parent wants the best education for their sons and daughters. Many see the grammar schools as superior.

However grammar schools creamed off less than ten percent of the population. Ninety percent were judged failures with all the self-prophesy that ensued. Ninety percent were written off as failures.

The psychological damage of labelling people as failures at 11, 16 or 18 years of age is a catastrophic disaster. It is a recipe for disaffection, underachievement and promotes a complete disregard for authority and society. I baulk at the unfairness of the system.

The next time you or friends and family are burgled or mugged you might stop and consider that it is likely to be a direct result of the failure of the education system.

I have seen enough over-bloated arrogance from some of our 'successes' to last a life-time. I infinitely prefer the failures. I detest the smugness of many academic successes who consider themselves better and more worthy than others. They are not. Many of them are lazy and supercilious.

It is not rocket science. If you want a happy, stable society you have to address inequality and injustice and ensure everybody is equally welcome and has a valued place.

The grammar school system is unjust and promotes inequality. As such it is divisive and destructive to a harmonious society.

It is not surprising that grammar schools produce great academic success. If you group all the bright kids in one area together and give them preferential treatment they should bloody do well. The surprise is that a significant number of these bright elite do not do well. That is reprehensible. In any comprehensive school they'd be the high fliers. The equal wonder is that so many of the 'failures', like myself, go on to achieve against all the odds.

Every child should be valued.

Every child should be able to achieve.

It is surely not beyond the wit of man to create fair education systems that enable all children to succeed and reach their potential without creating any failures.

Any system that creates failures is a disaster.

The answer is quite simple: we have to create a fair comprehensive system in which all students can achieve and be made to feel successful. Everyone has a place in society and feels valued. We have to put our comprehensive schools right and get them to work properly. Presently I do not think they have been given a chance. They have become political footballs at the whim of every half-brained, dogma driven politician. They need direction, stability and proper financing. They need to be made to work. If we put adequate support in for the students I am sure they will. My school had an explempary special educational needs department. That was the key to our success. We supported all our students who had special needs.

To get that maximum success we have to review our examination system to enable discrimination of abilities without promoting failure, and then properly finance our schools and found them on a sound philosophical basis. We have to wrest them away from politicians so that our children's futures are not subject to political doctrine in some arcane vicious football match where politicians of every hue are too eager to score goals at our kids' expense.

What is also apparent is that in order to function properly as a social unit size is critical. Schools should not be bigger than 800 pupils in size.

I believe we will never do this while we have private independent schools. All the time the rich can buy their way through the system our state schools will languish. If the education minister's daughters and sons had to go to the local comprehensive you can bet your last penny that overnight the funding and standards would be sorted!

One good solution is to provide a series of courses of equal status, some practical and technical, some vocational and some academic, and allow students to opt in according to their abilities and desires. If they all carried equal weight and there was genuine respect then it could work – as long as there was no selection and failure!

I also remain in favour of the current GCSE examination. They are a mixture of skills and knowledge and every child can pass. I see that as crucial. The A-C grades are tacitly seen as 'pass' grades by industry but in fact the G grade is a pass. I do not see any problem with this. We can easily differentiate the brightest students by simply looking at the raw scores. We do not have to label students failures in order to do that!

I am also in favour of coursework being part of the exam. Students learn and succeed in different ways. The more ways the better!

The GCSE exams might need tweaking to bring them into line with the modern world but they perform their function: they allow everyone to succeed and enables different abilities to be identified. That is pretty much ideal!

Chapter 28 – Restorative practice

'Restorative practice' is not only the way forward for schools but also the way forward for society.

It is fair, just and provides long lasting results. It avoids victims and resentment leading to grudges and further retributions or alienation.

As head of the pastoral system in the school I introduced restorative practice before the name was invented. I'm sure lots of reasonably minded pastoral managers did likewise. We did it because it made sense and it works.

One has to bear in mind when making a statement like this that nothing is one hundred percent successful. Sometimes we are human and don't carry the processes out well. Sometimes there are issues and personality clashes that make resolution impossible. Often there simply is not the time or will to get it to work. I am mindful of the individual who posted their report regarding my good self on Rate-your-teacher. He accused me of acting like the CIA when it came to dealing with playing field fights. He went on to abuse me for being short and having a long grey beard. Obviously he felt aggrieved and was not one of my greatest successes. You can't win them all.

However this is one where you can win most. Of that I am sure. All it takes is some time and a mediator with the skills and empathy to resolve issues. The chief skill is being able to listen.

The process is easy.

I used to bring all the involved parties in, isolate them, and ask them to write down what had happened from their perspective. I also gathered all the witness statements and personally read them.

When I had an idea of what had gone on I brought all the parties together in one room and talked things through. Each of them explained what they had done and why. Everyone else was asked to comment on this. My job was to tease out exactly what had happened and for all parties to see and accept what their part was and what they had done wrong.

In my experience nothing is ever what it seems at first sight. Hardly ever is there a clear-cut black and white situation. All incidents have multiple causes, misunderstandings and degrees of guilt. Rarely is there a completely innocent party. This particularly applies to staff. Often a teacher has had a bad day and found themselves wound up and furious. They expect you to instantly take their side and believe them without question. This has to be resisted. Often I found the teacher has a degree of guilt. They may well have misunderstood, misheard, or inadvertently contributed to an escalation. The pastoral leader has to stand up to the teacher concerned and be scrupulously fair. Teachers have a tough job and need support but each incident has to be dealt with objectively. If they are in the wrong to any degree that has to be teased out and accepted. The important thing is to rebuild relationships and find a way forward that all are happy with.

Once consensus has been achieved on what all parties have done and what was done wrong we move on to how to put it right.

This process involves accepting guilt and agreeing how to make amends. This normally involves apologies, handshakes and punishments.

When it comes to punishments I always asked the students what it was they felt they deserved. Invariably they would come out with a harsher punishment than that I would have given.

At the end the underlying issues have been resolved, a way forward established and suitable sanctions applied. The students leave without a sense of injustice, having been listened to and taken seriously and there is no ongoing resentment.

It is a system I applied successfully throughout my time in education. It worked.

The main objection has always been that it is time consuming. In the short term it is. In the long term it isn't.

There is a danger that resentment and alienation result in recurrence after recurrence. Nothing is resolved.

Restorative practice resolves issues. It could do the same for crime. Instead of using a hugely costly and lengthy process involving courts, judges and prisons, many cases could be resolved in a similar way. Fines, community service and even prison sentencing could replace the detentions.

It works and it is cost effective.

Of course it will never happen while the barristers and lawyers have a vested interest in maintaining such a lucrative system for themselves.

One thing is quite clear. Schools should always avoid any system that is inflexible and automatically aligns punishments to crimes. These can only be used as indicators.

Staff who like the reassurance of having a clear, black and white system should know there is no such thing.

In practice all crimes are nuanced by context and severity. Each incident is different. They have to be treated differently and punished accordingly.

Chapter 29 – Academies, Free Schools and Religious Schools

These initiatives all have to be political - don't they? No educationalist with an ounce of common sense would introduce policies like these.

Academies

What a stupid idea. You break away from your family of support with county and fellow schools. Branch off on your own under the distant support of the government represented by a small department in London. Great if everything goes smoothly. When things go wrong it becomes less clear. Where is that support?

In order to procure all the necessary services necessary to deal with disaffected students, legal, health and safety, attendance, subject support etc, previously supplied by county, it is necessary to build up partners and recreate the benefits of the county family.

The whole concept was ridiculous. Yet I introduced it in my school.

So why did we do it?

• Well firstly there was, as always, the need for money to ensure staffing levels. It meant an extra £500,000 only half of which was needed to provide the same level of services. We made £250,000 which could make a huge difference to provision.

• Secondly, county had been getting slack. In my opinion they took a slice of our money and did not spend it all efficiently. I felt that half of it was squandered. This needed addressing. We were not getting value for money.

• Thirdly, we did not get support when we needed it. This was clearly illustrated in my first year of headship when we had that series of unforeseen disasters with long-term staff sickness, a boiler breaking down, electrics condemned etc. I went cap in hand for a loan from their emergency fund to tide us over and received short shrift. Where was county support when you needed it?

The government knew all this and chose to exploit it. In the short term it made sense.

However the government has already gone back on its word and reduced the funding and so removed the only significant reason for becoming an academy.

The whole basis for this is political. It is an attempt to remove the power of the Local Authorities and return control to central government.

What a half-baked idea.

Free Schools

Another stupid political idea - allow any Tom, Dick and Harry to set up a school. They don't even have to be educationalists, not even a trained teacher. Anyone can set one up. This includes all those people with vested interests: Creationists who want to indoctrinate our children, religious groups who want to do the same; businesses who want to pervert education to meet their particular needs; disgruntled parents who have quirky ideas of what they want their children taught; disgruntled parents who are opposed to centrally organised school closures due to falling numbers.

Some of these parents may have a case; most do not. If a school is fundamentally uneconomical due to lack of students why would it suddenly become viable?

Of course the government reserves the right to veto the setting up of these schools. I'd sort that right away. I'd veto the lot of them.

It was a ridiculous idea in the first place. It panders to parents in order to win votes and again it is designed to undermine the local education authorities.

Religious schools

Historically all schools were religious schools. They were called grammar schools and set up to teach Latin grammar to upper class boys so that they could read the Bible and sing in the choir.

Poor kids did not matter. They were destined to be field and factory fodder. Poor kids did not need educating.

Once the rich kids had mastered Latin they formed an elite. The church was in control.

For much of our country's history the land was basically a theocracy. It was only when we moved to a secular basis following the enlightenment that state schools appeared. Up until then the rich commanded the top positions through their fee paying public schools and subsequent domination of universities. The poor were left largely illiterate and uneducated.

Religious schools have only one reason for their existence. They exist to instil their ideas and values in the heads of our children. In my opinion this is brainwashing.

Religious schools create intolerance, division and a belief in the supernatural. Religion has no place in education. Religion should be a personal choice made as an adult. Children should be protected from religious pornography. For the state to finance these schools is madness and a throw-back to the dark ages.

Parents like religious schools because they believe they value discipline and achieve high results. Could this be the result of extra funding?

All state schools should have good discipline and great results. They don't need religious indoctrination to achieve these.

The government and all concerned should be ashamed of this anachronism. The problem is that the people who make these decisions – on whether to continue with free schools and religious schools – are part of that elite. They have a vested interest in maintaining a system that favours them and gives them privilege.

Chapter 30 – Inspirational teachers

There are few professions where you can have the life transforming influence of teaching. Teachers have the power to inspire children and enhance their lives. In my own experience of teachers, as a student and as a professional, I have observed and been the victim of some atrocious teaching but I have also been exposed to inspirational figures who nurtured, inspired or cared for me; teachers who gave completely of themselves and took enormous risks in order to break down barriers and form nourishing relationships.

I look back on Mrs Horne at primary school who gave me warmth in a place of coldness. At secondary school there were a number who were good and interesting but there was one in particular who inspired me and made me think. He was only with us for a few terms and he was called Mr Trantor. He never taught me but I was still touched by his incredible personality. He was different. He was open and he was honest. What you saw was what you got.

Mr Trantor taught rural science. We had a large rural science department complete with vegetables, pigs and chickens.

Mr Trantor was a young man who illuminated the school with his brightness and energy.

I used to talk with him a lot as he intrigued me. He told me that he was only working for a short while in order to finance a boat that he was building and complete a navigational course at college. He and a friend were planning to sail round the world in it.

Mr Trantor did not believe in the rat-race. He had chosen an alternative life style and he also seemed to be the happiest, most contented individual I had encountered.

It was rumoured that Mr Trantor actually slept in with the chickens in order to save money and finance his schemes.

It was rumoured that Mr Trantor had slept with half of the female staff.

It was rumoured that half of the sixth form girls swooned over Mr Trantor.

It was rumoured that the French assistant had left early following encounters with Mr Trantor. It was rumoured that she was starting a family!

It was rumoured that Mr Trantor was a communist.

It mattered little if there was any substance to the rumours. It was all part of the mystique and intrigue.

Mr Trantor had few possessions. All I remember is his old bike. He had declared it public property. Anyone could use it. He announced that if you needed to get somewhere then use the bike.

The end result of this was that everyone did take his bike and rode it about. Mr Trantor did not care. They abused it. He laughed.

Every Wednesday the lower sixth were subjected to a lecture. They were usually incredibly boring and all but one have receded completely into the blankness of history without trace – except one.

They must have been at a loss for a speaker with Mr Trantor offering to fill the gap.

The Headteacher introduced Mr Trantor and his speech absolutely mesmerised me. I remember it vividly.

Mr Trantor told us a little about his life. Following university he rented a shed on Box Hill and lived in it for a number of years. The rent was £1.

In order to finance the rent he had a paper-round.

Each day he would get up with the sun, deliver his papers and have the rest of the day to himself. He grew vegetables on his allotment. He ate them and sold the surplus. He kept chickens and had time to think and learn. He read and planned a lot.

He and a friend had learnt carpentry and were building a boat. He produced a map and showed us exactly where they were going. They planned to stop and work to fund food and repairs and sail the world.

It was no idle pipe-dream. It was happening.

As Mr Trantor told me of his idyllic days on Box Hill, his thoughts, observations and emotions a world of possibility opened up to me. Life was an adventure with no need to follow the same old pattern. You could break away and do it differently. Nothing was ordained. You could make it up as you went along. Life could be full of wonder, awe and exploration or you could get a nine to five and work for your pension.

I happened to be reading Jack Kerouac at the time and this fitted in. It inspired me.

Well – I worked eight to six most of my life with evenings and weekends as an optional extra. So I didn't drop out. But in my head I did. In my head I promised myself that I would always keep a real, vivid life apart from work; one that was full of adventure, excitement, discovery, creativity and wonder. I've tried to do that. I chose writing, reading and travel. I made time to love and live, develop friendships, and get into crazy rock music. In my head I had a world of freedom every minute of every day.

I never told Mr Trantor how much he inspired me. But then we never think to, do we? We take teachers for granted.

As a Head I saw teachers who gave their souls to the kids, who brought the horrors of war to life, who made poetry live, who cared so much the kids fell in love with them. I saw kids saved.

Most of those students never said a word.

Thank you Mr Trantor. Thank you Roy, Pauline, Mark, Rebecca, Ruth, Chrystabel, Amanda, Lester, Rita, Mike, Jenny, Matthew, Sarah, John, Liz, Sean, Pat, Phil, Bev, John, Barry, Bill, Liz, Andrew, Sam, Trevor, Kathy, Steve, Ali, Tim, Pete, Dave, Martin, Ray, Guy, Gerry, Jo, Paul, Emma, Jack, Sharon, Alan, Debbie, Chris, Lee, Claire, Jim, Margaret, Rich, Gillian, Tony (I wish I hadn't started this list it could fill the book!)..... and the hordes of others who give your all for the kids and really care. On behalf of all the dumb students who were silently saved, transformed and inspired by you - I thank you. You have changed the world for the better.

Forget your teaching and learning, your exam results and league tables!

When I was in charge of biology I wanted wonder and awe. I produced a syllabus for year 7 that was all about discovery and investigation. We kept locusts and investigated how they lived. We hatched chicks from eggs. We investigated hair, snot and pond-water through the window into another world created by the microscope. We roamed the wilderness looking at nature. We investigated soil with a hundred experiments.

Every homework was written out on a slip, was a practical exercise and came with a joke. At the end of the lessons the kids asked for the homework slips and were laughing over the appalling jokes. They were corny but the kids were eager to take the slips.

The homeworks were practical. They had to dangle loo-paper into the toilet bowl and measure how high the water rose in half an hour. They had to put water in sealed bottles and put the bottles in plastic bags in the freezer. They had to collect woodlice and see what conditions they preferred etc.

Occasionally the parents complained. They couldn't see the point of dangling loo paper in the toilet. They did not appreciate the wonders of capillarity.

Every lunch-time the lab was full of excited kids feeding chicks and locusts, measuring, weighing and laughing. They were learning without toil. They didn't even know they were learning.

One summer one of my students camped out in the wood and carried out an intensive study of the local squirrel population. He caught and marked them, named them, boiled down dead squirrels to rebuild skeletons, stuffed the skins, examined faeces to identify food, marked drays and observed their habits. He produced a complete breakdown of his work. Rather gruesome but also amazing.

That was education. He'd done it himself. He'd lived it.

Then came the National Curriculum; overnight anything not directly described in the prescriptive strands was dumped by order of the government.

Science once more became a difficult chore to be memorised. Wonder and awe was banished.

As a Head I encouraged experimentation and active learning. I supported staff through complaints from governors and parents. I wanted that awe and wonder back again.

I rapidly began to see teachers reaching out and trying new things. I saw computer presentations complete with interactive learning that took my breath away. I saw the use of puppets, models, role plays and visits that opened minds. I saw kids buzzing.

I filled the checklists in because I had to. I did the observations but they were not important. What was important was that you could feel the electricity of learning. The kids were aglow with it. As long as that energy pervaded the classrooms and the kids were harnessing the power of their minds I knew the results, exams, league tables and inspections would take care of themselves.

When I was head of biology I had an eager young co-conspirator by the name of Sean Smith. He was a young student teacher who started on his probationary year and he was game for anything. Sean buzzed and the kids came to life when he was around.

Sean was a live wire in and out of the classroom. He had the same passion as me.

One December he came in to school with Christmas baubles as ear-rings. Barry the Head at the time did a double take. The staff and kids roared with laughter when he walked in.

Sean loved the kids as much as I did and had a brilliant sense of humour.

At the time I was developing my student centred modules in biology as Sean was mad keen to do a module. He tried it out and it was great.

Sean didn't come in to school one day. A member of the science department went round to his flat to see if he was alright. They found him dead in his bed. He had died of an epileptic fit.

That was one of the saddest days of my life.

There aren't enough Seans. He would have gone on to great things. I still miss him and his joviality. He was just the kind of teacher I would have been happy passing over the school to. I knew he had the right sensibilities.

Every Headteacher should wear Christmas baubles in their ears.

Education at BGS was alive. It was real and it wakened sleeping minds instead of dimming them; it opened up horizons for all students.

Chapter 31 – Safeguarding & Health & Safety

Safeguarding

It is widely reported that 10% of our students suffer some type of abuse. This is scandalous and tackling this should be a priority of every school and institution. We should always be vigilant and have systems in place to identify those being abused and then take action.

It is what is done about it that is important. I do not believe that a number of the safeguarding initiatives do anything to make children safer. In some cases they create a complacency that makes matters worse. I believe a number of the initiatives are political solutions introduced to create the impression that something is being done or are introduced as a knee-jerk reaction to a terrible incident.

There is a perception that all males are potential paedophiles and any touching is automatically wrong. I find this distressing and upsetting. As a normal male who has no paedophilic tendencies I find it disturbing that I am viewed suspiciously if I so much as smile at a young toddler in a café who is doing something amusing to catch my attention or if I were to pat a student on the shoulder in way of encouragement.

I believe we are impoverishing the lives of adults and children unnecessarily. We are primates and like all other apes we need the reassurance of gentle physical contact with each other in order to grow emotionally and psychologically healthy.

Because of abuse we have created an expensive bureaucratic system that cannot solve the problem.

When I was a kid the older men in my community were grandfather figures who would stop and talk with us and even join in our games. One I remember with great sentiment used to always have a pocket of boiled sweets to share with us. He would stop and show us a trick with a hoop or swap a genial greeting. Nobody thought he was after anything more. Nowadays actions like that would be treated with suspicion. I find it sad and I think it is a loss for everyone.

Children are growing up without that casual interaction with older men.

I am not foolish. I know there are paedophiles around who are adept at grooming children. It is more a question of what we can do about it and what is effective.

The fear of paedophilia has become hysterical.

Normal comforting human behaviour has now been sexualised. That is not humane. I would want my sons and daughters comforted if they felt upset. I see nothing wrong in that.

Naturally I think we need adequate vetting procedures for staff.

It is vital to have a central register of known paedophiles so that the caring professions can be warned when making staff appointments. This of course cannot alert to the unknown paedophile.

It is useful to have staff training on what signs to look for in children and indeed staff.

It is good to have a whistle-blowing policy if there are any suspicions.

As for the criminal records bureau checks; they are expensive and create complacency. What is required is a simple national data base. Any people working with children can be cross checked. It does not require a huge bureaucracy.

I do not agree with erecting huge fences around our schools in effect turning them into prisons. Neither do I believe that having staff and visitor badges makes anybody any safer. What good do they do?

The best form of safeguarding is vigilance and education. I am sure that most grooming goes on through the internet. That's what children need educating about most. Most abuse takes place in the home and is carried out by relatives. We need to actively look for the symptoms of that abuse and deal with it. It can take the form of sexual, emotional, physical abuse or neglect. Being trained and watchful is the best defence.

When I was young we knew where the flashers and perverts lived and took steps to avoid them.

It is not necessary to curtail the freedoms of all, impoverish everyone's life and create a massive bureaucracy to create a system that is ineffective.

What has happened in Rotherham and many other places is unforgivable. Hundreds of youngsters were abused and their abusers even caught in the act. Victims asked for help and were ignored. Families asked for help and were ignored. Nothing was done about the perpetrators.

What is the point of having all the safeguarding in the world if people are not listened to or helped?

Health & Safety

Health and Safety initiatives have worked. They have saved lives and prevented injury.

What gives health and safety a bad name is the heavy bureaucracy.

Sometimes there is no common sense.

Health & safety has a huge impact on science education. Over the years we have legislated to remove fun and interesting experiments from schools. Some were undoubtedly dangerous but most were not. We have ended up emasculating the teaching of science to the point where it no longer captures the imagination of students. It is not exciting. The smells, bangs and wonder of my youth have been replaced with tedium. Then we lament the lack of great scientists and technologists being generated by our British schools.

As a child I was attracted to science by the mysterious colours, explosions, and dissections. It was exciting, fun, and gruesomely fascinating. Science has been cleaned up.

I see nothing wrong in the dissection of organs – eyes, hearts, lungs, kidneys and the like from animals killed for meat. I can accept that some might prefer not to participate on moral grounds. That is easy to accommodate.

However I have always been opposed to dissection of animals in schools. I think that is ethically unsound. As a biologist I dissected rats, rabbits, dogfish, salamanders, snakes, frogs and numerous insects. I believe most of this was unnecessary. Some of these animals were on the endangered list and were live caught.

When working as a laboratory technician I had to unpack boxes of live caught frogs posted from Ireland eighty percent of which arrived dead and were simply thrown away. I found that most distressing. I could only imagine what those frogs went through as they were crammed into the cardboard boxes and chucked around on their journey.

It was detrimental when the blood work disappeared on the crest of the AIDS epidemic. The kids enjoyed pricking themselves, testing their blood groups, seeing agglutination and staining smears to find their own blood cells; likewise with cells from mouth linings.

When I was at school in chemistry our favourite teacher started each lesson with a series of explosions. We melted metals with bunsen burners. We set chemicals on fire. We created violent reaction giving off coloured fumes. We created evil smelling fumes that permeated the whole school. We added concentrated acids to sugars and watched as they spontaneously ignited and rose into blackened cones. We chucked lumps of sodium and potassium into water-baths and watched them ignite, explode, whiz around and burn dazzlingly. We ignited magnesium. We heated up flasks of acetone.

In physics we set about raising our hair with galvanometers. We gave each other static electricity shocks. We burnt all manner of substances with magnifying glasses. We created spectrums. We did fun experiments with magnets.

Science was exciting and fun.

A lot of us had pet animals. We collected caterpillars, newts, lizards and frogs. We learnt about the environment and what was damaging it first hand. We had chemistry sets that we augmented from the chemist who would supply us with alcohol, concentrated acids, sulphur and most other things on request. We mixed stuff up to see what it would do. We loved it when it reacted.

That exciting world has gone. It has been sanitised out of existence. It has been strangled by health & safety and political correctness. Science is now theory and highly controlled experiments which many kids find hard and boring.

Gone are the days when Tony went round frightening everyone with a cow's eye in his mouth. He'd go up to someone and slowly open his mouth so the eye opened.

Gone are the days where we built great big dams in the local ditch and blew them up with our home-made explosives.

Gone are the days of having a throbbing finger full of puncture wounds as Year 7 demanded you demonstrate one more time how to do that blood smear.

It's all gone super-safe and boring.

I remember the excitement back in my 6th form chemistry lesson I was merrily heating up a big round bottomed flask of highly inflammable acetone with a bunsen burner with the intention of seeing whether the introduction of solutes affected its boiling point.

I am not sure if I put a little too much acetone in or I merely enabled it to boil a little too fiercely but something went wrong. A spout of acetone spurted out of the safety vent in the top of the flask. I saw it spray up in the air and then seem to fall back over the apparatus in slow motion. As it hit the bunsen burner flame it ignited with a whoosh.

Immediately I stepped back.

A column of flame was now surrounding my apparatus. This immediately started to heat the contents of my round bottomed flask and further jets of boiling acetone shot up in the air and down over the apparatus. Within seconds there was a roaring inferno reaching up to the ceiling further fuelled by spurts of acetone from the super-heated acetone in the flask.

We all retreated in horror to the edge of the lab. It looked like it was going to explode.

Mr Bell sauntered over with his hands behind his back and casually surveyed the roaring conflagration. He calmly turned the bunsen off and picked up a damp cloth off the bench. He opened the cloth up and threw it over the apparatus dousing the flames.

Then he looked round at me and said: 'I would suggest a little less acetone next time.'

We were all well impressed.

I was teaching a science lesson with a lower school group. It was a practical lesson on food group testing in which they had to heat up Benedict's reagent with various types of food in a test tube.

They all had their goggles on and were heating away with great relish. There wasn't too much that could go wrong.

Boys like fiddling with things.

One of the boys had been absently twisting around a gas fitting that fed four bunsens. It had come loose and the taps twisted round.

The gas taps definitely should not have been able to twist round.

Much to his and everybody else's surprise the whole fitting came off with the accompaniment of a great blast of gas emanating from a now open pipe at least an inch in diameter.

It is quite incredible how much gas can come out of a pipe of that bore. It makes quite a noise.

It makes an even greater noise when it becomes ignited by a nearby bunsen burner.

The whole class rushed away in fright as a huge pillar of roaring, burning gas flamed up to the ceiling.

It was my big moment.

Mindful of Mr Bell I sauntered across and threw a damp cloth over the aperture of the gas pipe. The roaring flame immediately went out.

I then motioned one of the boys to pull the gas cut-off lever to off.

The ceiling was a little blackened but there was no harm done and my Red Adair impression was soon the talk of the school.

Those were the days!!

There is no doubt that we need health and safety. It is a question of getting the balance right!

Chapter 32 – Assessment and Marking

Assessment is crucial.

It is important to acknowledge the starting point, ascertain how much progress is being made, assist as and when necessary, and have achievable targets.

Every child deserves to maximise his/her potential.

I, like so many other kids, slipped through the net when I was at school. There were no rigorous tests and no interventions. All we had was the blunt instrument of an 11 plus exam, which was a glorified intelligence test, and that was it. Performance on one day at ten years old determined your future. Tell a kid he is thick and he will believe you. Tell him he is worthwhile, valuable, intelligent and going somewhere and he'll work his socks off for you.

No child at my school, when I was Headteacher, was ever written off. No child was worthless. No child was incapable. I believed in every last one of them. Even the most disaffected was important. It was our job to find out the reason for misbehaviour and its solution. Sometimes we fail. As an educator you cannot compensate for a lifetime of neglect or abuse, for the trauma of bereavement, or the frustration and anger of a divorce, but you can try to help and ease the situation with a dose of caring intervention.

Assessment is a tool. It is not brilliant. It is limited. It does not give the full picture. It is not the be-all and end-all of everything. It is merely a tool.

Basing school league tables on assessment data has to be flawed. They are not accurate enough. No two schools are identical. There are too many factors involved. To compare a school with other schools is only a guide. Assessments of this nature can only provide a rough indicator.

One of the limitations of all assessment procedures is that they can only measures the measurable. In my experience it is the things we do not measure that are the most important such as self-esteem and happiness.

However they are a start. We have to use them while trying to keep to the front of our minds that they are flawed.

Nowadays every child entering secondary school has a history of assessment that gives a rough picture of their capabilities. This is augmented by a detailed series of cognitive testing. These tests give further valuable information. They will indicate which students require intervention to help them succeed. Support is then deployed. This baseline of their ability assists with future judgements. If later on they begin to fall short of the level of progress we might expect we can intervene and find out causes and provide further support.

In addition there is a programme of assessments in all subjects. These should not intrude or be 'bolted on' but integrated into the system. Teaching staff will be aware of expectations for their students and note who is falling short. From these subject assessments student progress is monitored.

If this works no-one should slip through the net. Counsellors, support staff and outside agencies can be alerted to provide care and support.

The problems with assessment arrive when the government gets involved. Flawed assessment tools are used as a crude means of measuring schools against one another and of measuring progress of a particular school. This is simply not possible with assessments that are not accurate enough. We are not dealing with robots we are dealing with children. They have moods and illnesses. The tests are merely indicators. They are great if they are used to help students. They are poor if they are judged to be set in stone.

Assessments are flawed. Hence the league tables and judgements based on league tables are not only extremely limited but highly inaccurate. It is wrong to put so much judgement on them.

There is much more to a child than can be assessed in a few tests or examinations.

There is much more to education than can be tested.

The world has gone utterly mad trying to assess knowledge criteria and make judgements on schools and systems. It is in danger of destroying the more important aspects.

If we are to be judged on literacy, numeracy, student progress and the like I would also want to be assessed on how well we socially integrate students, develop their self-esteem, happiness, sense of humour, empathy, responsibility, helpfulness, pleasantness, truthfulness, tolerance and levels of respect. These are every bit as important!

I always reckoned that if a student were to leave school full of self-esteem and drive they would make their way in the world better than any student crammed with GCSEs and no personality.

As for marking - well I don't hold too well with it and yet I think it's crucial. I have seen teachers so burnt out with marking that they don't have the energy to teach. It can wear you down. To mark a set of 30 books thoroughly can take two hours (that is only 4 minutes a book). If you are teaching twelve groups you are looking at 24 hours of trying to focus on kids work each and every week in addition to the 'day job'. It piles up around you and you put it off. It nags away at you. You spend evenings trying to catch up with it. You spend weekends trying to fit it in. It is wearying. The last thing you want to do after a hard day at school is to start marking. Lesson preparation is onerous enough.

Diligent staff are doing sixty to seventy hour weeks which feels like you don't do anything else with your life.

Marking is important.

Kids need to get feedback and be monitored.

Teachers are expected to read work, write in spelling corrections, analyse and write diagnostic comments, write positive feedback, give pointers to help improvement.

I'm sorry but I don't think it is all necessary.

I was not diligent. I used to scan through, pick up the odd spelling mistake, tick every section to show I'd seen it, give a mark out of ten as an effort score and a short comment – usually a single word. I specialised in making up words such as: Superbo, Brillianti, Marvellessimo, Incredibilatto, and Excellento.

My main feedback was verbal as I returned the books. I used to throw the book back to each student with a positive comment such as 'That's superb James, much better, keep it going.' I used to spin the book so that it arced through the air and landed on the bench in front of the student. It became quite an art. I got hose books flying like boomerangs. The kids loved it. It got the lesson off to a great start.

That was very effective for me but obviously would be boring if all teachers did the same thing. The kids were eager to get their books back. They worked for the marks.

I always gave them the right of challenge if they thought I was marking too leniently or too harshly. Hardly anyone objected. The kids were extremely fair and honest when judging themselves.

The classes blossomed. Gradually the marks went up so that almost everyone was getting tens for effort. So I started eulogising over a few kids who were obviously trying like mad, saying they were trying so hard I was forced to give them eleven out of ten. I even gave a couple of twelves. It worked a treat.

From my observations they took no notice of any diagnostic writing. They weren't interested. They wanted to see that you had troubled yourself and cared to look at their books – the ticks, and what effort score you made – the mark out of ten, along with the subtlety of the single word comment. They worked out that Superbo was better than Excellento and Terrifico was better than Superbo. There was much competition for comments.

That was all that was important.

A set of books took me between twenty minutes and half an hour. That is more than enough.

Marking is crucial but detailed diagnostic marking is a waste of precious time and energy. I'd rather that energy went into the teaching.

I've seen other methods – such as stick in sheets of tick lists, 'records of achievement' and formulaic criteria. They are a waste of time. Kids hate them.

Chapter 33 – It's the little things that count

As with all things in life it is the little things that count. There are essentials. I don't believe in checklists but if I did this would be one:

- Greeting each student with a welcoming smile whatever you were feeling inside
- Standing in a prominent place to greet staff and students
- Touring the school and asking how students and staff are
- Offering help and standing in to cover if there is a crisis
- Always signing your name on certificates instead of using a computerised signature
- Always having your door open
- Always being available at the end of a phone line
- Answering all emails with a little comment or bit of praise and recognition
- Saying thank you when someone has done something well or beyond the call
- Recognising births and illnesses with cards and flowers
- Smiling
- Finding a positive comment
- Taking lenient view over absence or family needs
- Telling everyone how outstanding they are
- Telling everyone what an outstanding job they are doing
- Telling everyone that they are special, the school is special and everything they do is special
- Being compassionate with staff and students
- Practising a bit of give and take
- Never ducking the hard stuff
- Giving everyone the benefit of the doubt
- Learning to put up with less than perfection but striving for improvement
- Being lenient when you can
- Being firm when you need to be
- Being honest even when that is difficult
- Listening

- Consulting
- Empathising
- Saying sorry when you get something wrong
- Setting examples by demonstrating how to behave, dress, talk and relate
- Ensuring not to ask anyone to do anything you would not do
- Not kow-towing to anyone (governors, county, Ofsted, parents or government)
- Doing what is right despite the rules, public opinion or direct orders. If it is right it is right.
- Knowing what is going on
- Standing up and confronting your critics
- Standing up and leading
- Having a clear vision and keeping it to the forefront
- Keeping the momentum going
- Being able to manage change
- Publicising the school
- Being seen to work harder than anyone else.
- Being there first, leaving last, being off sick less
- Not letting power go to your head
- Cracking corny jokes

'Open, caring friendly' means just that. As a Head you have to exemplarise the philosophy. If you don't live and die by it who else is going to take it seriously?

Despite the pressures you have to be available to listen, accept criticism, explain, argue and if necessary demand. Your door, phone and emails must be open. All students, teachers and non-teaching staff must have access. That is 'open'.

When someone is upset, in a crisis, has made a mistake, is ill or feeling low and lost, a Head's job is to pick them up, make them feel valued, to comfort them and sympathise. A Head's job is to help solve the problems, find a way through for them and share some of the load. That is 'caring'.

If a member of staff needs a favour – their young child is in a play, there is a crisis or a need, be prepared to give time off. If necessary cover for them yourself. Most staff will really appreciate that and they will repay this ten-fold. Negotiate a deal. Be flexible. That is 'friendly'.

A school is often the greatest stability a student has in the whole world. Not all students are blessed with good home backgrounds, handsome features, athletic bodies, nimble minds, lovable personalities, endearing qualities or breath-taking skills. They need boosting up and helped to cope. Teachers are responsible for the welfare of their students. No student can learn while he is frightened, cold, hungry, abused or uncertain what is going to happen in their life. Those problems have to be addressed before good learning can take place.

Often a kind word makes all the difference.

Staff spend a large amount of their lives working. A school should be a welcoming place for everyone in which they can feel relaxed, cared for and loved. Work should be fun and something you can take pride in and go home feeling a sense of achievement. Being a teacher should be a as much a pleasure as it is a privilege. Education should be fun and school a refuge.

A smile, joke or friendly act makes the world brighter.

The ethos of a school is the result of how it is run. How it is run is the prerogative of the Headteacher and senior team. If they don't get the simple things right it will become ordinary. It is the little things that count. An ethos does not come about because you say it is there. It has to be carefully nurtured like a delicate orchid. You pour love and immense effort into coaxing it out of the ground. You cause it to blossom with the radiance of your passion. A Headteacher has to be the sunshine and rain.

The little things make the atmosphere that produces outstanding education.

There are no accidental outcomes involved. None of this is by chance. It is the end result of a philosophy.

The little things are what make the difference.

Chapter 34 – Starting School

The early days are crucial.

My first day at the big school was a bit of a disaster.

As I had failed my eleven plus I was informed I would be going to the local secondary modern which had a terrible reputation. I heard there were riots every day, total disaffection and hardly anybody achieved any examination results. My parents were furious. They had gone to County Hall to complain and got nowhere. I picked up on their anxiety and was frightened.

In disgust my parents took the family away on holiday and I was destined to miss the first week of my new school. I don't know what they were thinking off. That first week was important. To miss the first week would put me at an even bigger disadvantage; friendships would be established, seating arrangements, confidence built. I would come in as a stranger.

However on our return one of my friends came round and said I was in his class at the local bilateral school. This was news to us. I had the uniform for the secondary modern. My parents' ears pricked up. It was all they needed. I was whisked off to the clothing shop and a new uniform was bought.

The following Monday I started at my new school. There'd been a mix up and I'd mistakenly been enrolled at two schools.

My IQ test had been good enough to get me into the C Class - a class for children who had failed the eleven plus but never the less showed aptitude. That form group was full of many disturbed clever students. Many were from single parent homes, homes broken by death, divorce or alcohol. Trev was typical; he was the oldest of twelve, most of whom were boys. He had the job of looking after his youngest sibling who was a toddler. After school Trev would take the toddler around in a pushchair. Trev, by the age of twelve, was a 60 a day smoker. His fingers were stained yellow. His party piece was to share his cigs with his eager eighteen month brother. By eighteen months the boy was a seasoned smoker and would puff away merrily.

My form room was the technical drawing room. I turned up in my new blazer. The teacher had put pieces of wood with sandpaper glued on them for students to sharpen their pencils on. They were hung on nails around the room.

I had only been there five minutes when I got up to move to my seat and caught my new blazer on a nail. I spent the rest of the day with a triangle of material dangling down from my shoulder.

My second lesson was art. My class was not timetabled into a proper art room. We were housed on the stage behind the curtain.

The teacher selected me and two other boys to go across to the art room and collect the paint. The paint was powder paint that had been put in baking trays. Each colour was a heap of dust in one of the circular indents. We piled a number of trays on top of each other and set off back to the stage.

We negotiated the corridors, doors and road to the main block. We went through the door into the corridor leading behind the stage area. Unfortunately I had not accounted for the sunken mat inside the door. I could not see where I was going because of the heaped up trays, tripped and went flying.

I hit the floor. The trays went up in the air and came down with a great crash and huge cloud of powder.

I was a magnet for the powder. Most of the powder paint seemed to have come down on me. I was covered from head to foot.

I stood up looking like a dusty snowman and surveyed the wreckage. The trays were littered over the floor amid a desert of powder paint. It was disaster. The powder paint was like fine flour and I was coated with the pale dust.

The crash had brought the art teacher and most of the class rushing out to find me standing among the debris.

I was standing there and the tears started. As they ran down my face they mixed with the pale powder to create rivulets of rainbows.

It was not the most auspicious start.

During my first week in secondary school I met Ribena. She was a big year 10 girl who looked like an escapee from the Australian Cell Block H program.

Ribena was very friendly and explained that as a new first year I might meet up with problems. I did not quite catch on at first.

The next day two of Ribena's similarly built henchwomen were busy rounding up first years. They grabbed and marched me off behind the bicycle sheds.

Ribena had a girl's aluminium comb with a handle. She had sharpened the end of the comb handle into a sharp point.

Her two henchwomen held me against the wall while Ribena placed the point of the comb under my chin and pressed up until I was standing on tip-toe. She explained that schools were dangerous places and boys like me needed protection. For the modest sum of half my dinner money I would be guaranteed to live problem free.

So far the only real problem I had encountered emanated from Ribena and her gang but that was precisely what she was referring to.

For a number of weeks we all passed money over to the debt collectors and life was quiet.

Starting at a new school is fraught. The kids are told tales of all the bullying. They imagine themselves having their heads stuck down toilets. They come from a variety of different primary schools with different rules and ethos.

It is important that the new students are initiated into the new school ethos, looked after, have their fears addressed, and are taught how we operate.

In those first days they need caring for.

I ran the pastoral system in order to cater for the needs of students. There was always a dilemma. The problem was that there were two ways of going. You could assign tutors to forms and allow them to continue following their form through the school on the basis that they got to know each other well and could provide better care or you could appoint specialist tutors to different years and have the kids move between them.

I settled for a compromise. I figured that year 7 and year 9 required specialist tutors. In year 7 you needed tutors who would help their students settle, fuss over them, sort out problems, and care for them. Not all staff were suited. Some did not get on with the younger members of the school. Some were too cold and distant. Some were not organised enough. I put together a team of caring tutors who would operate with a corresponding head of year, someone who could form relationships with primary school teachers and organise the entire necessary liaison.

In year 9 students had to make subject choices that could easily affect their future careers. They needed guidance and advice. I put together a team with a head of year who were best suited to deal with that.

The tutors in years 8 & 9 and years 10 and 11 moved on with their forms and rotated.

Tutors always moaned. They had formed attachments with their form. They were reluctant to move on.

Every choice has a loss as well as a gain.

When I came to retire I had begun looking into solving all this through Vertical Tutoring. If it was carried out with proper training and preparation it could solve most of the problems. It addressed my concerns about students being artificially grouped in age groups and it enabled the older students to act as mentors and buddies. If done right, if the ethos was right, it could solve a number of issues. It could provide better care.

It required lots of planning and careful management to introduce it properly. Done badly it could be a disaster.

Chapter 35 – Individuality or uniforms?

I am not the best person to be discussing uniform. As a student I was at the forefront of protest. I pushed everything to the very limit and was in constant conflict with the authorities, particularly Miss McCoughlan, the deputy head at my secondary school.

I could not see how what I wore had any impact on how I learnt. I wanted to do my thing and they had a strict uniform policy and wanted me to comply.

From the age of fourteen I grew a beard. Every holiday I would grow it. Every time I went back to school Miss McCoughlan would tell me to shave it off. It became a ritual.

I tried to see how many days I could get through before she caught me. I remember once peering round this corner checking if she was about. A voice rang out behind me:

'Are you looking for someone?'

It was Miss McCoughlan looming over me with a wicked smile on her face. She knew I was looking for her.

I took to taking her literally.

She sent me home and told me not to come back until I'd shaved my beard off. I bunked off for three weeks until they sent the twagman round to find out what the problem was. I explained to him that I had been instructed not to come back until I'd shaved my beard off and I hadn't shaved it off yet.

It caused a bit of a rumpus.

On another occasion I was instructed to go home and shave my beard off and come straight back. I went home and shaved off a half inch tract from my lip to my chin and went back. It took a further three days for Miss McCoughlan to catch me.

'I thought I'd told you to go home and shave that beard off!' She exploded.

'I have,' I replied indignantly pointing to the narrow strip of bare flesh. 'These are side-burns and this is a moustache.'

The new edict was that sideburns could not be below the earlobe. I grew them in big bushy masses in front of my ears.

In a strange way I bet Miss McCoughlan enjoyed our battles of wills as much as I did.

With some of the other staff it was all rather nastier. Mr Morrell, my biology teacher, took rather a dislike to me. He did not like the way I always came top in his group without doing any work. My priorities at the time were more focussed on my social life. School was a social event. I spent my time chatting to the girls, sorting where the action was, arguing about rock music and lining up who to take to which party at the weekend. Lessons got in the way. Mr Morrell had a group of diligent, hard working students who achieved moderate success and me. He was Welsh and I suspect had a strict chapel background. My attitude, chirpy disregard and care-free ability went against his ethic. He preferred achievement to come out of sober hard work and applied industry. I flaunted that.

It came to a head when I turned up for my O level in jeans. I'd taken the opportunity to flaunt the dress code on the basis that they couldn't fling me out of an exam, could they?

Well they didn't, that is apart from Mr Morrell. He went to the Headteacher and demanded I be sent home to change. I was sent home and consequently missed half an hour of my exam. Still it was worth it.

Whether it was pointed shoes, hipster trousers, beards, fluorescent socks, bushy sideburns, long hair or coloured shirts I was the rebel and I loved every moment of it, particularly my duels with Miss McCoughlan and Mr Morrell's apoplexy.

I did not change much when I went into teaching. I was the one member of staff with the shoulder length hair, huge bushy beard and rainbow coloured hand-crocheted ties. I enjoy pushing the limits.

However, from a teacher's perspective, and particularly a Headteacher's, I can see some of the benefits of uniform.

It does not, as claimed, remove social class. It is amazing how a group of kids all wearing the same clothes can look so very different. If anything it exaggerated the differences between the kids from the council estates and the kids from the posh houses.

It can produce tribal ownership and give a bit of pride in the school.

It does aid the discipline of the school.

You cannot teach in a disorderly environment. There can only be one person with power in a classroom and that has to be the teacher. No matter how pleasant and friendly you want to make that classroom there has to be a power base. When students came into my classroom they were coming into my area, my personal zone. I was in charge. I controlled it. I did not do that through rigid discipline, distance, or threats. I did it through insistence and consistent demands. I made sure I had their full attention before starting. I waited. I made eye contact and non-verbal communication to let them know I was waiting and I was expecting them to comply. I called them in to me so that I had them close to me. They hated this but you cannot have a good discussion if they've got a desk between you. It's a barrier. It creates their space. I wanted them in my space.

In order to get to that pleasant, friendly and hugely positive relationship you have to work at it. This means all the friendly greetings, the giving of your personal self, the opening up, sharing jokes, talking honestly and treating each other like human beings. My students were friends. They were also kids and I was in charge.

Uniform can be an important element in this. As well as the pleasantries there are the constant little reinforcers that show who is in charge.

'Hi Max, how's it going?'

'Pretty good, sir.'

'Let's just get that shirt tucked in and the tie a bit straighter.'

I wait while he does it. We both grin. If it is done in the right way it doesn't create resentment. It's a little game, a ritual we go through.

Asserting control becomes part of the relationship. With thirty students in a classroom they have to know who the boss is ultimately. There can be no grey areas. If you have set the precedent with a thousand little demands all pleasantly met you have established the parameters of the relationship.

Uniform can be useful.

However, ideally I would do away with it altogether. Having experienced classrooms on the continent and having taught in the USA where there was no uniform I prefer it without. I did not find any discipline problems, or less student concentration due to the lack of uniform. I did appreciate the more relaxed environment. I found it more conducive to learning.

Ironically the students at my school, as I came up to retirement, were voting to bring back school blazers.

Is there no end to rebellion?

Chapter 36 – Parents!!

Parents!!! But hey, I don't mean you. You are OK. It's those others, the tiny minority. They are the ones that cause the problems.

When little Danny steps out of line and gets punished for it most parents are OK with that. They know the score. Danny was naughty. Danny gets punished. There's no problem.

Yet for some there is a problem. Their little angel could not possibly do anything wrong. It has to be a mistake. It has to be some other kids fault. It has to be the teacher picking on him. They simply cannot accept that their child has done anything wrong. They come into school all guns blazing.

'Why has he been put in detention?'

'Show me the paperwork.' They search for the slightest error in the procedure. They demand the school disciplinary policy. They threaten legal action and bring in solicitors to back up their claim. They demand the punishment be removed. They get exceeding belligerent and nasty.

The only way to deal with belligerent parents is to stand your ground, ensure procedure is followed and quietly and calmly insist that Danny will either do the punishment as prescribed or they can find another school for him.

Every parent wants the best for their child. We all know that.

Every parent thinks they know their child better than anyone else. That is not always the case. Children can be extremely manipulative. They can act as brilliantly as any Oscar winner. They have learnt over many years what to say and how to say it. They can spin their parents round like a ball on a finger.

I know. I used to do that with my parents. I could play one against the other with the best of them.

When I was doing my A level chemistry, and doing it rather badly, I was approached one break-time by my chemistry teacher.

'Do you know how many homework essays I have set so far this term?'

I considered this in very bad taste. He was encroaching on my free time with questions about work. Break-time was essential chatting up time. How was I supposed to sort out my weekends if I kept being interrupted with questions about work? I had high maintenance hormones to take care of.

'Not off hand, sir,' I said politely.

'Twelve,' he replied softly.

I blinked waiting for a reason for this outrage.

'Do you know how many you have handed in?'

'No idea sir.'

'None.'

'They must be about somewhere, sir,' I scrambled around for an excuse. 'I'll have a hunt round for them.'

'Hmmmm,' he said frowning and nodding his head slowly. 'I don't suppose you know what is happening next week?'

'No idea, sir.'

'Next week we write reports.'

That was a bit of a low blow. I peered at him.

'Unless I receive all twelve of those essays in by Monday I shall be writing your report accordingly.'

That was bad news. My Dad tended to take reports very seriously. He thought they were an indication of my progress. It could trigger a bit of a lecture. I didn't like lectures. They rather spoilt my day.

I spent Sunday scribbling out twelve essays. I can't think the quality can have been very good. An essay per half hour with very little research does not bode well for quality. However they might serve a purpose – they would at least fill in the gaps in his mark book.

'I've hunted out those essays you were after, sir,' I said with a deadpan expression, handing over a wadge of paper.

'Oh,' he said with a degree of consternation, looking really taken aback. 'I didn't think you could possibly do all those over the weekend. I'm afraid I've already written your report.

The report arrived home and my Mum read it. It never made scintillating reading at the best of times because, according to my mother, all the teachers were wrong. They failed to recognise that I was a genius. The reports were their failing not mine. My Dad had slightly different views but for the sake of marital harmony would usually take a back seat. On this occasion the report was worse than usual.

'Your chemistry teacher has given you a really bad report,'
Mum remarked, looking very concerned. 'Dad won't be happy with
this.'

'Really?' I replied innocently. 'What did he say?'

'He says you haven't handed any work in at all,' she said.

'But that's complete nonsense,' I exclaimed indignantly.
'He's set twelve essays and I've done every single one of them and
handed them in. He doesn't know what he's talking about. He's
obviously got me muddled up with somebody else.'

That evening Dad read the report. He was of the opinion that
my hair was too long and I should smarten myself up and think
about careers instead of girls. We used to have a few contretemps.

'The man's a complete nincompoop,' my Mum told him in
no uncertain terms. Chris has done all the work. He doesn't know
what he's talking about!'

Job done.

It even had the added bonus of deflecting away from the
mediocrity of the other subject reports.

For a Headteacher parents can be extremely difficult.

On one occasion I found myself dealing with a particularly
nasty fight. It involved three boys. One lad had completely lost it, hit
one of the boys and battered the other kid quite badly. There was
blood everywhere and he'd had to be dragged off by a member of
the duty team. The lad on the receiving end had a severely split lip,
swollen eye and bad nose bleed. He wasn't a pretty sight.

In good old restorative practice fashion I took the three of
them to my study and set about finding out what had been going on.

After much questioning it turned out that this had been
brewing for a few weeks. There had been some goading from the
two victims. The boy had put up with the name calling and then
exploded.

We ascertained exactly what had happened and who was to
blame. The two victims were clearly out of order for winding him up
and he was out of order for snapping and attacking them.

We went on to discuss what they should have done. When it
started it should have been reported to the form tutor who would
have got to the bottom of it and sorted it out, or they could have used
the 'bully box', or gone to their head of year, or their parents, or any

teacher they felt comfortable with. There were no shortages of avenues to turn to in order to sort problems out before they escalated into violence.

They all accepted this.

We then discussed what punishments were appropriate for the things they had done wrong. The two 'victims' accepted their guilt and we decided that name calling deserved an evening detention. The aggressor accepted that he should have used the correct procedures and not punched the boys.

We all agreed that this was severe enough to warrant a two day suspension.

The boys all shook hands, made up, apologised and went off home.

School had finished. I wrote letters and phoned home. There was no reply.

I thought no more about it. I had a hundred and three things to be getting on with. As far as I was concerned it had been properly dealt with and there was nothing more to be done.

The next day both the mother and her suspended son were sitting in the waiting room. I could tell from her scowl and body language that she wasn't happy. I invited her up into my room where she exploded.

When the tirade had subsided I gleaned that in her eyes her son was the victim and should never have been excluded. He had been bullied for two weeks and nothing had been done about it. The two boys concerned had got off with detentions and her poor son had been victimised and put out of school for defending himself against the two of them. She wanted the suspension lifting and taking off his record.

I explained to her that her son should have told somebody about the name-calling. If he had done that we would have dealt with it. We cannot deal with things we do not know about.

She irately claimed this was incompetence on the school's part. We should know what is going on with our students.

I pointed out that the school did not condone violence and her son had to learn that resorting to violence carries a severe penalty. There are better ways of dealing with things.

She claimed he had not been violent. He had merely defended himself.

I pointed out that there had been some verbal taunting but nothing sufficient to justify the ferocity of the attack her son had carried out. One of the boys had been punched hard in the head and the other had severe injuries from a number of hefty blows. His mother had had to take him to hospital to have his nose checked for a break and his lip seen to. If our duty staff had not arrived quickly on the scene it would have been even worse. Her son had lost control of himself.

She refused to accept this and wanted the suspension lifted and expunged.

I told her that this was not going to happen. We had discussed it together and all the boys had agreed that the punishments were appropriate.

She claimed I had bullied her son. He had been too intimidated to speak up for himself.

I repeated that the school did not condone violence and that the punishment was appropriate for the crime committed. If she was still unhappy I suggested she contact the chair of governors and appeal my decision in the usual complaints process. I also pointed out to her that if it had been her son assaulted in such a manner she would probably be looking for the perpetrator receiving more than a couple of days suspension.

She left in a fury telling me that I hadn't heard the last of it. She was right.

The next day I received a call from the chair of governors and a call from the director of education at county hall. The woman had sent legal letters in, quoting chapter and verse, stating that I had flouted regulations and was victimising her son. There was a string of offences listed.

I had failed to contact her personally by phone within the stated time. I had not sent a letter informing them. Her husband had not been informed – they were separated and he had equal parental rights and responsibilities. We had failed to care for her son and deal with bullying issues. We had victimised her son by not dealing with all three boys equally. She wanted the suspension lifted and expunged or she would proceed to sue through the courts.

The chair of governors implied that it might be best to concede. I told him 'over my dead body'. The lad had been vicious. He deserved the punishment. It had all been done properly. I had tried to phone there was no reply. Letters had been sent including to her husband. We had a system set up to do precisely that. I said the same to the director when she rang. They were both concerned and alarmed at the legal nature of the letters they had received. It was all in legal jargon.

I checked with the office. A letter had automatically been sent to her husband. I noticed that neither of the addresses were in our catchment area. That sent alarms ringing. We were heavily oversubscribed. Nobody had a place in the school from out of catchment. We couldn't even take everyone from the catchment area let alone the hundreds of others who applied from outside. I asked the office to check on admissions data.

I wrote back to the woman explaining that the punishment was appropriate for her son and for the other boys that all procedures had been followed and the punishment stood and would remain on his record. I ameliorated this a little by explaining that if there were no future instances of violence the record would neither be passed on to anyone else or inform any references.

The next day I received a letter from the father, written in similar legalese, citing a series of offences I had committed in the course of dealing with this. One of them was that I had not informed him by post.

I wrote back to inform him that a letter had been sent to his address and gave times.

Another letter arrived by hand from the woman demanding access to her son's file and all paperwork involved with the case including the witness statements. She quoted chapter and verse of her rights under various acts.

I wrote back and told her I was happy to show her the files. She should arrange to come in and go through them. I also said that if she was so unhappy with the school perhaps she should consider taking him elsewhere. We had a strong anti-bullying policy and did not condone violence. Perhaps there was a school out there that could meet their needs better than we could. They might, for instance, tolerate her son battering other boys.

Another letter arrived the next day demanding the files be copied and sent to her. I replied that she was at liberty to see them but I wasn't copying and giving them to her.

A letter arrived from the father with another set of claims. He had moved but we did not have a record of a change of address. This address was also outside the catchment area.

I checked with the head of year and requested the file so I could check all was in order. I found the witness statements were missing. I checked with the head of year, they had been misfiled and accidentally shredded.

'Damn', I thought to myself. 'Of all the cases to accidentally shred statements - we had reams of files all stored away in perpetuity and we had to shred these.' I intimated as much to the head of year. He was extremely apologetic.

The mother came in with a 'friend' and they pawed over the files making notes. They demanded copies. I refused. They demanded the witness statements. I told them they had been accidentally destroyed. They went apoplectic.

The next day another letter arrived with demands and accusations. They were going to start court proceedings.

I wrote to both of them and enquired as to the validity of the address they had used to get their son into the school. I checked with named primary schools as to the address used when they had attended. The primary was out of our area. They had created similar trouble before and moved schools a number of times. I made some enquiries and found the grandfather lived at the address given. I suspected they had fraudulently used this address to get their son into our school.

They were undeterred by my shot across the bows and came storming back with more demands and accusations.

Despite the fact that I had quite enjoyed the exchange I had had enough. I was too busy to bother with such petty matters. I bundled it up and sent it off to the legal department. They came up with very bland replies.

I talked to the solicitor about the threats. He said it was all pseudo legal stuff. The mother was obviously trawling the internet and considered herself a legal expert. She was probably writing the letters for the father as well and was in contact with a variety of parent support groups who were extremely biased. It read very legalistic but was really quite amateurish.

This case reminded me of another parent who had created havoc whenever his son was punished. He used to chain himself to railings and on one occasion super-glued himself to a window at county hall.

There are parents who try too hard to be friends with their sons. One father used to buy crisps and beer and spend Saturday night watching porno films with his twelve year old son. He saw nothing wrong with it.

The most belligerent parents I ever had to deal with resulted in me ordering them out of my room and banning them from the school premises.

We used to end the academic year with a two day festival. This involved numerous activities around the school and a number of trips to various places.

One of these trips was a day at the bowling rink. The boys would receive tuition if they wanted it and could then bowl for the rest of the day. They could eat on site and there were lots of other activities to do apart from bowling. It was all self-contained and easy to organise. Under no circumstances were the boys allowed out of the centre. That was mandatory. Not even at lunch-time.

This group of year 10s had, for reasons unknown, decided to bunk off and walk a mile to catch up with a group of their friends who were going to the cinema at a nearby multiplex. The big question was why had they decided to do that when they could have opted to have gone to the cinema in the first place?

Anyway, they had waited until everyone was checked in and settled and then sneaked out the back door and ran off. They had even planned it so they kept their outdoor shoes with them.

I received a phone call from the member of staff in charge of the film group. They had caught the four of them trying to sneak in to the film.

I had them collected and brought back to the school. I gave them a dressing down, phoned their homes to have them picked up and banned them from the next day's activities. They had to report in to school instead.

I considered this quite lenient considering the amount of trouble they had put us to.

However the parents did not agree. Within minutes they were in my office. They considered the whole situation was due to the poor organisation of the school trip.

I pointed out that the boys had planned the escapade in advance and deceitfully sneaked out. That we had a limited number of staff in the correct ratios but they could not be held responsible when boys of fifteen, who were supposed to be mature, behaved so deviously and disobeyed clearly explained orders.

They did not agree. They had paid for two activities. They wanted him reinstated.

I would not relent. I pointed out the danger involved in walking alongside a busy dual carriageway to get to the film group. An accident could have occurred. Staff had spent time searching for them. Staff had had to sort out the problem at the film end. Staff had to go and pick them up. They had caused a great deal of trouble.

Voices were raised.

They were furious.

I rose from my seat in a very deliberate manner, opened the door and ordered them out. I informed them that if they did not remove themselves from my study and the school site I would summon the police and have them arrested.

They left.

Chapter 37 – Public and Private Education

My parents came from working class backgrounds. My father's father was a meat porter at Smithfield market. My mother's father was a water meter reader and later a spiritualist healer. Neither of my parents were well educated but both were highly intelligent.

My father had to leave school at fourteen and go out to work to bring in a pay packet. He brought his unopened pay packet to his mother and she allocated him pocket money. The irony was that he had passed the exam to go to grammar school but his parents claimed they could not afford the uniform. If he had have gone his future earning potential would have been greater.

My mother suffered ill health at around eleven years of age and was parcelled off for a prolonged convalescence. On returning she had missed a significant period of school and was subsequently placed in the remove class with the remedial students. Her teacher, on finding that she was a very able child, used her to coach the other students. Thus it was that she never escaped the remove and never matriculated from school. She also left school at fourteen years of age.

They both pulled themselves up by their bootstraps and took courses in typing that enabled them to get jobs working for the newspapers in Fleet Street. They did this through their own determined efforts. They saw education as the key to escape from poverty and a working class background. My father ended up being in charge of an office of telephone reporters on the Evening Standard newspaper – quite a prestigious job.

My parents wanted the best for me and my sister and misguidedly sent us to a small private school. They had to scrimp and save to pay the fees. However, because they could not afford much, the school was of a rather poor standard that in no way helped us prepare for the future. It had a veneer of gentlemanly behaviour overlaying an old-fashioned ethos, even by the standards of those days, and paucity of real learning. It was all froth and no coffee.

I took the eleven plus at ten years of age. As we could not sit it at my school – there were only four of us taking it, we had to go to the big junior school. I had no idea what the eleven plus was. I had not received any preparation what-so-ever despite going to a private school. All I knew, picking up on my parents' immense anxiety, was that it was incredibly important and would alter my life.

Consequently I was in a frightened mode when I went to the strange big school to sit my exam. This was made worse by the fact that there was a real pea-souper fog and I became totally disorientated going to the outside loo prior to the exam. It seemed sinister and frightening.

We were overseen by a very stern lady who glowered round at us and who instructed us to write in pencil as biro ink faded and disappeared. I had a mental image of all my answers fading into oblivion.

I don't know what happened as I concentrated on the test and time whizzed by. It finished well before I did. I still had a lot of questions to answer. Time had caught me out.

The results came to school. The Headmistress came in and announced them. She praised Ann and told her she had passed, she should pack her things and go home to tell her mum the good news. She turned her glinting eyes on the other three of us and surveyed us with a granite expression that made me feel that I had let her and the school down and should be thoroughly ashamed of myself. She informed Billy and me that we had interviews. She told Liz that she had failed. Then she walked out.

We sat there with a desperate sinking feeling.

I knew this was bad but I did not fully comprehend what it actually meant.

The interviews were held in the Headmistresses front room weeks later. This was her living room and was normally absolutely off-bounds, a more terrifying place I could not imagine.

They had cleared the room of furniture. The interview was carried out by three people each with a clipboard. They placed a chair in the middle of the room. One interviewer sat directly in front, the other two were to the side. This meant you were aware of them out the corner of your eye but could only look at them one at a time.

My Headmistress ushered me in. I cannot remember what happened apart from them firing questions at me.

It was the most terrifying experience I have ever had. All the interviewers saw was a scruffy, terrified little boy who did not have a clue what the hell was going on apart from the fact that it was so important it was going to change his life and that his parents were scared stiff of how it was going to go.

That little boy floundered, mumbled, failed to make eye contact and was bewildered by the whole thing.

I failed.

That was my brush with the supposed benefits of private education and the vagaries of an absurd examination system that tried to separate lambs from goats at the foetus stage. It was truly horrendous. But how many other equally intelligent children were sacrificed at this age?

Until a time comes when people cannot purchase privilege and are forced to use the same path everyone else they will perpetuate an unfair and unequal system. The sons and daughters of the rich will buy their way into better education and, more importantly, better contacts and all the dubious benefits of the 'Old Boy Network'.

One only has to look at Oxbridge to see this working in practice. Then there are the various high earning professions and high status careers, such as politics, where you see the long term effect of the private school advantage.

This is made worse by the way that state Education is left in the doldrums and under-funded.

Why, perhaps one should ask, are public schools exempt from Ofsted and all the initiatives that flood over state schools in such a disruptive manner? Surely these establishments should be subjected to the same rigour and have all the benefits of state schools when it comes to the imposition of TVEI, ROA or the wonders of deep learning, specialisms and the three part lesson?

Why are private schools exempt?

Perhaps it is the simple explanation that all those wonders of initiatives are reserved for the plebs? The true ruling classes do not need these new initiatives. They can sail along in their pristine glory untrammelled by political intervention and this year's flavour of the month. Their alumni rule and make the decisions. It is no wonder that they remain wrapped in cotton wool and preserved as the best of British.

So it is that state schools are slated for having too short a school day, too short terms, teachers that are inadequate and students that are lazy when their private school counterparts have even shorter terms, shorter days, less contact time, teachers that are not worn down with extreme workloads, bureaucracy and government initiatives, and students who can be dealt with easily with a word to mummy and daddy who are footing the bill.

That is possibly another factor: you do not value what you don't appear to have to pay for.

But imagine this:

At the next election the electorate miraculously gives a mandate to a government that is not made up of upper class twits, public school boys and those with privilege. Instead they elect a cabinet that is representative of the people for once. And this new government decides to do away with privilege and bring in a level playing field. They banish private education.

Overnight the children of all the privileged classes have attend the same schools as everyone else (true this would be affected by where they live and wealth and poverty would still create pockets of privilege). Do you think it is now conceivable that these schools would be allowed to suffer leaking roofs, inferior equipment, and poor standards of teaching or inadequate leadership? No. Finances would appear, demands would be made and standards for all children would miraculously rise. All our children would find their prospects greatly enhanced.

Then, and only then, when schools have the full spread of intelligence in their students, when they are properly funded, when they are properly run and overseen, will we have a comprehensive system that will not only flourish but will be the envy of the world.

If I ever came to power this is the first action I would take.

Chapter 38 – Training

I have seen some good staff training and a lot of sessions that were an excruciating waste of time.

It is incredibly frustrating to go to a three day course and find that the whole thing could have been condensed into one morning session.

My previous Head Gerry used to send me along to courses to check them out to see if it was worth him attending. Even when he did attend if he felt it was a waste of time he would simply get up, make an excuse and walk out. He walked out of a lot of training sessions.

The problem was that the government was keen to bring in initiatives to be seen to be doing something to address the perennial thorny bush that was education. Each initiative required staff training. The staff would be issued with great glossy packs. Planning and lesson plans would be adapted, techniques learnt and materials purchased. It would last a year or two and fade into oblivion. Where are 'records of achievement' or 'technical and vocational education initiative' etc now?

Things come and go. What is flavour of the month now will be forgotten tomorrow despite all the millions spent on it. The more cynical staff dig their heels in, pay lip service and wait for it to go away.

Instead of following trends, or even diktats, a Head should evaluate what fits with the vision of education they have and then seek to justify their choices and actions accordingly.

Going against trends is not a disaster.

The current trend in education has been towards selection, streaming and setting. I think that is ridiculous. It runs contrary to my philosophy of fairness and equal opportunities. No matter how it is done there are winners and losers. The tendency is for the winners to become arrogant and lazy and the losers to feel worthless.

There are no perfect answers. Whatever you do has good and bad points but I am a firm believer in mixed ability teaching and have demonstrated quite clearly that it works. The results at my school could hardly have been better. With a year group who sat squarely on the national average, one hundred percent of them achieved 5 or more GCSEs and 80% achieved 5 passes at A-C grades. You can't argue with that. Academically it works.

When Ofsted came in they could not argue with it. They came in to promote selection and left acknowledging that we had made mixed ability teaching work.

I presented them with behavioural data. Over 80% of our student behaviour withdrawals from lessons came from the two subject areas that still insisted they had to set students – maths and languages.

The fact that we stood up for what we believed in and did it our way was noted and accepted. It worked for us and not against.

At present we have a backward looking government who are promoting retrograde steps such as selection, the English baccalaureate, and a toughening of the GCSE examination.

I do not agree with any of this.

They want to recreate the far from halcyon days of the 1950s. We have been there and been failed by it.

If we look at each of these in turn:

Back at that time when the country needed lots of unskilled work in factories secondary modern schools met the needs of the country. That is not true anymore. Industry needs skills and brains. Things have become much more technical. My mixed ability comprehensive school addressed this. All our students were stars and all of them succeeded. Only a few of the most socially damaged failed to reach their potential.

What Britain needs at this moment in time is an education system that promotes creativity and skill development in all subjects especially science and technology. We seem to be blithely heading in the wrong direction in the pursuit of knowledge.

Initiatives such as the poorly thought through, politically inspired, English baccalaureate are an attempt to force students through a robot factory by limiting their choice of subjects. It would force them to take subjects they hate and are useless at. It will also reduce the importance of many significant subjects. These would include geography, history, art, music, PE and ICT some which could be squeezed out of existence. Some may only survive as after school clubs.

Ironically I am all in favour of an English baccalaureate that is well thought through and encourages our students to take a broad selection of subjects including arts, science and languages. This can be done in a way that recognises a broad range of subjects that accommodate student preferences. The model proposed by the government is too restrictive and forcing students down too prescriptive set of choices could be catastrophic. Students who have no interest in a lesson disrupt education for others who want to learn. Putting students into an academic straitjacket is not a good idea.

Exam systems have always been a favourite political football. We have ended up with a mess. Instead of one set of nationally set exams there is a whole panorama of different exam boards with varying ethos. How can they possibly be standardised? Instead of celebrating the success the students have earned they are proposing to make exams more difficult because too many people are passing. Students have never put in as much effort as they do now. I certainly didn't when I was at school. The truth of the matter is that teachers have become so much better and students have never worked harder.

The problem is that people do not compare like with like. The world is different now. The knowledge based curriculum of the 1950s with its essays has been replayed by the computer skills age of the 21st century - essays are obsolete and knowledge is available at the press of a button. The country's needs have changed. Education has changed. To go back to knowledge based exams with high failure rates would do everyone a disservice.

As educationalists we want a hundred percent of our students to pass and succeed. Why not? The not too big leap of imagination is to devise an examination where a hundred percent can pass and yet we can still differentiate levels of achievement within this so that employers and universities can ascertain aptitude. The GCSE raw marks could do just that. With a bit of tweaking the GCSE examination can fit the bill. The last thing we need are people becoming demoralised by failure. I for one do not want to live in a society where the rich successes languish in opulence within their gated communities while the disenfranchised masses mooch about in dark alleys looking to mug and burgle. I want a fair society with opportunities for everyone and a place for everyone, where everyone is valued.

The best training I ever witnessed was carried out by a head of year Lester Jones on how to deal with students. It was based round an old black and white film. I always wanted to redo the whole thing and perform it as a drama.

In featured a student who was leaning up against a wall in an empty corridor. A teacher rounded the corner and approached the boy. He berated him, told him to stand up straight, take his hands out of his pockets, and tuck his shirt in. The boy reacted angrily. The teacher bellowed in his face. The student bellowed back. They both ended up enraged and furious.

The scene was repeated with different teachers, different approaches and totally different outcomes.

In the last one the teacher approached the boy, smiled and stopped to chat. They shared some words and a joke and went off laughing together.

That's all I remember. It seemed to summarise my philosophy. If you treat people with respect and care they will open up and respond to you. If you treat them with arrogance and disdain they become distant, resentful and angry. It's not rocket science.

If you want a friendly school then you have to be friendly with everyone. Not only is it good sense but it pays off handsomely. You don't seek major confrontation and conflict.

Teaching is about relationship.

The worst training I ever went on was for the new biology GCSE. I was head of biology at the time. The government of the day had, without adequate consultation, imposed a new examination on us. They had thrown out the old O level and CSE examinations and melded the two into a new exam that was supposed to be the great panacea for the country's troubles. It would solve everything that was wrong in education.

We in teaching would probably have agreed with them. The O level was obsolete. It no longer served a purpose in the modern world. It was too memory and content driven and the world had moved on. We needed modern skills such as ICT. Likewise the CSE was seen by students, employers and staff as a lightweight exam of little value. The GCSE might well solve this. It was the way it was brought in that was the problem. It was rushed and ill thought through – typical of politician driven initiatives – highly flawed.

Overnight the O level and CSE were discarded. The boards were instructed to come out with a new exam to replace them with a more skills based syllabus.

This would have been fine if they had the time in which to do the job. They didn't.

September came and we had no syllabus to produce our lessons from. Undeterred we went ahead and followed our normal pattern incorporating the sort of skills that we had heard rumoured were going to be required - finally the syllabus appeared along with sample examinations. They were radically different to anything we had been doing. We adapted the lessons accordingly, at huge time and effort, and turned our attention to the practical element. After many panicking calls to the examination board we were told not to worry, help was on its way. We were to undergo training. All would be revealed.

On the day 60 heads of biology gathered for a two day course on how to deliver the practical element. I can remember sitting there discussing it with other Heads of Biology. We were all shocked. We could not see a way of doing it.

The trainer arrived late and told us they had come straight from training at the examination board centre. We had two days to bring us up to speed so that we could cascade it down to the teachers in our departments.

He started the session off by asking us for our concerns so that they could all be addressed in the course of the two days.

'I have done the calculations,' I started. 'It doesn't add up and it does not look possible.'

He looked nonplussed.

'We have been told we have to assess thirty two practical skills for all of our students. We can only assess, because of the challenging tasks, eight students at a time and we should test each skill twice. Is that right?'

'Yes,' he confirmed, not appearing to recognise the inherent problem this represented.

'Right,' I continued. 'I have one hundred lessons in my Y10/Y11 GCSE biology course. I have twenty eight students. Just do the maths.' There was a general muttering of agreement from the audience. We had all seen the problem.

He still did not seem to cotton on.

'If I assess each skill with only eight students and have 28 students so have to do it four times that is already 128 lessons. If I do it twice it is 256 lessons.' Heads were nodding round the room. It was obvious. Yet it was equally clear that nobody at the examination board had seen this. 'There is still a huge amount of content to teach so even if I wanted to I cannot just do practical lessons geared to giving me assessment opportunities. We have been given the task of fitting a gallon into the pint pot. It is not workable.'

There was general agreement.

The government had rushed it through and imposed it and the boards had not had time to come up with a working model. The kids were going to be guinea pigs in a highly flawed experiment – as usual.

Everyone waited for the trainer to come up with an answer to the problem we had all clearly seen but they apparently had not.

'There are sixty highly experienced heads of biology in this room,' he announced. 'We have two days to share ideas. Between us we will come up with a solution.'

With dismay we realised that there was not going to be any training. We were expected to solve the insurmountable problems ourselves. The board had no panaceas. We were on our own. Once again the politicians had dumped on us.

We spent two days ranting and venting our spleen but nobody seemed to be able to come up with a solution.

I went back to school with an insurmountable problem. We had to try to solve it as best as we could.

The examination board set about solving it. They sent inspectors round the schools to see if anyone had the answer so they could share it with the others. In other words they didn't have a clue either.

I got round it by cheating.

I created multi-skill practicals with differentiated worksheets to enable all abilities to access and achieve. Each lesson took about thirty hours of preparation. There were multiple instruction sheets, assistance sheets, record slips and tick lists for the teacher. It was a nightmare. Each lesson had about twenty separate bits of paper and the organisation was horrendous. However it meant that I could assess many skills simultaneously with all the students in my class so I actually had time to do a bit of real teaching.

An inspector came in to see how I was getting on. She was knocked out with what I had produced and suggested I had them published She gave me a contact at Oxford University Press.

I went to Oxford and they loved the practical multi-skill worksheets. We produced them to a professional standard. Being Oxford University Press they weren't content to get them done quickly and out to meet the needs of teachers. They took their time. They wanted to get them one hundred percent right. Then they sent them round schools for comment. By the time they got it together the market was saturated with similar solutions that had been eagerly snatched up by desperate teachers. I'd missed the market and was not rich and famous – ho hum.

The two lessons to be learned are:

Politicians should never be allowed near education.

Training is often a waste of time but can occasionally be brilliant.

Chapter 39 – Rock 'n' Roll Head

When I was in the throes of retiring one of the English staff and film maker Mark Richardson came to see me requesting to make a documentary film of my educational philosophy. It was a lovely compliment and I jumped at it.

He told me that I had once said that my philosophy stemmed more from rock music than education.

That is true.

My sensibilities were honed and sharpened more by Bob Dylan, Roy Harper and Woody Guthrie than any educationalist or politician.

They sang about fairness, justice, humanity and freedom. They shared visions of a world without hatred, full of love, not riven by war, exploitation and racism. They voiced their concerns about tyranny and the dystopia that modern society was descending into.

That is what education meant for me. It was the stepping stone to a better world. It was the only way to free people from the shackles of their backgrounds and opening their minds up to new horizons.

Education for me was not about exam results and league tables; it was about the joy of emancipation.

Education had to be a broadening, liberating experience or it had failed.

It was no good churning out damaged human beings with handfuls of certificates; it was about repairing them and equipping them for a fulfilling life, a life of wonder, experience and participation.

Rock music made me revel in the wonder of poetry, politics and philosophy. It gave me intelligent objectivity. Those singer/songwriters focussed on real issues and sang with passion about real life and creating a better future. They exposed the hypocrisy of the present day and made you think.

I took all that joy and passion into my teaching. I wanted my students to think about real issues and explore solutions.

I was idealistic and full of zeal.

I always reckoned that education should be a good mixture of skills, knowledge, quality development, mind expansion, awe inspiration, self-esteem raising, passion, enthusiasm and experimentation. It should promote creativity and investigation. It should develop the whole child. Anything less is a travesty.

My Rock 'n' Roll students should be empowered to go out into the world with a swagger, grab it by the scruff and put it all to rights. They should appreciate that life is not a selfish, greedy experience where they grab more than their share and not give a damn; it can be better than that. We can build a better way of doing things that is fairer and more fulfilling.

Chapter 40 – Finance

Finance is the crucial life-blood of the institution.

Finance determines staffing levels. With more money there will be more staff and reduced workload so teaching becomes more effective; you can afford better equipment; you can decorate and repair so providing a better learning environment.

These things raise morale in staff and students and create a positive, happy vibe. That vibe makes people feel good and that affects the quality of education.

There is a balance to be made between staffing, equipment repairs and decoration. There is never enough finance to do it all properly.

Finance is allocated according to the number of students and the funding formula for your area. The East Riding is one of the worst funded regions in the country. Hull is much better because it is a city. If my school had been just five miles down the road we would had received an extra £600,000 a year. Imagine what I could have done with that money?

As it was, the only ways of gaining extra money was to join in with silly government initiatives, such as specialisms, or attract in more students. It was essential to get each year group up to maximum and encourage students back in to the 6th Form. We had money for each and every bum on a seat.

This created a bit of friction with the teaching staff. More students mean bigger classes. The bigger classes meant more difficult lessons and more marking. Some teachers actively discouraged students from coming back into the 6th Form. They only wanted the really bright ones who were bound to pass. They felt that students with behaviour problems or ones that just scraped the grades were too much trouble.

I had a slightly different perspective. If students had a chance of achieving a pass then I felt they should be given a chance.

I managed to get all the year groups to capacity and a large sixth form which secured our financial situation for the short term. By the time I left we had secured a third 'outstanding Ofsted' and were receiving accolades from Ofsted, the government, as well as both Oxford and Cambridge Universities. Our results were very good and we also had a reputation for being a friendly, caring establishment, free of bullying and full of happy kids. I could have filled the school twice over. Families were moving into the area to get their sons in and we were turning students away.

The governors were keen on expanding.

I was not.

At a size of 890 we were larger than I would have liked to be. I think small schools can create that family atmosphere that is lost when they get too big. If it was not for the finances I would have restricted numbers to around the 800 mark. That would have been ideal.

Chapter 41 - Publicity

One of the major roles of the Headteacher is to publicise the school. As most of what happens is pure psychology you have to play the game. My aim was to get the school operating on a very high profile. I wanted lots of positive stories going out highlighting our achievements.

There were a number of reasons for this:

- I wanted the students to feel great about themselves and take pride in their school
- I wanted staff to feel that everything was going well and they too would take pride in their achievements
- I wanted students and staff to receive public recognition for their efforts
- I wanted parents to feel that the school was performing brilliantly
- I wanted the public talking about how well the school was doing
- I wanted the governors feeling that everything was going great
- I wanted prospective parents thinking it was the best school in the area
- I wanted the local authority and Ofsted to get the impression of a school at the top of its game

There were a number of positive outcomes. The students felt good about themselves and that fed into relationships with improved behaviour and learning. The staff felt good about what they were doing and were relaxed about the direction the school was going, the vision and leadership. This took the wind out of the sails of the dissidents. The governors and parents were confident and more likely to take a back seat. The school was seen as highly successful and people wanted to send their sons to us and when Ofsted loomed on the horizon they could check out the great press coverage we were getting.

To function optimally you need as much unity as you can achieve.

I fostered good relationships with the local press and knew the major writers and photographers. I fed them with stories and they printed my information. It worked well for all of us. I even supplied them with the photos. It was a great example of mutual benefit.

I produced a weekly bulletin for the staff. I did as many warm fuzzies as possible, high-lighted all the things that were going on and continued the positive picture.

I also produced a termly newsletter with plenty of photographs. It was always thirty plus pages and full of what was going on, what had been achieved, student success, lots of named students and staff, lots of warm fuzzies and recognition.

I was aware that it had numerous audiences. I geared it towards students, staff, governors, parents and Ofsted. It painted a positive picture. I put in jokes and tried to keep a nice light informal feel. I saw this as a chance for me to put a slant on the school's successes. There was no way I would farm this out to anyone else. What I portrayed was my vision of the school. This was the school from my perspective. It was the opportunity to nudge it along in the direction I wanted, give out the praise and recognition for the things I favoured and make that clear to all.

My vision was instilled throughout. It permeated every story. I sent a copy through to the local press and they selected the stories they wanted to run with. It made their jobs easier and secured great publicity for the school.

The other major way of publicising the school was through public speaking. We had Speech Day which meant I could stand up in front of governors, parents, staff and students and give a glowing picture of achievements throughout the year. It was an opportunity to praise staff and students to the heavens.

The visitor's comment book was placed in the front waiting room and all visitors were encouraged to write a comment. They read each others and invariably made more that could be displayed, put on the website and quoted. Ofsted always read these comments.

The web site is crucial. This is often the first contact Ofsted or prospective students have with the school. I had it well designed and ensured that it reflected the 'open, caring, friendly' ethos. I put someone in charge to ensure that it was kept up to date as a priority. There is nothing worse than an out of date web-site. It sends out a message that the school is not on the ball.

Publicity is the life blood of the school. Everyone who is part of a succeeding enterprise receives a big 'feel-good' boost.

Chapter 42 - Back your staff

If your staff are going to extend their reach, experiment and take risks they need firm ground to stand on. The Headteacher is that firm ground. Trying new things sometimes results in failure and when you fail you need support.

I always to supported my staff in public.

When a parent rang up with a complaint I always informed them that I would follow it up, ascertain the full picture and get back to them.

I would then interview the member of staff and find their side of the story.

I would interview the students and find their side.

If necessary I would interview witnesses.

Usually the accusations were out of proportion or just wrong.

If the member of staff had made a mistake I would try to resolve it through restorative practice. I would bring the parties together and go through the facts. I would try to find a resolution. This would usually result in apologies and handshakes and a new start.

If the member of staff had done something serious I would take the necessary action – a verbal warning – written warning etc.

Only then would I get back to the parent and inform them of the action taken. Usually they were delighted that something had been done about it and the problem addressed.

It was not a question of sweeping things under the carpet so much as taking the heat out of things, supporting staff so that they felt able to take risks and make mistakes, and getting things in proportion.

The student and member of staff both left feeling that the matter had been resolved.

If the parent was still unhappy and wanted further action taken I then asked them, to put it in writing and felt quite able to back the member of staff.

If the parent was wrong I informed them that I had investigated and reported my findings.

I would back my staff to the hilt. They had to know I would not hang them out to dry.

A good Head should always take the blame!

I have never allowed a parent to openly criticise or castigate a member of staff. If there is a complaint that is valid it is the Head's task to chastise or take the appropriate action with the member of staff in private. There is often a learning experience but that's OK. That's how we get better.

My staff knew I would support them even if the matter was serious. That enabled them to experiment more and take those risks that make teaching exciting and raise it to a higher level.

Playing safe produces boring mediocrity; I wanted exciting excellence!

When I was a Head my chair of governors rang me up to say he'd received a complaint. One of the parents, who happened to be employed by him, had written to him, enclosing an English script which was littered with swearwords. He assumed that I would not have known what the English department was sending home with students. He told me he wanted it pulled and the staff responsible cautioned. I told him I'd look into it.

It turned out that the script was for a play that was being produced within the class. It was a script on the exam board's approved list.

I talked to the staff concerned and we discussed the validity of the script. We all decided that it was appropriate. The kids loved it and there were no words they did not hear on a regular basis. I gave them my approval and told them I'd sort it with the governors and parent.

I informed the parent and chair of governors of my decision; neither of them was happy but I refused to budge and they did not pursue it.

Chapter 43 – Attendance

Attendance is the barometer of success.

If you have a caring supportive environment, then attendance will be high. It shows that staff and students are happy and want to be there.

Staff attendance is crucial. Staff absence means the use of cover staff and no matter how good they are the students will lose continuity and suffer. Staff will be absent if they are too stressed, too overworked or unhappy. Consequently it is an idea to have a staff welfare group that is completely open and able to criticise management. Their views should be taken seriously, addressed and listened to.

Steps should always be taken to keep staff contented. They are at the cutting edge. I attempted to create good work conditions by reducing contact time as much as possible. I considered it essential for all the senior team to carry a high teaching commitment. They were supposedly the best teachers and they needed to set an example. Staff are always cynical if they see lots of free time on a time-table. If the senior team are not pulling their weight then why should the rest of the staff? - As a senior teacher responsible for the curriculum, pastoral, attendance, biology and PSHE. I was on a 14 period out of 20 teaching commitment. As a deputy head I was on 12.

As a Head I always tried to provide facilities and support. I would provide food when we had an evening event. We had an entertainments committee and regular staff outings. Staff welfare is paramount.

My school's student attendance was always above 95%. I don't believe a school can get attendance much higher than that. There is always some level of illness and genuine essential need for absence.

I encouraged attendance with a huge drive on recognition and reward. I gave out certificates and talked them up to the students. I told the students that they were as valuable as qualifications to an employer. I held celebration assemblies and gave it the highest profile possible.

Attendance is crucial. If students are absent they cannot learn.

There is often confusion regarding attendance and strike action. Some parents complain whenever there is a strike and their children miss out on a lesson. Now I would prefer that we never had to take strike action at all but sometimes it is necessary. But it is not so much the time lost by missing a lesson that is important; it is the continuity. If a child misses a lesson that other children in their class have accessed then they sometimes do not have the knowledge to access the next lesson. It is like missing an episode on a drama. Many children get lost and fall behind. If they all miss a lesson they are all at the same place. It is not so much of a problem.

If it wasn't for strikes the quality of teachers and teaching would have gone through the floor. We've had to fight every inch of the way for proper funding and funding means quality. For children to be missing a few days school is neither here nor there as long as the continuity is there.

I'm all in favour of fining parents who take their children out of school for a cheap holiday though I can appreciate the problem; tour operators really ratchet up the prices in the holidays. I would sanction absence for clear compassionate reasons such as bereavements or family illness and even the occasional educational type trip. I used my discretion. It was up to the parent to lay out their case and convince me. A week in Benidorm did not tick my box.

Chapter 44 – Student Voice

Students are not immature kids; they are intelligent consumers of the education in your school. They have a valuable perspective. They know what works and what does not. If they feel powerless they will not feel involved. They need empowering.

With empowerment they can become a tremendous force for improving the school. They have great ideas and can bring everyone on board. A unified school is a motivated school. When students are empowered they become inspired!

They are not stupid; they know when you are paying them lip-service.

A great student body requires a great 'Student Voice'.

That Student Voice is not merely a student council. It should be a force that permeates all aspects of the school. It should be democracy in action.

The student body democratically elects a representative from each Form. These should be representatives – bringing forward the views of their fellow students. They need good organisational skills, eloquence, debating skills, self-confidence and intelligence. They do not just represent their own views.

This body should meet regularly to discuss school policy and suggest improvements. It should have a budget, discuss planning and bring forward suggestions. The Student Voice should hold assemblies to inform the school of their deliberations and activities. It should meet regularly with the Headteacher. It should have a say on appointments of staff, planning, finance, policy and decision making at the highest profile.

Ideally the Student Voice should have a representative in senior management (not present during sensitive discussions such as staff discipline) and the governing body.

A good, high profile, vibrant Student Voice, that is listened to and acted on, is a sign of a confident, secure school.

Chapter 45 - Governors

I have never really understood the function of governors. Why would you want a bunch of amateurs running the school? That is surely the job of a highly professional senior team?

I can see the need for an overseeing body to ensure that things are being carried out in a legal, professional manner; that finances are tight and practice is tailored to the needs of the students. But surely that should be carried out by a highly professional, educational body who knows what they are doing?

One problem with governors, apart from the fact that they are amateurs and largely ignorant of the mechanics of education, is that many of them have vested interests. There are parents and staff with various agendas that are not always helpful or correct.

I was quite happy to report my policies, actions and progress to the governors. I was happy for them to be fully up to date on issues like finance, safeguarding and health and safety. They had an oversight of the school. I was not happy to have them involved with the day to day running of the school, the planning or appointments or decision making. I do not consider them qualified or well enough informed.

Shortly after my appointment I went to a Headteacher's conference in Birmingham. It was a three day event. Gerry had eulogised about it and told me I must go along. It was packed with thousands of Headteachers. I enjoyed it but already had a head full of ideas. I wasn't looking for more.

In the course of the three days I bumped into another East Riding Head and we had a chat about things. During this conversation he asked how many days I had come along for. I told him I was there for all three. He was surprised; he told me his governors had only let him go along for one day. My governors did not even know I was there. I'd tell them how good it was when I saw them next!

Chapter 46 - Specialisms

What nonsense. Where do they get their ideas?
The government brought in Specialisms to meet a need.
What need?
Instead of educating all children and allowing the innate ability of children to find a path through the curriculum that meets their needs, desires and wishes in a balanced way we were channelled into specialisms.

We could decide to specialise in one distinct area out of a limited choice. If and when we met the criteria we would receive a package of money to help us develop it.

In these days of extreme financial deprivation there was no option but to go for a specialism. We chose engineering on the basis that it was an area we had wanted to develop.

A team of staff, under the Head and a deputy set about putting in a bid. It took hundreds of hours of time. We were successful and received our £110,000.

We still had to meet all the national curriculum needs. What we did have was a big board saying we were now a specialist engineering college, hundreds of wasteful meetings that took good teachers out of the classroom, and a slight change in emphasis that upset a lot of staff – oh – and £110,000 that we now had to justify spending with detailed accounts of every penny.

In our town, if you were male, you had only two options. You could go to us as an engineering college or the other school which was a performing arts school. Heaven help you if you were not gifted in either of these as there were no other easily accessible options apart from shipping out to another town up to forty miles away. Did that mean we did not cater for linguists? mathematicians? computer experts? budding artists? historians and the rest?

Or was that our fault for living in a small town?
Obviously we should all move to a city!
Specialisms, like all the other crazy government schemes – TVEI, ROA, and a host of others I have blotted out of my mind – have cost a fortune in wasted time and energy, produced no results other than those concocted by bureaucrats to justify the colossal expense, and will eventually go into oblivion where they belong.

These schemes were hatched by political think-tanks somewhere in London. They use London as a model and think it can work everywhere else. It might stand a chance in a big city where there is a large population, a number of schools within walking distance and choice. It doesn't work in a small town.

What percentage of the population lives in small towns and villages?

Please Mr Politician - try taking towns and villages into account when drawing up your crazy schemes.

Somewhere there is a basement room in Whitehall stuffed full of filing cabinets containing the paperwork of myriads of stupid dead government initiatives in education.

Once again I say to politicians – stay out of education!

Give us adequate funding.

Stop wasting enormous sums of money on gimmicks.

Leave it to educationalists to deal with education. They are the experts.

Chapter 47 – Politics, Education and Austerity

It is manifestly obvious to everyone connected with education that having politicians running the show is a disaster.

Politicians think politically. They have their own agendas and political dogma. They are in the business of winning votes not improving education. They are subject to lobbying from vested interest groups. They have preconceived views and are intransigent. They always think short term (political office is 5 years). They bring in too many initiatives, which are poorly thought through, and based on dogma and ideology. They believe whatever the other party did was wrong – whether it was or not – and set about doing something completely different and to hell with continuity. They believe change is necessary; it produces headlines and makes voters think they are doing something. The new initiatives cost large amounts of money and divert finances from where they are most needed.

That is the last thing education needs.

We have just seen this in spades with this latest administration. We were faced with a need for austerity so what did the government do? They brought huge rafts of change throughout the public sector. Any sane person knows that change costs money. It has a snowball effect – training, resources, books, equipment, rooming and upheaval. What is needed in times of austerity is stability and a trimming of the fat. If they had merely cut all the training, conferences, glossy brochures and bureaucracy they could have saved a fortune. Huge numbers of highly qualified teachers are taken out of the classroom to service these political initiatives. They are put into offices producing bumf that I used to put straight in the bin. Every day my mail arrived and there was a heap of superfluous glossy brochures that I had to sort through and dump. All of those teachers need to be put back into the classroom. It would have saved a fortune and improved education.

We could have managed a couple of years without training, initiatives, conferences and glossy products. We would have survived. A moratorium would have addressed the austerity agenda. At least they could have done this for a few years until we were back on our feet.

It wasn't just education though, was it? Look at the same pattern in NHS, police, fire service, local authorities etc.

They are politicians. They can't help it. They do not understand the services they are running. Rarely are they qualified to any level within those public services.

Look what we are now lumbered with: free Schools, unqualified teachers, academies, restricted curricula, religious schools, streaming, banding, poor pay, worsening of work conditions and pensions and a change in examinations to a 1950s model. It is a time-bomb that is going to explode a little down the road and will take a generation to put right. We will find that teaching will no longer be attractive to the best graduates and standards will drop.

I ask you – did that address austerity or was it another expensive application of political dogma?

Good teaching requires stability and the time in which to develop teaching resources and plan lessons. A lesson may take five times as long to produce as to deliver. To bring in interactive resources, practical work, group work, video input, and good question and answer sessions requires time and expertise. There is nothing more frustrating than having spent years perfecting one's resources to have them thrown out because some minister has been on a trip to the USA or Scandinavia and had the wool pulled over their eyes.

Politicians are motivated by the absurdity of PISA world league tables which are dominated by countries that cram their students down narrow curricula in limited subjects. Those countries focus on knowledge above all else and do not have the time to develop the whole child, lateral thinking, creativity or skills. My daughter, who is a chemical-engineer worked with the products of this system in China. They were fine with day to day operations as long as things were proceeding along the proscribed linear path. As soon as there were any deviations or problems to be solved they were useless. What are we in Britain renowned for? - Innovation, creativity, problem solving and lateral thinking. Do we really want to sacrifice all that on the altar of limited PISA league tables? Do we want the suicide rate of Japan or the social exuberance of Korea? The PISA tables are a red-herring. I want to foster the more important things. That is our strength. I also want happy students who are well rounded, well adjusted and are full of passion and enthusiasm to take on the world.

Politicians are not experts.

1950s schools were extremely rigid and limited. Students were force-fed knowledge to regurgitate in exams. They sat in rows, were told to shut up and ruled with a rod of iron. That is fine if what you are after is a very narrow view of education. It carried out a number of the basic functions of education:
1. It disciplined kids
2. It enabled them to be graded
3. It filled their heads with knowledge that the brighter students would be able to manipulate
4. It suited some types of learners

But where were all those other things we have come to expect from schools? Where is the social care? The skill development? The teamwork? Where's empathy? Tolerance? Responsibility? Computers? Sex education? Being fitted for life in the 21st century?
Are students meant to develop those through osmosis?

If you brought one of those students from the 50s into the light of the 21st century you would see how well they coped. Put them in front of a computer, place a mobile phone in their hands, ask them to operate as a team to investigate a hypothesis.

Instead of returning to the formula of sixty years ago we need to look to develop the skills of the future. Our students might not be good at essays but they can multitask and delve into new technology like nobody's business. They are bright, alert and imaginative. They are outgoing and tolerant. Those are the skills we need to build on.

Forget your restrictive baccalaureates, the ending of coursework assessment, your essay writing and a return to streaming, grammar schools and war-damaged soldiers masquerading as teachers, this is the 21st century not the 19th. We've moved on.

Chapter 48 – My own Classroom Ofsted Inspections

As a Headteacher I made sure I did more than my share of cover lessons. It was part of that principle to ensure that nobody would work harder in that school than me. It meant that I taught many classes.

It was always great meeting new classes. I would often use it as an excuse to get to know them, to listen to them, and to gain a different perspective on my school.

One of my favourite lessons was to organise the class into small groups and ask them to pretend to be Ofsted officers. Their task was to review all the teachers who taught them, without naming any; and decide how to grade them. I asked them to organise them into outstanding, good, satisfactory and poor. I also asked them to identify four outstanding features of the school and four things that needed to improve.

The students loved doing this. They always took it very seriously and it created a great deal of heated discussion.

This gave me a snapshot of how teaching was in the school, what was working well and what needed attention.

Forget Ofsted inspections. The kids know what the score is. They judge things far better than Ofsted ever will.

Chapter 49 – Appointments and Promotions

You'd think this was easy. It is not. It is incredibly difficult and complicated.

Promotions in particular are fraught with complexity.

Appointments

You have a position for a subject teacher. What should your criteria be?

1. They support the ethos of the school.

This is head and shoulders above any other criteria. I don't care if they are the world's best teacher who can do wonders in the classroom, if they do not support my philosophy I do not want them. I do not want someone who shouts and intimidates kids, who is arrogant and aloof, who doesn't value all abilities equally, who does not value effort, and who does not care. I'm not interested if they know their subject backwards and are as charismatic as hell. They would be pulling the school somewhere I didn't want. I'd rather not appoint.

2. They care about students.

If they do not have a caring personality I don't want them near my students.

3. They have a sense of humour.

I have to work with them. I don't get on with miserable gits. I want a happy, pleasant work experience.

4. They are brilliant in the classroom.

As a deputy when I had the task of taking the interviewees around the school on a tour. I'd chat a little; explain how things worked and what we stood for. I watched them. By the time we reached the interview room I had sorted out who would fit in with the ethos and who wouldn't.

Ethos is King!

I am extremely suspicious of all the new fangled criteria that interviews have to be conducted around. I think they are complete rubbish. You cannot judge an applicant solely through a tick list. Yet another formulaic scheme designed to avoid taking responsibility and to act as a safeguarding mechanism to prevent candidates from suing the school for unfair interview practice.

In my experience the best interviewers of all are the students. Our Student Voice panel always did a great job and were spot on.

Promotions

It is not just who is appointed but who is not and why.

Promotions are really complicated. They are useful if they send out a clear message to staff. These are the people I am promoting because they are doing the things I want and they reflect my values.

Why would anybody think I would promote them if they were working against the ethos I was trying to create? I want the school all pulling together. Promotion is a tool to get things done my way.

It is not quite as simple as that. Only one candidate can be successful. There are usually a number of worthy applicants with different skills sets and personalities to bring to the post. They would all do the job in a different way and probably all succeed. It becomes a question of weighing up the advantages of one over the other.

After the appointment follows the task of picking up the unsuccessful candidates and getting them back on board as motivated positive forces. This can be transformational for them if you get it right. It all comes down to the skill involved in the debriefing process.

A good debrief builds someone up with all the good things they are doing. It then outlines some of the aspects they need to address. It should point a clear way forward and give them optimism for the future.

Someone should come out of a debrief feeling disappointed but knowing that they are valued and with a clear view of what they need to do in order to improve and progress.

This was particularly difficult when it came to interviewing colleagues of long standing who had become friends. Some of my worst practice was dealing with some of these promotions in my early days of Headship. I found it the hardest part of the role. In trying to deal with things dispassionately I may have appeared cold and uncaring. In actual fact because I cared I had to control my emotions. I handled some of these situations badly but became better at it.

Sometimes you evaluate the situation and decide that the job requires a completely new start which means bringing in someone from outside. That is hard to take for colleagues who have supported you. They feel betrayed. I can understand that. But c'est la vie. The school and students have to come first.

Chapter 50 – Leadership & Management

There is no doubt that a Headteacher is paramount to the success of a school. No matter how wealthy a school is, what brilliance of staff, quality of students, the most important ingredient is the Headteacher. This is not to decry all the others. It is just a fact. A good leader sets the tone, epitomises the vision and sparks the drive.

The Headteacher epitomises the ethos of the school. They represent the philosophy that unites and drives the school. Their presence is like the pheromones of a queen bee; it permeates the school and affects everything within it.

If the Headteacher is passionate and clear their ideas will set the tone for everything that happens in school. Their appointments and promotions reflect this. People will find favour and gain promotion if they support the ethos and are industrious in promoting it. People will be passed over or ousted if they oppose the ethos. The school will gradually change to project the Headteacher's vision.

A weak Head has no clear vision or fails to communicate it. They merely reflect current government doctrine and slavishly follow every new initiative. They are not prepared to stand against the flow and promote what they believe in. Staff sense this and become disillusioned. They expect fire and fury.

Weak Heads are a disaster.

Not that a Headteacher should operate as a tyrannical dictator and run roughshod over everybody's views. Far from it. There has to be collective ownership in order to bring everyone on board. Without some semblance of consensus initiatives are doomed to failure.

Strong Heads are also a disaster.

There is a middle way.

The Head's job is to sell ideas to the staff in such a way that they will support the ventures. That takes skill and time. To short-cut this and impose ideas, or go through a sham of consultation will ensure failure.

At the end of the day it is the staff and students who will determine whether something works or not. If the Head has failed to enthuse them the initiative will peter away into history. If they become enthused it will flourish. That is no mean task in this day of initiative fatigue. The cynics on the staff are all too keen to let things wither and fade. They have seen it all come and go. If you work hard to put it in place you will only see it discarded in a year or two. It is much easier to drag your feet and let it pass without putting any effort in particularly if it is another crazy scheme put in to place with the sole purpose of satisfying Ofsted.

Heads have to be approachable, listen and incorporate good ideas from all strata. Good ideas do not just emanate from the management team. Sometimes the office cleaner or gardener can come up with a gem. They need the opportunity. What is certain is that most of the guff coming from above is usually political dogma or unsound education garbage produced from think-tanks of public schoolboys. The Head does not have to be the font of all knowledge. What they have to do is select the ideas that are in sympathy with the over-riding philosophy.

Chapter 51 - The precariousness of Headship and tyranny Ofsted has become.

The pressure on a Head is enormous. You are responsible for all the students in your school and all the staff. If anything goes wrong their lives are affected and your job is gone.

The problem is that not all of this is in your control. Things can change so rapidly and the present system is so unforgiving.

The reason for this is the power, vagaries and affect of Ofsted coupled with the devastating effect of budget cuts, student numbers and freedom of choice. You are only as good as your last Ofsted and your last set of results.

Every Head is constantly aware of this. If things dip you are pitched into a spiral that is impossible to get out of.

In the 'old days' before freedom of choice and Ofsted there was stability. You knew what your numbers looked like. You knew what your funding was. There were no huge curriculum changes. Everything ticked along in a nice safe pattern year after year. Teachers were left alone in their classrooms to teach in a style suited to their personality and there was time to develop positive relationships with students. Parents did not panic about moving kids about from one school to another. The 6th Form was made up of students who moved through the school and eased their way to the next level. They didn't shop around like they do today in the hope of finding somewhere better.

Back then if there was a dip in results one year it would likely come back up the next. It was of little consequence.

Of course there were faults – there were some lazy teachers and a lack of rigour. But have we replaced it with something better?

As a Head you always have to push for better exam results because Ofsted demand constant improvement. The statistics are pawed over, comparisons are made with mythical schools that are supposedly identical to your own (though nobody can ever identify where these schools are and everyone knows that no two schools have identical circumstances) and your performance is judged.

If the results do not show that you are constantly adding more value to the student's performance you are subject to an inspection.

A school can be outstanding one minute, with resultant full role and adequate funding, and in special measures the next with redundancies, poor staff morale, teacher flight, falling roles, falling results and utter crisis.

It is so easily done.

A dip in results one year can result in an Ofsted inspection.

The Ofsted inspection team studies the data and give a 'need to improve'. The confidence of the staff is knocked for six. They are inundated with work and instructions. They are observed, tick boxed and analysed to death. They work themselves into the ground vainly trying to meet the standards set by Ofsted for preparation, marking, testing and teaching the perfect 'all singing all dancing' lessons. Unfortunately this cannot possibly be maintained because it would take a superhuman. They are working sixty hours a week. They are stressed to the ceiling. They are not sleeping. They have no social life. Their self-confidence has gone and they feel inadequate. Regardless of their personality and teaching style they are poured into the standard Ofsted model for the perfect lesson. Unfortunately this is not their style. The standard of their lessons dive. More pressure is applied. Staff are placed on the dreaded 'capability'. There is a climate of tension and fear. Teachers are off ill with stress. Teachers are cracking up. There are tears and arguments. Outstanding teachers find themselves becoming poor teachers. There is conflict between unions and senior team. The senior team have to up their observations and pressure in order to drive results back up. The effect is the opposite. Parents apply their right of choice and move their children to other schools. Students exercise their right of choice and go elsewhere to the 6th Form of their choosing. The numbers drop. The funding drops. Redundancies are thrown into the mix. The best teachers give up and leave. There is early retirement, long term sickness, a flight of top staff and a severe budget crisis. Redundancies kick in, preparation time is cut further and the remaining staff have yet more pressure. Student behaviour has gone through the floor. The pleasant ethos has become open warfare. More staff leave, more students go elsewhere, the curriculum has to retract, the results go through the floor, the funding is dire and the Ofsted team heads back in. The school is in special measures. The Head is sacked. The school is wrecked and the governors are blamed for not acting sooner.

All of this can happen in a single year – from hunky dory to despair.

Who'd be a Head?

Well if you are a Head worthy of your salt you can show your leadership by standing up to the ridiculous system.

You can stand before your staff and say 'We are not here for Ofsted! We are here to teach the kids. I have faith in you. I know you are brilliant teachers. Go out and teach your students adventurously and with experiment and fun. I want every student to come out of your lesson shining. Value them. Praise them. Give them your care and love. Recognise their efforts and reward them. Do not be afraid to fail – just try your hardest. We in the senior team will come in to help. My door's open. I will support you all I can. Drop in for a chat. Give me your ideas. If we stick together, support each other and go on doing our best for the students we will come through this.'

Then it is a question of getting support in for the weaker staff and helping them develop. It is about telling your senior team to go round accentuating the positives and providing that support, the shoulder to cry on, the kind words, advice and the praise. You instruct your middle managers to go in and support their staff, to concentrate on the good things and offer praise. Every observation should have at least one aspect to praise and have no criticisms – just a few pointers for improvement.

It's not rocket science. Everyone responds to praise and recognition. If you tell them they're good they will respond.

If you tell them they're rubbish they will get depressed, think they are rubbish and become rubbish!

Getting on the positive will maintain morale. It will get a positive response from the staff. It will bring people together against the common foe.

You make a point of throwing your clipboards out of the window.

If you fill out your observation sheets you do it after the lesson and away from the staff.

You use you observations (often just a head round the door and bright hello) to inform where to target support.

You constantly tour the school, smile, talk and support your staff.

It's not about statistics – it's about basic psychology!

You tell Ofsted what you are doing and why.

At least you'll go down fighting.

Teachers are not robots. There is no 'one size fits all' type of lesson. What children need is diversity of styles and characters. Teaching is not about detailed planning; it is about relationship!

While Ofsted focus on the tangible, objective criteria I value the things you can't assess far more. If you haven't got them going in your school you've failed whatever the standard of results!

There is no doubt that Ofsted inspections did bring back rigour and helped drive up standards. What we have now is a tyranny that creates terror and destruction.

Ofsted have become the rottweilers of the government. They exist to drive through government dogma.

To hell with Ofsted!

Long live good education!

Chapter 52 – How to pass an Ofsted Inspection

Gaining Outstanding in an Ofsted inspection is easy.

To start with put Ofsted in perspective; they have no importance what-so-ever. What is important is that your students are properly educated. That should be your only objective. Anything that gets that job done is good; anything that gets in the way is bad.

You pay lip service to the silly gimmicky things and focus on the important stuff. You never, ever, ever, pander to Ofsted.

You keep your vision firmly to the fore and you fight to implement it with all the energy and power you can muster. You explain your logic and demonstrate that it works. You are prepared to stand up and argue your case in the face of a hurricane of resistance.

This is where a Headteacher has to have that strength of character.

If you do not believe you are right you should not be in that position. If you don't have a vision worth fighting for you are a fraud.

When Ofsted come in you show them that your vision works. Show them happy, creative, eloquent, empowered students full of self-esteem, clutching certificates, pride and determination. Students ready to set the world alight with their compassion, empathy and desire.

Students who care about the world and are full of love.

Students who are motivated to make a difference.

Nothing else matters.

In my experience Ofsted will recognise excellence when they come in. They know when a school is outstanding.

Chapter 53 - The Future of education

Britain is renowned for its innovation, creativity and invention. It was not for nothing that the industrial revolution started up here. That is what we are good at. That is what our education system needs to foster.

We seem to be at a perennial cross-road.
We have people harking back to the past and people looking forward.
I'm in the forward thinking group. I believe the world has changed. There is a whole new technology out there. We need an education system that reflects this and prepares students for that world. We must enable our students to compete with the rest of the world. Our country's economy depends on the skills of its citizens.
This is the age of computers, I-Phones, Wikipedia and the World Wide Web. There is no need to remember information. It is there at your finger tips. There is no need to write up experiments; you can record them on your phone, fill in tables on your phone and look up whatever you need.
This is an age that really favours creativity, innovation and invention. All we have to do is harness the technology and free the imagination. We let all that passion and enthusiasm lose on the world and help guide it. Students love to learn. It is human nature. We have to nurture that enthusiasm. All too often it is present in primary school and dies the death in secondary. That is because the students are stifled by the process of education.
Free them!

I am all for seizing the future. I wish I had access to those resources when I was in the classroom.

Some schools are banning phones because they see them as a distraction. I argue the opposite. I would embrace them whole-heartedly. I would have the students using phones in every lesson. I can imagine science lessons with endless investigation and experiment; with students recording on their phones and beaming their results and conclusion through to the teacher.
How exciting!

How motivating! Newton would have loved it!
What fun!
That's the future! Surely that's the future!!!

Chapter 54 – Retirement

One minute you are working flat out putting in your 70 hour weeks, worrying your head off and striving to get everyone behind your vision and then you wake up and it is over. There is no way to further influence what happens in your school. Your power has gone. It has ceased to be your school. You have passed it on to someone else.

You are no longer a Headteacher. You are a pensioner.

It is amazing how quickly it drains away. One minute your views carry import and the next they are perceived as worthless.

You can feel it.

You can see why people may crave power. There is dynamism to it. You are valued.

As a retired Headteacher you may have to sit in the wings and watch impotently as all the things you valued and fought for are systematically dismantled. You see the school you love changed. Your vision is no longer the guiding principle. All you can hope is that some of it will be valued and will continue and that someone else's vision is not as bad as it could be.

That can be distressing.

All a Headteacher can do is hope that your successor shares your values.

You can also to use all that free time to write down your thoughts and philosophy in the hopes that it might just inspire a few other potential Headteachers to take up the challenge to make their own extraordinary schools; or a few classroom teachers to fight against the hierarchy of their schools to bring in change. Power is not the exclusive prerogative of Headteachers. Any impassioned person prepared to fight for what they believe in has power to change things for the better.

All our brilliant students deserve nothing less.

This book is one small product of my retirement. It is why I went a little early while I still had a few brain cells, energy and enthusiasm to want to inform future education and change the world for the better.

This is what gets me up in the mornings.

I can only hope it has some small effect. Thank you for reading it.

Chris Goodwin - October 2014

Appendix 1 - What qualities a Headteacher needs

- To really care for the education of all children

- To have a clear vision of a philosophy they are prepared to fight for

- To have excellent communication skills in verbal, written and non-verbal

- To have a sense of humour

- To be able to handle pressure and remain resolute

- To be stubborn in the face of opposition to their vision

- To have leadership skills

- To have management skills to plan a route through to the goal of their vision

- To practice care, understanding and deploy latitude when dealing with staff and students (everyone can make a mistake or two and deserves a second chance)

- To be flexible yet firm at the right times

- To be an agent of change

- To have the welfare of staff and students at the forefront of their mind

- To respect all students, staff and parents

- To seek excellence in the widest sense

- To refuse to compromise to Ofsted, governors, local authority, unions, politicians and pressure groups but remain true to ones own ideals and do what is best for the education of their students and the success of the school

Appendix 2 - What really works in the realm of education.

Over the course of five decades working in education I have a good idea of what is successful when educating students:

- Making education **Fun** – school should be welcoming and friendly. Education should be enjoyable.

- School should be a sanctuary for students. Outside may be full of violence, grief, bullying and chaos but inside the school we can protect, nurture and love.

- Relationship is the key to teaching. A brilliant teacher gives of themselves and shares.

- Equality is essential. No person in the school (including the Head) is of greater value than anybody else. It is their role, position and the way they behave that is worthy of respect. That respect has to be earned. All students are of equal value regardless of behavior, attitude, gender, race, ability, disability or culture.

- The GCSE is an example of a good examination. It enables students of all abilities to gain a pass and thus creates no demoralized failures yet it enables (from raw scores) the students to be differentiated by ability. The last thing we want to create is failures.

- Restorative practice is the way to deal with disputes. This works for staff as well as students. Bringing all participants in an incident together, talking through and resolving issues are fifty times better than making knee-jerk judgments and applying sanctions.

- SEAL – social, emotional aspects of learning is a great initiative. If you do not understand the baggage a student arrives with you cannot find the way forward.

- Celebration of success – for individuals, forms, various groups, subjects and the school. If there is good practice, improvement or achievement it needs shouting about and rewarding (The nature of the reward may be a word, certificate, special assembly, bulletin, newspaper report, mention in the newsletter, a handshake, a call to the office, or a party. It needs celebrating! Rewards work wonders!

- Inclusion to provide access; to enable progress. This is where good targeted support is essential, good teaching materials and outstanding teaching.

- Child centered multi-skill, practical, investigative, hands on, experiential, role-play, drama and practical approach. What else?

- The deployment of integrated IT. In this modern world students are immersed in IT; they love and it should be deployed and embraced. The modern world runs on IT.

- The interactive whiteboards are an example of the deployment of good technology. In the hands of an expert they are a world away from chalk and talk and provide a range of experiences that were unimaginable.

- Firm, fair management of students. Within the classroom there can only ever be one person with power. They should be strong, confident and visionary enough to empower their students and facilitate as well as direct. If that power is exercised too fiercely it can become a negative despotic tyranny that does not promote learning. It can become bullying and while remaining a rigid control is detrimental to student education and personal development.

•   The Student Voice is potentially the greatest power for good. If it involves students in the day to day running of the school, the policies, rules, management, events, promotions and appointments it can create a democratic force for change and improvement. I would love to see student representatives on the senior team, departmental teams and governors. Then we would get positive drive!

•   Mixed ability teaching. I have taught in streamed, banded and mixed ability settings. Mixed ability is extremely hard to do, requires great support systems and a lot of teacher and support staff expertise but it is head and shoulders better. Selection promotes a feeling of failure, inadequacy and lowering of self-esteem. Selection is self-prophesising. Students who feel incapable give up and do not try. Those selected become arrogant and feel superior. Those rejected feel of less value. Despite providing lessons that are tailored to their abilities the "B band' feel that they cannot be bothered. These classes become a nightmare to teach. The school becomes socially split with divisive antagonism often resulting in bullying, aggression and violence. Even if there were academic benefits (which I do not believe is the case) the social ramifications make it unacceptable.

•   The deployment of variety in a lesson to address different learning styles. The psychologists understanding of the learning process has identified that students fall into different categories regarding their preferential style of learning. By addressing this we can enable better access and student progress.

•   Informal, regular lesson observations by managers and colleagues with a view to support and providing positive encouragement. What we do not need is formal, negative observations.

• Integration of students from different ethnic backgrounds into the values and freedoms of British culture while allowing respect for difference, other traditions and culture. The over-riding ethos must be the British secular tradition of freedom, democracy, respect and the law of the land. Abhorrent practice such as indoctrination, cruelty, inhumanity, violence, and intolerance must be countered via good PSHE.

• Pastoral support for the classroom, using SEAL to inform staff and assist with effective methodology, managing behavior, student recognition and reward, exclusion, inclusion, monitoring progress, attendance and effort and promptly dealing with incidents with the deployment of restorative practice. Pastoral support should be positive and heads of year foster good relationships and understanding of their students.

• Careers advice and guidance is brilliant at focusing students on the future and helping them find a path through to a fulfilling life. It can help promote much more effective student decision making and thus inform better progress.

• A broad, balanced curriculum that delivers a range of subjects, skills and quality development that enable students to grow as individuals, hone their skills, gain knowledge, develop social skills, gain qualifications and develop as fulfilled citizens. A curriculum is not just about gaining lots of academic passes. There is much more than academic success. I always said that a student who leaves the school with no qualifications but a huge amount of self-esteem is better equipped than one who leaves with a huge number of A grades but no personality (ideally of course they would leave with both!).

- PSHE is the most important subject in the school. Anybody who does not understand that is ill-informed. This is the subject that enables students to think, reason and form their own views on politics, religion, sex, health, careers, relationships, finance, and life. Nothing is more important. To teach this, instead of facilitating it is a farce. To make an exam for it is absurd! PSHE done properly is pure, awe-inspiring, liberation. It is the epitome of all that is good.

- The use of the student's own personal technology to enhance lessons has a huge potential for furthering educational developments. Enabling and empowering students to work in groups using their phones to record, film, interact with the internet and process data is potentially the greatest advancement in education. Throw out your text books, exercise books and written reports. This is the computer age – get real!

- Creativity is as important as literacy and numeracy. We should teach it, facilitate it and recognize it! Creativity is what makes this country special! It does not happen by chance!

- Empowerment is exhilarating. Staff should be empowered to experiment with their teaching and if they mess up they should be supported one hundred percent by the senior team. Students should be empowered to interact, and be involved with their learning. Teachers should facilitate as well as teach.

- Addressing the little things prevents them escalating into bigger things. No instance of bullying is too small to be processed. No incident should be allowed to go unaddressed. By dealing with them, often with a word, escalations can be avoided.

- Dealing with difficult situations one to one. The most challenging aspect of all, at all levels, is to deal with staff or students you may not like or behavior you may abhor. Talking things through one to one in private often solves a lot of problems and nips things in the bud. It is always good to talk. If it doesn't work or you are unable to do so then move to mediation through a third party.

• Effort is the only way to judge students. Attainment judgments are demotivating and create self-fulfilling failure and demotivation.

• Detailed diagnostic marking is a waste of time and energy but checking work, providing praise and a simple pointer on how to improve is essential. It shows you care.

• Adding the personal touch – signing certificates by hand, knowing names, sharing a joke, personalized praise, being personally warm and friendly is crucial. They have to know you care for each and every one of them.

• Diagnostic testing and regular monitoring of effort, behavior and attendance is key to targeting recognition, praise and support. If someone starts underperforming there is usually a reason. Your job is to find out why and provide support. We have to pick up problems quickly and deal with them effectively.

• Good attendance is the key to good education. It shows the health of the school. If students are enjoying school, making good progress and being recognized and praised they will attend. If they have personal problems they may fall down in their attendance. That needs addressing.

• Counseling is effective. If behavior, attitude, attendance, effort or performance drops then counseling should be applied. A trained counselor is worth their weight in gold.

• Staff rewards are essential. All staff (teaching and non-teaching) require a pat on the back when they do a good job. They need to feel valued. This extends to such things as sending flowers when they become parents, are bereaved or are unwell, cards, public praise, private praise and incentives.

• Ofsted has been effective at raising standards, beating out poor practice and driving schools to greater progress. I fear it has run its course and has now become draconian and a tool of the politicians. What it promotes is no longer good practice. Schools are being put through hoops, teach to the exam, narrow their curriculum and restrict teaching and learning. That is reprehensible. Ofsted needs replacing with something more supportive and flexible.

• Three year planning is effective at creating direction, cohesion and impetus if well implemented with democratic involvement of all concerned and an overarching whole-school framework. If everyone buys into it and it unifies staff behind good policy and practice it will be effective.

• Whole school planning must be democratic. If it is shared and owned it will be instrumental in bringing about effective beneficial change.

• The coordination of planning and policies into whole-school and departmental handbooks is effective in creating impetus and direction.

Appendix 3 - What is neither effective nor desirable.

• Streaming, banding and setting. These are excellent at creating social division, demotivation, reducing self-esteem as well as creating displacement aggression but have no place in a school. They produce arrogance, superiority and failure. Only two areas of my school were set and they were responsible for 80% of the behavior problems. That says it all.

• A knowledge heavy curriculum. In this day and age, with web access, the last thing we need is too much focus on knowledge. All knowledge is available at the flick of a finger. We need skills and the ability to relate things together and process knowledge. A good curriculum is an active and balanced one. Knowledge has its place but it is not the be-all and end-all of education.

• A narrow curriculum focusing too much on too few subjects is a poor curriculum that will not meet the students' needs.

• Intimidation from teachers is counter-productive. It results in resentment and displacement aggression.

• Corporal punishment is applied violence. It is totally undesirable. It results in resentment, anger, aggression and violence. It never solves problems. I am glad it is illegal.

• Inflexible rules that do not take into account the variables such as emotional state of people concerned and provocation etc.

• A tick box culture that fails to address the feelings and subjective elements of education that are less assessable but equally important.

- Heavy handed management that seeks to solve problems by imposition.

- Teaching to the exam.

- Operating the school to satisfy Ofsted.

- Detailed diagnostic marking.

- Too much interference of governors in the direction and running of the school. The senior team are the professionals. They should be left to get on with it. Only if things starts going wrong do the governors need to get involved. Personally I would do away with governors and replace them with a professional body of education experts from the local authority who would oversee the functioning of the school. Why have non-professionals with vested interests?

- The interference of dogma driven politicians who bring in rafts of pointless change and ill-thought through policies. These initiatives are attempts to try to create the idea that they are solving problems. They rarely do if ever. What would improve education is more funding, highly motivated teachers and support staff, well thought through policies based on educational psychology and educationalists' theory and not having the top students creamed off into private education.

- Grammar schools. They cream off the top ten% and fail 90%. They are socially unacceptable. All our students should be equally valued and catered for.

- Private schools – while these exist the state system will not receive the funding it requires to succeed. If there were no private schools then the state system would flourish.

- World comparisons such as the PISA League tables (programme for international student assessment) are positively harmful. They are severely limited and based on small samples. To compare the worth of our education with other countries that cram and pressure students on extremely narrow parameters is driving our own system into equally restricted folly. Our strengths have been our creativity, innovation and flexibility. Products of this restricted practice are narrow minded and unable to function outside of their linear processes. This is not what I would recognize as a good education system at all! We're much better than that!

- Ofsted. It is my opinion that Ofsted served a purpose and helped raise educational standards. I do not believe that is the case anymore. Ofsted has become too much of a political tool of the government and is promoting harmful doctrines that are restricting the development of good education. The effects of Ofsted are draconian. Schools play along to Ofsted and exam results to the detriment of a wider, balanced education. Only aspects that can be measured are focused on. We have lost the joy in education and the tyranny of Ofsted has played a large part in that. Ofsted need overhauling to become a mechanism for positive development, support and advice. The climate of fear and stress they create, the public humiliation and drastic effects of their reports, have a detrimental effect on schools.

My advice is to believe in the kids! They are the future!

Printed in Great Britain
by Amazon.co.uk, Ltd.,
Marston Gate.